The CONJURING of AMERICA

The CONJURING of AMERICA

MOJOS, MERMAIDS, MEDICINE, AND 400 YEARS OF BLACK WOMEN'S MAGIC

LINDSEY STEWART

LEGACY
LIT

New York   Boston

The third-party trademarks used in this book are the property of their respective owners. The owners of these trademarks have not endorsed, authorized, or sponsored this book.

Copyright © 2025 by Lindsey Stewart
Jacket images by Shutterstock and Getty Images
Jacket illustration of flowering plants, grasses, sedges, and ferns of Great Britain courtesy of the Biodiversity Heritage Library
Photos of women by Albert Henschel/Collections of Leibniz-Institut für Länderkunde
Cover copyright © 2025 by Hachette Book Group, Inc.

Hachette Book Group supports the right to free expression and the value of copyright. The purpose of copyright is to encourage writers and artists to produce the creative works that enrich our culture.

The scanning, uploading, and distribution of this book without permission is a theft of the author's intellectual property. If you would like permission to use material from the book (other than for review purposes), please contact permissions@hbgusa.com. Thank you for your support of the author's rights.

Legacy Lit
Hachette Book Group
1290 Avenue of the Americas
New York, NY 10104
LegacyLitBooks.com
@LegacyLitBooks

First Edition: July 2025

Legacy Lit is an imprint of Grand Central Publishing. The Legacy Lit name and logo are registered trademarks of Hachette Book Group, Inc.

The Hachette Speakers Bureau provides a wide range of authors for speaking events. To find out more, go to hachettespeakersbureau.com or email HachetteSpeakers@hbgusa.com.

The publisher is not responsible for websites (or their content) that are not owned by the publisher.

Print book interior design by Taylor Navis

Library of Congress Cataloging-in-Publication Data has been applied for.

ISBNs: 978-1-5387-6950-8 (hardcover); 978-1-5387-6952-2 (ebook)
Library of Congress Control Number: 2025935534

Printed in the United States of America

LSC-C

Printing 3, 2025

To my great-grandmother, Margaret "Booie" Lindsey Perkins, an amazing Candy Lady. I'm so grateful I got to witness a little of your magic early in my life.

The work of our time is maintaining that hard-won freedom, and to do that, we're going to need the truth—the whole truth—about our past. We must teach it to our children and preserve it for theirs. Knowledge of the past is what enables us to mark our forward progress. If we're going to continue to move forward as a nation, we can't allow concern about discomfort to displace knowledge, truth, or history. Knowledge emboldens people. And it frees them.

Justice Ketanji Brown Jackson
Birmingham, Alabama,
16th Street Baptist Church
September 15, 2023

We can't know how American we are until we know how Black we are.

Robert Farris Thompson, art historian

Contents

Introduction: How to Keep That Shit off You 1

PART ONE: THE HERBAL CURES OF NEGRO MAMMIES

Chapter 1: An Alternative History of Vicks VapoRub Salve 17

Chapter 2: "An Old Woman, Who Doctored Among the Slaves" 23

Chapter 3: Negro Mammies, Botany, and American Home Remedies 32

Chapter 4: A Doctor's Visit in the Nineteenth Century 44

Chapter 5: What History Will We Choose to Remember? 49

PART TWO: THE VOODOO QUEEN'S MERMAID

Chapter 6: Why Can't Disney's Ariel Be Black? 57

Chapter 7: Juliette and the Voodoo Queen 60

Chapter 8: Mermaid History 66

Chapter 9: Conjure Fuels Rebellions 75

CONTENTS

Chapter 10: Oshun, Mami Wata, and a Pantheon of African Water Deities 82

Chapter 11: The *Gris-Gris* of the Downtrodden 90

Chapter 12: "She Was Hard on the Men" 96

Chapter 13: Our Mermaids, Our Stories.. 104

PART THREE: THE MOJO OF AUNT JEMIMA

Chapter 14: Aunt Jemima's Grand Debut, the Chicago World's Fair of 1893 109

Chapter 15: From Negro Mammy's Hoecake to Aunt Jemima's Pancake Mix 118

Chapter 16: Sarah Byrd's Cakewalk............................... 127

Chapter 17: Aunt Caroline Dye's Mojo 136

Chapter 18: Aunt Jemima, the Black Power Revolutionary 150

PART FOUR: THE QUILTS OF GRANNY MIDWIVES

Chapter 19: Our Ancient Textile Tradition....................................... 157

Chapter 20: Enslaved Midwives as Weavers............................... 164

Chapter 21: Black Midwives and the Nineteenth-Century Brawl over Abortion 179

Chapter 22: The Quilt of Motherwit 197

Chapter 23: The Midwife's Bag, a Tool of Rebellion 215

Chapter 24: Black Women's Hair, the Everlasting Textile 226

CONTENTS

PART FIVE: THE CANDY LADY'S SOUL FOOD

Chapter 25: Oshun's Legacy in the New World 241

Chapter 26: The Candy Lady 253

Chapter 27: From Black-Eyed Peas to Red
Beans and Rice 263

Chapter 28: Wild Lettuce, the Greens in
My Gumbo Pot 274

Chapter 29: Black Women Put Their Foot in This 289

Conclusion: Where Did All the
Conjure Women Go? 294

Acknowledgments *303*
Bibliography *307*
Notes *337*
Index *369*

INTRODUCTION

How to Keep That Shit off You

If you're on social media, you've probably come across the hashtag #blackgirlmagic. Maybe you've also seen it scrawled across a T-shirt, featured on a wine label, or referenced in popular television shows like *Scandal* and *Queer Eye*. As ubiquitous as the phrase "Black girl magic" is in American culture, its historical origins are less well known. The viral hashtag emerged in 2013 and quickly became a social movement. By 2014, the hashtag had become a fixture in our world, from apparel lines to a trademarked podcast and television show. But the scope of Black girl magic is much broader than the various merchandise sold under its name. And Black girl magic is much older than the social media feeds that turned the hashtag into a global vibe.

For as long as Black women have been in the United States of America, we have used our magic to battle the racism and sexism that plagues our lives. We have used our magic to identify and commune with one another and to build a world where we are valued and seen. The features of the world we made with our magic is the skeleton upon which American culture hangs. Black women's magic laid the foundations for the American staples we still enjoy now: popular home remedies, like Vicks VapoRub salve; powerful female icons, like mermaids; blues, the bedrock of all contemporary American music; blue jeans, a major building block of American fashion; and soul food, America's first fusion food, born of African, European, and Indigenous cultures.[1] Our magic has informed all aspects of our lives, from the practices that bring babies into this world to those that help the dying pass in peace. And while "Black girl magic" is often used as a catch-all phrase to celebrate the staying power of Black women, our magic is more than our accomplishments or our resilience. Black girl magic also refers to a specific cultural tradition that is very real.

Our magic began long before America was founded. When she first coined the phrase "Black girl magic," Joan Morgan, author of *When Chickenheads Come Home to Roost*, suggested that our magic stretches all the way back to West Africa.[2] At a time when she, like so many of us, needed to be reminded of her self-worth, Morgan turned to the comfort of the sea so that she could "breathe again—unafraid of [her] tears or fragility."[3]

By the sea, Morgan "heard Oshun's laughter twinkling like bells, urging [her] to recapture the feminine and discover the fierceness of a black girl's magic." The sea gave her solace and strength and ultimately "saved [her] life." Because, in the mirror of the sea, Morgan saw that she was connected to generations of powerful women who wielded their magic to make a way out of no way. With her reference to Oshun, Morgan hints at the historical basis of the phrase "Black girl magic" and the rich cultural heritage that is captured with it. Oshun belongs to the pantheon of gods called *orishas* in Yoruba religion, which has been practiced in West Africa, primarily Nigeria, for thousands of years.

Oshun: Nigerian goddess; the most beautiful woman in the world; the eye's delight and the tongue's savor; the sweetness of honey and the sharp bite of ginger; the innocence of first love and the wariness of imminent betrayal; the peacock that so desired to save the world it burned away its beauty and became an ugly vulture in an old Nigerian tale; ruler over the rivers that carve up continents and the tiny torrents of blood, streaming through our bodies; fierce warrior; protector of women; mother of abundance, called upon when love and money and wombs run dry; mirror that lets women see themselves as worthy of every good thing in life; symbol of Black girl magic.

There's an old Yoruba tale about Oshun that explains how Black women and girls got their magic.[4] It happened long before the advent of the transatlantic slave trade, and it begins with an important question: *What would happen if all the women in the world vanished?*

That's what sixteen male *orishas* were left to find out when they colluded to leave the female *orisha*, Oshun, out of their decision-making. Late one night, these male *orishas* met with all the men of the Earth to make a secret pact of power. This secret pact was designed to give the men ultimate power over the women in their lives. Drunk from the power they gained from this pact, the men began to mistreat the women. Some husbands began to beat their wives. Some fathers began to enslave their daughters. Some brothers began to starve their sisters.

This was not the first time that Oshun's brother *orishas* had left her out of the decision-making around the fate of the world. During the creation of the Earth, Oshun's brother *orishas* had erroneously believed that her input was not needed because she was young and a woman (so what could she know about such serious matters as these?). She objected to her brothers' exclusion. Their belief that she was not needed in the creation of the world was tantamount to disrespect of her status as a god.

But Oshun knew that she was fully equal to her brother *orishas* in power and strength. She understood that sometimes the only way to show someone how much you're needed is to remove your presence, to let their world fall apart in your absence. So, Oshun decided to teach her brother *orishas* a very important lesson. She took her essence—all the fresh water, rivers and waterfalls and creeks—from the burgeoning Earth. Soon the land began to crack for want of moisture. The plants began to wither at their roots. The animals started to faint for thirst.

The brother *orishas* were dismayed by this outcome. As a result, Oshun's brothers complained to Olodumare, the supreme god of the Yorubas faith. To their surprise, Olodumare informed the brothers that they must make peace with Oshun. Her sweet waters, Olodumare informed them, bring a necessary balance that the Earth needs to sustain living things. So, the brother *orishas* went to Oshun and apologized to her. They were forced to admit how much Oshun's essence was needed for the survival of the world. Persuaded they had learned their lessons, Oshun returned the fresh water back to the Earth. The soil became dewy, the flowers began to bloom, and the animals grew plump.

As painful as Oshun's lesson was, her brother *orishas* soon forgot it in their quest for power. When Oshun learned of the secret pact her brothers were now making with the men, she realized they were excluding her, yet again, from their plans. And worse, they were trying to oppress the women of the Earth, which would create a major imbalance and social discord. But Oshun knew exactly what to do. Last time, she'd taken the water from the Earth. This time, Oshun simply took the women. All of them.

The next morning, the men woke up to find the women missing from their beds and their homes. They began to check with their neighbors, but their neighbors were just as amazed. At first, the men rejoiced, thinking that there was now no one to stand in the way of their whims and plans. But very quickly, they learned their mistake.

For the things the men depended on the women to do were no longer getting done. The stench from houses left uncleaned and the hunger from meals no longer cooked drove the men mad. Worse, there was no new human life brought into the world. And with that loss of new life, the men could no longer envision a future. Without the women, the world was thrown into an even greater imbalance.

The male *orishas* returned to Olodumare to complain. And once again, Olodumare pointed out that their exclusion of Oshun had led to the destruction of the world. Olodumare told them they had to make peace with Oshun to return the world to its rightful balance.

By this time, Oshun had learned that no matter how many times she removed herself from the Earth, her brother *orishas* would suffer for a while, sure, but they would ultimately try to exclude her again. What was to stop the men of the Earth from following suit and attempting to oppress the women again? Oshun did not want the women to be powerless under the foot of men if another pact was made.

So, Oshun went to Olodumare and asked the supreme god to give the women of the Earth a portion of the god's own power, the same power used to create the universe—a power called *aje* or magic. Olodumare obliged, and with *aje*, the women gained "power over men."[5] Oshun became the leader of these special women, called *iyami aje*, which translates roughly into "my mysterious mother."

In Yoruba culture, these women were called witches, at worst, and "our mothers," at best. They were believed to be a "secret society of powerful old women" who had the power to "transform into birds at night" (like Oshun) during secret meetings in the forest, where medicinal herbs and roots and flowers are found.[6] (Elderly women were thought to belong to the *iyami aje* because the Yoruba considered it "a sign of women's power that they live to be very old, often outliving men."[7])

The *iyami aje* played a vital role in the community. They were believed to be powerful women who held the health of the community in their very hands. Through their vast knowledge of herbs, they corrected the imbalances that brought about illness in the sick. And they used their power to balance their social world against oppression, as their origin tale describes.[8] They observed three simple rules: Respect the herbs, don't show off wealth, and share everything you have with the community.[9] In Yoruba thought, the *iyami aje* were humans who held a power similar to the gods.[10]

When the Yoruba were kidnapped and forced to take the journey across the Atlantic to enslavement, they carried stories and rituals of Oshun. These stories were soon enmeshed with the other religious traditions that West and Central Africans brought with them to the Americas. In fifteenth-century West Africa, Islam was widely observed alongside local practices, such as the worship of *vodun* (deities) by the people of Dahomey. At the same time, in Central Africa, Christianity fused with the indigenous worship of *minkisi* (objects possessed by spirits) by those from the Congo.

These religious traditions carried blueprints for solving problems. They contained herbal knowledge for healing physical ailments. They offered spiritual wisdom to navigate social conflicts. They provided guidelines for the prosperity of their respective communities. So when newly enslaved Africans faced problems in the

New World, from heartaches caused by lovers to the torture meted out by their slave masters and the illnesses they suffered as a result, they did what their relatives and ancestors had done for centuries. They turned to the divine for help to meet these challenges.

But remembering and passing on the religious traditions of their loved ones from Africa was not an easy feat for the enslaved in the New World. Some slaveholders violently prohibited enslaved Africans from worshipping their gods. And at times, slave owners forced the enslaved to worship in their churches, where pastors preached that God wanted slaves to "obey their masters." By the nineteenth century, many enslaved Africans in the New World had forgotten the names of the gods with which their ancestors had traveled over, like Oshun.

But enslaved Africans did not forget their ancestors' ritualistic use of herbs for medicine or their overall relationship to the divine, where all manners of spirits could be called upon for help. Over generations, enslaved Africans passed down these aspects of West and Central African beliefs, adapting them to their new environment. So by the nineteenth century, enslaved Africans had incorporated new flora from the Americas into their West and Central African herbal remedies and cooking styles. They had channeled the *minkisi* of their ancestors into the mojos their descendants would later sing about in the blues. They had incorporated the religious and folk beliefs of people they encountered in the Americas, like the Indigenous who lived near plantations and even the Europeans who enslaved them. They had fully meshed the African gods of their ancestors with those they met in the New World—their *orishas* became saints of Catholicism or the Holy Spirit of Protestantism.

In this process of religious innovation, enslaved Africans transformed the West and Central African religions of their ancestors, birthing new spiritual traditions in the New World that had very old African roots: Haitian Vodou, Jamaican Obeah, Brazilian Candomblé, and Cuban Santería. In the United States, enslaved Africans created conjure—a mix of spiritual beliefs, herbal rituals, and therapeutic practices. For four hundred years in this country, West and Central African spirituality has lived on in customs of conjure that run through the whole of African American culture like an aorta.[11]

Across America, there were many arteries that flow into conjure. Along the Gulf Coast, like southern Louisiana, there is Voodoo, a unique blend of Yoruba religion, Haitian Vodou, and Roman Catholicism. In the Deep South and lower East Coast, there is hoodoo or rootwork, which combines aspects of Yoruba religion (such as herbalism) with the *minkisi* of the Congolese and Protestantism. But no matter where you are in the United States, to lay hold of our conjure is to feel the pulse of Black women's magic that has been thrumming in America since the country began. And to understand how Black women have shaped America, you must learn how to recognize this pulse, how to feel the rhythm of our conjure, reverberating across centuries.

Slavery is the most salient place to pick up the pulse of Black women's magic in America. During slavery, the Black women who used conjure in their communities became powerful leaders. They were especially renowned on plantations for their ability to successfully treat cold and flu symptoms, a widespread problem since viruses had yet to be studied or understood by scientists. It was not until the 1890s, long after slavery's official demise in 1865, that doctors grasped how viruses transmitted diseases and the importance of hygiene practices. So an enslaved woman who could heal you when you had a cold, or better yet, keep the cold off you all together, was powerful indeed. And this was not all she could do.

To the enslaved, conjure was a way to manage their "luck"—their overall spiritual condition, which they believed could influence all aspects of their existence: births and deaths, illnesses and health, love and heartbreaks, slavery and freedom.[12] Conjure women were considered experts in luck management.

What did it mean to manage your luck successfully, according to the enslaved? Good luck did not mean gathering riches, for most of the enslaved could not legally hold property. Nor did it mean opportunities to advance in your career, for the enslaved were often forced to do work they would not have chosen for themselves. Rather, good luck meant preventing an already bad situation from becoming much worse. Conjure women were believed to be especially skilled in treating an abundance of mishaps that, left unmanaged, would greatly increase the misery of the enslaved.

So the common cold was just one of the many kinds of misfortune conjure women could treat with their skills: The grip of croup when you're young or flu when you're old. The swelling of wrists and ankles and hips. Measles and mumps. The evil eye of a neighbor. The straying eye of a slave master or his lingering hand on your bottom as you passed out plates for supper. The revenge of a past lover or the eager wishes of a new one. Snakes in the field where you harvested cotton, rice, or cane. The master's cat-o'-nine-tails or the leather strap of his wife, when the tea was just a little too cold for her taste. The eyes of other nosy slaves who would betray your plans to run away. The dogs and pain and fear and confusion that would slow you down while you ran. Spirits that wrecked your dreams or vermin that wrecked the itty-bitty patch the master let you have right alongside your slave quarter. You know, the patch that yielded the cotton that you raised and sold in town on Sundays, the only day to yourself, in order to buy the freedom of your mother or brother or daughter or lover. In essence, conjure women knew *how to keep that shit off you.*

Conjure women had this incredible range because they saw the social suffering and physical ailments of those under their care as intimately linked. Within the healing traditions of conjure, illness was believed to be the result of more than merely physical causes. Illness suggested a profound imbalance in your life, an indication that something has also gone awry in your relationships, whether with the recent dead or your ancestors, your family, your lovers, your friends, your enemies, or even your relationship to yourself. Seen in this way, divination became much more than reading tea leaves; it became a special skill akin to lay psychology. So the conjure woman's treatment of your illness included not only methods to remedy your physical pain but also an assessment of the social imbalance that made you susceptible to that illness in the first place.

Within enslaved communities, conjure women were deeply revered for their knowledge about health and illness, births and deaths, spirits and plants. They were skilled herbalists, healing the sick with teas, baths, and salves. They were spiritual advisors who counseled those troubled in spirit. They assisted women in their reproductive health by supporting births, providing abortions, and empowering them with social rituals to gain power over their male lovers. And conjure women were heavily engaged in the struggle for emancipation. It was often conjure women who motivated rebellion and inspired dreams of freedom in their communities.

Enslaved conjure women, like the *iyami aje*, were constantly involved in a struggle where those in power sought to reduce them to nothing. And like the *iyami aje*, enslaved conjure women drew upon magic to even the scales and regain a little power. And when conjure women, like the *iyami aje*, were denied respect by those in power, they used their magic to command it.

Throughout American history, conjure women have been a force that was greatly feared by slaveholders and their generational oppressors, even as they were begrudgingly admired. The expression of this fear has transformed over the centuries: whippings from masters during enslavement; the barbaric treatment of women by doctors in the emerging field of gynecology during the antebellum and Reconstruction eras; and the oppressive laws passed against conjure (especially the conjure practiced by midwives) during Jim Crow and the Civil Rights movement.

We find the conjure woman doing a delicate dance during intense racial conflicts that mark our national history, from slavery to Jim Crow. She rises to assert the power of Black women; she, in turn, gets pushback from those who would oppress Black women. Despite this pushback, in each era of our national history, she has managed to stamp her conjure onto American culture, in our medicine, our heroines, our music traditions, our midwifery practices, our clothes, and our food.

In these pages, I will tell the story of how these conjure women first emerged during slavery in the US South, how they were thrust into the heart of national conflicts, and how they have shaped our American culture in response. Black women in America have always had to live in a world that was hostile to them. Conjure is one way that our foremothers survived and at times, defied that world. Conjure reminds all of us that even when things are most dire, it's possible to drum up power in unexpected places.

I'm drawn to this story and want to share it with you because there have been countless times, over the last few years, when I have felt powerless. Throughout the COVID-19 pandemic, seeing such senseless deaths brought on by disease; witnessing murder after murder after murder of Black people at the hands of the police, most notably the case of George Floyd; the Supreme Court's overturning of *Roe v. Wade* with *Dobbs v. Jackson*, reversing a decision that to many, including me, was a landmark of women's empowerment; being subjected to laws introduced by state legislators that whitewash our history, like Florida's revision of its curriculum in grades K–12 to include instruction on how "slaves developed skills which, in some instances, could be applied for their personal benefit"; and the moments when, as a Black woman, I am often underestimated, discounted, and, like Oshun, excluded from matters that directly impact me.

Sifting through such personal feelings of loss and disempowerment, I got to wondering how my ancestors got through, and even managed to flourish in, much tougher times than these. I wanted to know how my great-grandmother, Margaret "Booie" Lindsey Perkins (1921–2014), after whom I am named, managed to maintain a steadfast sense of self-worth, even as she lived through the bulk of Jim Crow, a time when Black women were publicly demeaned and belittled in America.

What came to me again and again were these conjure women. In their conjure, a sanctified blend of West African spirituality and Christianity, I saw an unshakeable faith that enabled them to grasp real possibilities when all else seemed hopeless. Their conjure built a platform of power that later generations of Black women could step upon to voice the woes of racism, sexism, and classism that have plagued us for centuries.

THE CONJURING OF AMERICA

The Conjuring of America is the epic story of conjure women, spanning five historical periods: slavery, antebellum, Reconstruction, Jim Crow, and the Civil Rights movement. These five periods trace the transformations of the conjure woman, moving from the Negro Mammy of slavery to the Voodoo Queen of antebellum, from a mojo-wielding woman of Reconstruction to the Granny Midwife of the Jim Crow era. I end with the Candy Lady, who has been with us well before, during, and after the Civil Rights movement. In each period, we find Black women wielding a powerful weapon through conjure to address the problems of racism, sexism, and classism they faced.

The story of Black women's empowerment through the evolution of the conjure woman—the national problems she faced and the resources she found in conjure to do so—urges us to reflect on the history of America in a new way. Conjure women have had a tremendous impact upon America, but Americans know so little about them. Without this knowledge, it's hard for us to fully grasp not only the world we live in but also who we are. Because to learn the history of conjure women is to learn something vital about ourselves at a time when we need it most: that even when those in power rise to threaten our freedoms—even when we are killed with impunity by the police and denied control over our wombs—we are not powerless.

PART ONE

The Herbal Cures of Negro Mammies

CHAPTER ONE

An Alternative History of Vicks VapoRub Salve

Let me guess what's in your medicine cabinet. There are probably painkillers like aspirin or Aleve (especially if you have menstrual cramps as debilitating as mine), rubbing alcohol or hydrogen peroxide and Band-Aids for minor scrapes and cuts, leftover masks and COVID-19 tests, probably Prozac (or any of its generic brands) if you're a millennial, since we understand that there's no shame in getting a little help sometimes, and honey-lemon drops for pesky coughs that linger long after colds. And I'm willing to bet at some point in your life that little blue bottle with the Vicks green triangle was in your cabinet too: Vicks VapoRub, or what my family still calls Vick's Salve.

Can you remember the smell? The withering woody sweetness of eucalyptus under ever-burning menthol. The scent is as unforgettable as its texture, greasy like the BB Super Gro or Vaseline the women in my family applied lovingly to my scalp. For many of us, Vicks VapoRub was love made tactile, spread under our noses, down our throats, over our chests, and landing straight in our soul when we were ill and in need of comfort.

Vicks VapoRub had humble beginnings. It was originally sold

as Richardson's Magic Croup and Pneumonia Cure Salve, a popular cold and flu remedy in North Carolina. During the 1918 flu epidemic, Vick Chemical Company launched an aggressive marketing campaign, offering much-needed public health advice. Their efforts were hugely successful, sending what had now become Vicks VapoRub flying off shelves around the world. And now, over a hundred years later, it is not only an American staple but also beloved around the globe, especially in Latin and South America, as well as India. Proctor and Gamble, which now owns Vicks VapoRub, considers the salve to be one of its billion-dollar products.

Lunsford Richardson (1854–1919), a southern white man born in Selma, North Carolina, is credited with the development of Vicks VapoRub in 1894. His story seems quintessentially all American. He experienced certain hardships: His father died when he was but two years old, his mother died when he was a teenager, his family home was decimated during a war, and he was left with very little money after this war to start his own business. And then, with a stroke of luck, he went from rags to riches when his experimental drug salve saved the day during the 1918 flu epidemic. It is estimated that sales for Vicks VapoRub jumped from $600,000 in 1917 to almost $3 million (about $67 million today) during the 1918 flu epidemic, making him the instant millionaire so many Americans dream of becoming.[1]

But there is a dark underside to Richardson's American success story. Slavery is part and parcel of his particular dream. His family home was a plantation. The war that ravaged his family home was the Civil War. And he grew up among enslaved Black women who had an extensive knowledge of the plants and herbs that formed the basis of and were indeed the key active ingredients found in his original "magic" salve.

Recently, the medical contributions that enslaved Africans made to this country have been in the national spotlight.[2] You may have heard the story of Onesimus, the enslaved Yoruba man who, in the eighteenth century, helped the city of Boston stave off a widespread outbreak of smallpox with the vaccination method from his homeland. But there is also a lesser-known story to be told about the countless, anonymous enslaved African women who toiled on plantations and cured the sick, day in and day out, for centuries. They were women who wielded conjure, a mix of spiritual beliefs, herbal rituals, and therapeutic practices that emerged among enslaved Africans along the Gulf Coast and lower East Coast of the United States. During the seventeenth, eighteenth, and nineteenth centuries, enslaved conjure women were largely responsible for the day-to-day care of colds, flus, and other minor ailments on plantations.

Some important questions emerge from this history. What did Lunsford Richardson learn from these women who were also responsible for taking care of him? How did the healing traditions of these Black women shape the medicine—both preventative and curative—of the nation during slavery?

When you look up the history of Vicks VapoRub online, you will note very little mention (if any) of slavery in the discussion of the salve's origins. I want to propose a story that puts slavery front and center in the development of this American staple. A story that centers enslaved Black women who'd been using very similar salves to treat colds and flus and congestion long before Richardson was born. A story about the conjure women who were essential in getting this American staple into your medicine cabinet.

One of Lunsford Richardson's relatives describes the following scene from Richardson's childhood.[3] *In a prominent cabin* in the slave quarters on the Richardson family's plantation, there was *an old woman who minded enslaved children while their mothers were busy in the fields.** Every day, without fail, this woman would *come to the cabin door* at noon and *call out "bread and licker."* The children would come running *with little wooden bowls to hold their soup [while] each was given a pone of corn bread.* Among those enslaved children was often a little white one. Richardson thought upon these times fondly, and he *used to say often that he considered it a great privilege when he was allowed to run along with [the enslaved children] and get the same portion [of food] that always tasted much better* than the lunch waiting for him up at the Big House.

This "old woman" was described as Richardson's "Mammy." Negro Mammies were enslaved Black women who did domestic work and who also knew about and drew upon the herbalism within conjure to treat illness. Richardson's Mammy was a *tall, middle-aged colored woman, who, at times administered a much-needed spanking when out of sight of the family.* From his relatives, we find that Richardson spent quite a bit of time with the Negro Mammy on his family's plantation during his childhood—enough time to be disciplined when needed!

In the slave quarters of this Negro Mammy, Richardson would have seen treatments that were far different from those administered by his doctor father (like bloodletting). He would have seen flowers and roots and bark and leaves used for teas to treat colds, coughs, and fevers. He would have seen salves and poultices administered for congestion. And he would have especially seen this Negro Mammy employ the various uses of one of the main active ingredients in his original recipe for Vick's Salve, turpentine. Present in her

---

* Throughout the book, I have italicized quotes that are historical primary sources and folklore. I have used quotation marks for contemporary writers and academics.

teas, salves, and cough syrups, she likely gathered the turpentine herself from his family's plantation, bordered by the large forests of pine trees his father owned. Along the edges of these forests, she would have found a variety of mint plants (like mountain mint and horsemint) that are native to North Carolina and have a natural supply of menthol, another key active ingredient in Vicks VapoRub.[4]

Down in Selma, North Carolina, there is a family that would give this anonymous Negro Mammy a name. Crystal Sanders, a historian at Emory University, told me that her great-great-grandmother, Wiley, was owned by Lunsford Richardson's family. The healing traditions that Wiley passed down through generations in the Stancil-Shepherd family—knowledge of herbs and plants, recipes for teas and salves, and methods for curing colds, burns, and child illnesses like thrush—suggests that Wiley, in fact, had been a Negro Mammy on the Richardson plantation.[5]

In mainstream lore, the story of Vicks VapoRub is that the salve was developed out of desperation, with a bit of luck. In 1894, Richardson had a very sick son on his hands. His young child was suffering from a severe case of the croup, an illness that swells the airways, making it hard for children to breathe. So, with a degree in Latin, a budding interest in chemistry, and all the medical knowledge granted by having a doctor as a father, Richardson retreated into the office of the little drugstore he was running to experiment on something that would save his son's life. What he came up with, just in the nick of time, was the aforementioned Richardson's Magic Croup and Pneumonia Cure Salve, eventually renamed Vicks VapoRub.[6]

But for generations, the Stancil-Shepherd family have passed down a completely different story of the salve's origins that goes something like this: Richardson spends much of his youth under the eye of Wiley, his Negro Mammy, who has an extensive repertoire of knowledge and skills for treating common ills and ailments. Richardson goes away to college while Wiley gives her daughter, Miley Stancil, just a few years younger than Richardson, another kind of education: how to gather herbs from the forest, the recipes for teas, the benefits of salves.

When Lunsford Richardson returns home from college and sets up a local apothecary, his son falls gravely ill. And there was one fateful night when a very worried Richardson took his young, sick son to Miley's house. Miley was known in the county for treating sick children, both white and Black. Richardson's son got well after Miley's treatment, and he was so impressed that he returned to Miley for the remedy. Then, according to the family, he passed her salve off as his own.

During the nineteenth century, many enslaved Black women passed down their herbal recipes for cures the same way they would heirlooms, as Wiley did to her daughter, Miley Stancil. The Stancil-Shepherd family claims that the recipe for the magic salve that earned Richardson millions was stolen from Miley. The drama of these two American families, the Stancil-Shepherds and the Richardsons, is like so many others in the annals of our country's history, where race plays a factor in determining not only the generational wealth a family is able to accrue but also how our lives and contributions are—or are not—remembered.

CHAPTER TWO

"An Old Woman, Who Doctored Among the Slaves"

LUNSFORD RICHARDSON'S LIFE MAY HAVE BEEN THE CLASSIC AMERican dream, but the reality of enslaved Black women who labored on his family's plantation, just outside Raleigh, was an American nightmare. Thanks to Harriet Jacobs (1813–1897), we have a detailed depiction of what slavery in North Carolina was like in the nineteenth century.[1] Jacobs, who wrote under the pen name Linda Brent, was an enslaved woman who made a harrowing escape from her slave owner, Dr. Flint: She hid for seven years in the dark, cramped, insect-infested attic of her grandmother, Martha. Her story tells us about the role Negro Mammies often played in facilitating escapes from slavery.

Conditions were often so bad during slavery that, to escape, the enslaved risked poisonous snakes and alligators that lay in wait in marshes, flesh-ripping bites of hunting dogs, and even death. Throughout her narrative, Jacobs recounts stories of slave masters who routinely whipped, sexually coerced and raped, and withheld adequate food and clothing from the enslaved. Jacobs tells us that these stories of cruelty are *not exceptions to the general rule*; rather, *humane* slaveholders are *like angels' visits—few and far between*. When the enslaved showed even the slightest resistance to such mistreatment, slave masters responded with even more viciousness.

If an enslaved person who was sold on the auction block refused to go with their new master, Jacobs tells us that the enslaved person was *whipped, or locked up in jail, until he consents to go, and promises not to run away during those years.* If an enslaved person tried to run away and was caught, *the whip is used till the blood flows at his feet; and his stiffened limbs are put in chains, to be dragged in the field for days and days!* And if an enslaved woman dared to tell the truth about her light-skinned child's parentage—such as a slave master who raped her—she was liable to be sold to another slave owner and separated from her children.

Sometimes slave owners even took simple acts of care among the enslaved as a challenge to their authority. Jacobs tells us that she was punished when her loving grandmother gave her shoes. Mrs. Flint, Dr. Flint's wife, took exception to the *horrid noise* they made and told Jacobs to *take them off*, threatening that if she ever saw Jacobs *put them on again*, she would *throw them in the fire*.

These shoes were important. Many enslaved people complained about the lack of shoes, a seemingly small thing that had massive consequences for their overall health. Shoes could prevent insect stings and snake bites and various abrasions to the skin from leaves and sticks and pine needles and stones that could cause infections. The care of Jacobs's grandmother, a free Black woman, got under the skin of Mrs. Flint, *grat[ing] harshly on her refined nerves.* Putting Jacobs in her place as a slave, Mrs. Flint made Jacobs remove her shoes, and then Mrs. Flint commanded her to walk *a long distance* in the snow. Jacobs, of course, got sick.

It is heartbreaking to read that Jacobs, then a fourteen-year-old girl, not only went to bed that night believing she would die but was also aggrieved to find out, upon waking the next morning, that she had not passed away.

In her narrative, Jacobs describes how rape, too, was one way that slave masters could attempt to break the will of their slaves. From age twelve, for seven years, Jacobs suffered insults, threats, and even beatings by Dr. Flint for refusing to sleep with him, a man *forty years [her] senior.* When Dr. Flint attempted to seduce her, he also reminded Jacobs that, according to the law, she *was made for his use, made to obey his command in [every] thing,* for she was *nothing but a slave, whose will must and should surrender to his.* Dr. Flint took seriously the power granted to him by the Constitution of the Carolinas in 1669: *[e]very freeman of Carolina shall have absolute power and authority over his negro slaves, of what opinion or religion soever.* For an enslaved girl like Jacobs, that absolute power and authority extended to sex.

Jacobs consistently refused Dr. Flint's advances, but she also understood that there was *no shadow of law to protect her from insult, from violence, or even from death* and that, upon enslaved Black girls, these horrors were often *inflicted by fiends who bear the shape of men.* She also knew she could not trust Dr. Flint's many promises that he would be kind to her if only she would give in to him. Throughout her teenage years, she had observed, time and time again, how slavery *corrupted* white slaveholders: *it makes the white fathers cruel and sensual; the sons violent and licentious; it contaminates the daughters; and makes the wives wretched.* And so, she found herself between a rock and a hard place concerning Dr. Flint's demands. She was doomed if she said no, and she was doomed if she acquiesced. So she decided to escape.

WHEN JACOBS FLED THE PLANTATION run by Dr. Flint's son on a warm, still night, it was a conjure woman who kept Jacobs's escape from ending when it had only just begun. Jacobs had fled to a sympathetic neighbor's house to hide. But when dogs and men rounded the house in search of her, she got so spooked that she jumped out a window. She landed in some bushes, and soon she felt something cold and slimy grab hold of her leg. Without thinking, she struck at it blindly for release. She was bitten in return, rewarded with a painful swelling that weakened her ability to stand.

She waited in the bushes until the men and dogs looking for her had left. Even though she was in dire pain, Jacobs retained enough composure to instruct the friend who harbored her how to treat her leg. Jacobs told her friend to make a poultice of warm ashes and vinegar to reduce the pain and swelling. The poultice brought some relief but not nearly enough. So, her friend turned to *an old woman, who doctored among the slaves* for help. Jacobs's friend was told by this old woman to *steep a dozen coppers in vinegar, over night, and apply the cankered vinegar to the inflamed part*. The old woman's remedy worked. Jacobs was able to stay in hiding for a few more days.

Jacobs then hid for several nights in the Snaky Swamp, which lies on the border of the Great Dismal Swamp. Stretching across the coasts of Virginia and North Carolina, this network of trees and water and islets was home to many enslaved runaways—including those who fought alongside Nat Turner in his 1831 rebellion. (This was the deadliest slave revolt in American history, killing over fifty white people who lived along the shared border of Virginia and North Carolina.) The swamp was a haven for runaways due to its dense foliage, which provided cover. But it was also home to animals that presented significant threats, such as the poisonous snakes after which Snaky Swamp was named.

While Jacobs hid in the swamp, her uncle Philip built a shelter for her in the attic of her grandmother's house. For seven years, Jacobs would live in that shelter: a nine-by-seven-foot-wide space with no airflow and no light (until she bore two small peepholes into the floor). At its tallest point, the shelter was only three feet high, which meant Jacobs could neither stand nor sit up straight. Her children were frequently permitted to visit Jacobs's grandmother. So Jacobs often passed her days lying upon a makeshift bed on the floor, listening for the voices of her children below. At night, rats and mice ran over her limbs, disrupting her sleep. The only relief from the stifling air was her meals, which were passed through the trapdoor of the attic to her by her grandmother Martha, her uncle Phillip, and her aunt Nancy.

While she was in this dismal space, Jacobs tells us that she was *tormented by hundreds of little red insects, fine as a needle's point, that pierced through [her] skin and produced an intolerable burning.* It sounds like, after all she had been through, the poor woman was also suffering from a bedbug infection. Jacobs tells us her grandmother helped her clear up the infection by giving her *herb teas and cooling medicines.*

In the creeping, crawling dark of that cramped attic, Aunt Nancy helped Jacobs maintain her sanity. As the current Negro Mammy of the Flints, Aunt Nancy was *the [factotum] of the household.* Since *nothing went on well without her,* Aunt Nancy was able to pass along crucial news to Jacobs. And it was Aunt Nancy who first emboldened Jacobs to escape. Jacobs tells us that *[w]hen [her] friends tried to discourage [her] from running away; [Aunt Nancy] always encouraged [her].* And it was Aunt Nancy who told Jacobs *never to yield* when she thought *there was no possibility to escape* and considered returning to her master. *A word from [Aunt Nancy] always strengthened [Jacobs],* and it was many a time that Jacobs *kne[lt] down [from the attic] to listen to her words of consolation.*

HARRIET JACOBS'S DESCRIPTION OF *AN old woman, who doctored among the slaves* joins a mighty chorus of others provided by the previously enslaved in interviews compiled by the Federal Writers' Project in the 1930s:

> In South Carolina: *I don' remember what kind of medicines dey use in slavery time, but I know my mamma used to look after de slaves when dey get sick.*
>
> In Georgia: *dere was three old 'omans what Old Mist'ess kept to look atter sick slave 'omans. Dem old granny nurses knowed a heap about yarbs (herbs).*
>
> In Alabama: *dere was always a nurse on de farm, and when a slave got sick dey was righ' dere to give dem treatments. Back in dose days dey used all sorts of roots and yarbs (herbs) for medicine.*
>
> In Mississippi: *when we was sick the old women, they made tea out of some kind of herbs that would cure any little ailment.*
>
> In Texas: *when we gets sick, master he would first go get old negro mammy. She would get her gunny sack and go to the woods and go to getting several kinds of herbs, brings them in and boil them all together.*[2]

These women who disappeared into the woods to make medicines—Jacobs's grandmother, Jacobs's Aunt Nancy, and the *old woman, who doctored among the slaves*—drew upon the herbalism within conjure to treat illness. Another ex-slave in North Carolina, Sarah Louise Augustus, explains that these women who treated the sick with their herbs were called Negro Mammies because one of their primary roles on the plantation was nursing all the children on the plantation—both enslaved and slaveholder. *She was called black mammy,* Augustus informs, *because she wet nursed so many white children. In slavey time, she nursed all babies hatched on her master's plantation.*[3]

When they weren't minding the children whose mothers were off working in the fields, Negro Mammies tended the sick, cooked for the enslaved or in the Big House (the house where the slaveholders lived), assisted births as midwives, or produced textiles such as clothes, quilts, or other household linens. Negro Mammies were often assigned these roles when they were too old to work in the fields any longer, usually in their forties.[4] They learned their trade by apprenticeships that often began in their childhood. Harriet Jacobs herself was being trained as a wet nurse by her aunt Nancy and her grandmother, both of whom had served generations of the Flint family in this way.

As skilled herbalists, Negro Mammies served as the first line of defense in medical care on the plantation. Doctors were usually the last resort, called in if the illness was grave, if the methods Negro Mammies had already tried didn't work, or if there was a bone problem, such as a broken limb. Although some men also knew how to heal with plants, in the nineteenth century this type of care was largely seen as the province of Black women, whose knowledge had been passed down through previous generations of women in their family line.

Enslaved people by and large preferred the medicine offered by Negro Mammies to the care provided by doctors.[5] In their interviews, the previously enslaved also complained about how often slaveholding doctors used medicine to exert even more control over their bodies, like administering medicines to make them vomit to exact punishment for "stealing" food from the master.[6] And Negro Mammies often had a better track record of healing illnesses—especially the chills and fever that came with the flu, the most dreaded ailment on plantations.[7] The massive archive of the Federal Writers' Project is full of stories of how Negro Mammies were able to successfully treat people at times when doctors couldn't. There are stories of fevers that lasted so long doctors gave up, leaving the enslaved for dead.[8] There are stories of births so complicated that doctors walked out on the mothers in despair.[9]

Negro Mammies held a unique position on the plantation in relation to the other enslaved. They were often considered valuable by their masters since they spared their masters an immense loss in "property"—the severe bodily impairment or death of an enslaved laborer. At times, that value spared them from some of the harshest experiences of enslavement, such as whippings.[10]

But Negro Mammies had to negotiate their position carefully. When their advice challenged that of nineteenth-century medical doctors—property-holding white men—they were placed in an impossible bind. If Negro Mammies chose to defy the medical doctors and do what they thought was best for their patient, they often faced punishment.

Even free Black women who practiced medicine were precarious at this time. Eliza Foote, a free Black woman who practiced medicine in Cockeysville, Maryland, was closely watched by the whites in the community. When some enslaved runaways were seen leaving her house, Foote was thrown into jail by these whites. She was *ordered to leave Baltimore County or to be sold into slavery.*[11]

For many white people in the nineteenth century, there was always the fear that Black women could use their knowledge of herbs and roots to harm them when they were most vulnerable, sick, and ailing. And worse, these Black women might use their knowledge to help the enslaved escape, just like the *old woman, who doctored among the slaves,* Jacobs's grandmother, Martha, and Aunt Nancy all did.

But slave masters knew how skilled and effective Negro Mammies were, so they continued to rely upon their labor as healers. And as they worked, negotiating this tense and harrowing contradiction at the heart of American slavery, Negro Mammies managed to develop the recipes for many of the over-the-counter medicines for cold, flu, fever, and minor aches and pains that Americans would continue to rely on for generations.

CHAPTER THREE

Negro Mammies, Botany, and American Home Remedies

To heal, Negro Mammies largely depended upon what they could find in the woods. They cultivated healing traditions from Texas all the way to Virginia, states that form the Coastal Plains of the United States. As part of the same region, the woods that Negro Mammies foraged had similar compositions. Along the edges of these forests, there was often mullein, a fuzzy-leafed weed with bright yellow flowers, and poke roots, a shrub with a cluster of purple berries on red stems that poke out from bright green leaves.

Within the forests, there were pine trees, red oak, and sassafras, which shaded weeds like horsemint (also known as bee balm) and bushes like black cohosh (also known as black snake root). Weaving through these trees and underbrush were freshwater sources, such as waterfalls, creeks, and streams. Sometimes this fresh water swelled and swelled until it produced swamps, like the Great Dismal Swamp in Virginia and North Carolina or the Atchafalaya Basin, a swamp in Louisiana. The similarities of landscape, which included plants, trees, and water ecosystems, helped to yield a consistent tradition of treatment that Negro Mammies employed across both the Gulf and Atlantic Coasts.

Of all the people on plantations, Negro Mammies were the most intimate with the land. From their childhood, they had worked in fields, drawing upon agricultural techniques from their homeland to grow difficult crops like rice.[1] They had snatched bolls of cotton from their prickly ensconce of leaves, dripping blood into soil as they moved from plant to plant. They had cut down walls of sugarcane and shimmied shy ears of corn from their emerald wrappers.

Negro Mammies learned early in their lives that the woods offered a source of solace from the horrors of slavery. There, they could hunt and fish and forage to supplement the meager food rations their slave masters allotted. There, they could worship their god(s) away from the watchful eyes of their masters. Unlike their European counterparts whose folktales paint the woods as a wilderness of evil witches and wolves, big cats and bears that needed taming, Negro Mammies were at ease in the woods. And in this symbiosis of woods and spirituality, Negro Mammies developed medicines for healing.

Their relationship with the woods helped them gain a wide range of botanical knowledge that their slave owners did not possess.[2] As one previously enslaved person put it, white folks during this time would *jest' go through the woods an' [they] don' know nuffin'*. They couldn't identify the plants used for common illnesses like fevers and chills or colds and coughs. White folks did not understand that these plants were *good medicine when you be sick an' dey bring you good luck an' dey gwine git you outten trubble effen you smart 'nuff to use dem*. These white folks—including nineteenth-century medical doctors—were cut off from the language of the forest, rendering the cures they offered subpar to those of Negro Mammies.

HARRIET COLLINS, A NEGRO MAMMY in Houston, Texas, provides insights that help us grasp how conjure influenced enslaved women's botanical knowledge. In an interview with the Federal Writers' Project in the 1930s, Collins tells us that she learned about conjure, which she called *doctoring*, from her mother, an enslaved woman. As with many other Negro Mammies, the healing traditions in conjure were passed down from mother to daughter through generations in her family line. What Collins's mother knew about doctoring, she had learned from *de ole folks from Africa, an' some de Injuns taught her.*

Some of what the Indigenous had taught her mother, as well as Negro Mammies across the South, was knowledge of the local flora. It's likely that the sassafras Harriet Collins uses in her cures was taught to her mother by the Choctaw people in the area.[3] Her mother was able to learn from and expand upon what the Indigenous taught her because her ancestors' West African traditions held similar views about healing, illness, and our relationships. And the Indigenous had comparable language about the land, which made Collins's mother especially attuned to the forest.

Collins's understanding of plants—how to harvest them, when to use them, which ones were toxic, and how much of them to use—was spun within a delicate web of practical experimentation and spiritual mysticism. Her West African ancestors, such as the Yoruba, might have described the threads of this web as the *ashe* that connects all living things. *Ashe* is the divine energy or power to make things happen, a portion of Olodumare (also known as Olorun), the supreme god of Yoruba religion, that flows through everything.[4]

Plants and animals, waterfalls and rivers, humans and the lesser deities called *orishas* all have *ashe*. And for the Yoruba, illness is an imbalance that results in a lack of *ashe*.[5] That imbalance can have many causes: natural causes, such as an imbalance in the blood; social causes, such as falling out with an elder or a sibling; or spiritual causes, such as offending an ancestor or an *orisha*. So a healer has to be prepared to correct imbalance in all areas of a patient's life—natural, social, and spiritual.

This is why Yoruba healers used methods that address the physical symptoms a patient exhibits as well as the social dimensions of their illness. So, if you were seriously ill, your treatment would typically include medicinal herbs, offerings to *orishas*, and a sacrificial meal that was to be shared with your neighbor.[6] The meal with the neighbor was to shore up social support, as the Yoruba believed that interpersonal relationships also play a factor in the patient's health.[7]

In Yoruba society, there were a variety of healers who cared for the sick in the community. You might be treated by a local woman healer, often a priestess or follower of an *orisha*, like the *iyami aje*.[8] It was believed that these women possessed magic or *aje* (due to Oshun), and in Yoruba society, healing is a crucial way that *aje* is expressed.[9] *Aje* also gave these women access to plant knowledge, especially how to use plants for healing or harm.[10] If the sickness was chronic and sustained, you might visit expert diviners, called *babalawo*, or specialized healers, called *onisegun*.[11]

In their attempt to grasp the *ashe* of their medicinal plants, Yoruba healers amassed an extensive array of botanical knowledge. They believed each plant has its own *ashe*, its own "mystery, caprice, and even individual psychology that must be known by the person who is about to pick it."[12] Yoruba healers understood that plants, too, "behave" in certain ways. How you handle and prepare a leaf or stem or flower of a plant—the methods you use to extract their beneficial properties—affects the levels of potency the plant will have when it is administered. So the power for healing sought from plants cannot be harvested without respect for and recognition of the plant's unique *ashe*.[13] Failure to understand the plant's *ashe* can result in harvesting the plant at the wrong time, using the wrong part of the plant for an illness, or, worse, administering a part of the plant that is toxic.

For the Yoruba healer, the plant's *ashe* must be considered not only in relation to the *ashe* of the patient but also the *ashe* of the *orishas*, or lesser deities, as well. The interrelationship between the *orishas* and plants in Yoruba beliefs is shown by the catalog of different herbs, fruits, and roots that are assigned to each *orisha*. Yoruba healers believed that the *orishas* have a special partnership with their associated plants, which results in even more power when they are paired appropriately in rituals. Most notably, Osanyin, the *orisha* of herbalism, inhabits the forest, giving the woods "a spiritual life and power of its own."[14]

Oshun was even more central to healing with herbs. Oshun is the river goddess, whose cool, sweet waters support life on Earth. But Oshun is also a master herbalist, and so, too, are her adherents.[15] The *orishas* Osanyin and Oshun are a powerful duo when it comes to healing. It is said that without Oshun's blessing, the effort to make medicines will fail.[16] Without Oshun's fresh waters, Osanyin's plants cannot heal.[17] There is, perhaps, an even deeper connection between Osanyin and Oshun—forests are a major source of fresh water on the planet. This may be why in Yoruba lore, as Nigerian scholar Oyeronke Olajubu points out, Oshun's eyes *sparkle[s] in the forest, like the sun on the river.*[18] Oshun holds both *the wisdom of the forest* and *the wisdom of the river.*[19]

To heal effectively, the Yoruba healer must balance the *ashe* of Osanyin and Oshun (and any other *orisha* called upon in the healing ritual), plants, the family line of the ill, and the larger community in which the ill lives. To ensure alignment of these various entities, healers must closely observe how each being expresses their *ashe* and reacts to the *ashe* of others, much like a chemist does with substances and primary elements. If the Yoruba healer was successful in this delicate rebalancing, it was believed that the *ashe* of the ill will increase, boosting their recovery.

The need for close observation and recalibration according to the *ashe* of these various entities fostered holistic treatments, where the patient's health was understood within an entire ecosystem of physical, spiritual, and social strata. The Yoruba healer's model of healing—which stressed the interconnection of all aspects of life, a cardinal respect for *ashe*, and a wide range of methods and diagnoses, from skillful herbalism to lay psychology—encouraged a kind of experimentation and empiricism that we often associate with the scientific method. This is why, in some cases, their descendants in the Americas were often more effective than nineteenth-century medical doctors.

ALTHOUGH HARRIET COLLINS DID NOT refer to Oshun in her interview, she did retain West African beliefs about the sacredness of the forest and fresh waters. The bonds Collins developed in the enslaved community through their secret worship and festivities in the forest were just as central to her understanding of health as the herbs and roots she gathered for healing.

Collins learned that when slavery brought on a spell of despair, the forest could fortify your soul. In special clearings of the forest, along with the other enslaved, Collins could engage in the Ring Shout, a counterclockwise dance of African origin. Within this dance, the West African belief in spirit possession was translated into a Christian context. The spiritual and physical world met sonically at the center of the ring, in the joyful dancing of the enslaved person, who was believed to be possessed by the Holy Spirit. And in that moment, away from the eyes of the slave master, the power of their ancestors and their god(s) were drawn upon for strength.

Collins's mother passed down to her this sacred relation to the forest through songs the enslaved sang as they danced the Ring Shout. Collins tells us that, in the forest, her mother sang songs such as "Steal Away to Jesus." This song also served as a code for escape in the Underground Railroad. One need not dig too deeply into the conjure woman's repertoire to find elements of rebellion.

In the fresh waters of the forest, the enslaved were also baptized, dipped into the sweet waters of Oshun. For example, Collins had a deep connection to the Brazos River, which ran along the forest bordering the plantation where she grew up; it was a place of joy. In its waters, she tells us, *I had er lot ob good times. I went fishin' an' to dances an' ter 'vivals.* The bounty of fish, the sensual dances, and the spiritual ecstasy of revivals are all things associated with Oshun's essence, her *ashe*: the sweetness of rivers and streams that bring a lushness to life.[20]

In worship and baptism, dances and fishing, Collins learned the *wisdom of the forest* that Oshun brings. During these forays into the forest, Collins learned how to look for *signs*—strange events, irregularities of nature, riveting dreams or visions—which drew relationships between physical world and spiritual cosmos, plant life and illness, social interaction and misfortune.[21] Under her mother's tutelage, Collins learned that the land, too, had *signs*, and if you knew how to interpret them, you could read the forest like a book, coax healing from the bark of trees, cull poison from leaves.

When she struck her hoe at the base of a tall black cohosh bush, Collins learned to hear the slither of its roots and delight in the snake that gave this plant its nickname: black snake root. She came to feel the hope thrumming through bees as she picked through horsemint and dug under privet bushes. She started to trust in the murmur of weeds like jimsonweed and mullein when she prepared poultices and teas for the sick.

Her West African ancestors would say her mother was teaching her the *ashe* of the flora in the forest. Collins demonstrates this type of knowledge in her instructions for how to deal with mullein, outlining uses for different parts of the plant: the flowers for salves to cure inflammation of rheumatism, the leaves for colds and coughs. The temporal strength of the plant's *ashe* also plays a role in determining when it is best to harvest. Throughout the seasons, the *ashe* of some plants wax and wane in potency. Collins informs us of this dynamic when she instructs that black snake root is to be gathered *in de spring w'en de sap is high*.

Collins also seemed to grasp a relationship between forest plants and fresh waters in the healing traditions handed down to her by her mother. She primarily used water methods—teas and baths—to administer the plants and herbs. Such teas were also a major component of a salve that she made to cure rheumatism. She tells us *you can make er linermint from er tea made by bilin' mullein flowers, poke roots, alum and salt all togedder*.

Even more striking, Collins also observed this relationship between forest plants and fresh waters in her own intimacy with the moon. *When I plant anything I plant it in the moon*, she said. If it's a root plant like potatoes, she planted them *in the dark of the moon*. If it grew *on top of the ground*, like peas, she planted them *in the light of the moon*. It was believed that just as the moon raises the water of the oceans, it also raises the water of the soil during certain phases. Plants that benefit from this extra moisture, like peas, were placed in the ground when the light from the moon is at its fullest. (Some gardeners today still swear by this ancient practice.) While the waters of the ocean are associated with the *orisha* Yemaya, the waters beneath the soil that facilitate the growth of Osanyin's plants are also the sweet waters of Oshun.[22] Perhaps these life-sustaining relationships between the soil and the waters below and the moon high above is why Collins insisted that you ought to treat the moon *lak er lady*. Pay attention to the moods of the moon, from waxing to waning, just like you would a lover.

Collins's understanding of plants went well beyond the piecemeal application of herbs to diseases. She treated the plants as if they existed in an ecosystem, much like her West African ancestors did. She understood that healing was something that must be negotiated in a series of partnerships. For her, these partnerships were wide ranging and included relationships with the sick, with the soil, with the moon, with fresh waters, and, ultimately, with the divine.

WHAT HARRIET COLLINS'S MOTHER LEARNED *from de ole folks of Africa* is not necessarily the term *ashe* but the model of health—of balance negotiated in relationships among humans and the Earth and the divine. *Ashe* framed how Negro Mammies related to the woods, priming them to observe, experiment, and accrue extensive botanical knowledge of all the flora that lived there. And from that base of knowledge, Negro Mammies created recipes for medicines to treat the colds and flus that could kill you in the nineteenth century.

For colds and flus, Negro Mammies turned to teas of various barks, roots, and herbs, including red oak bark, wild cherry bark, dogwood bark, black cohosh, peach tree leaves, chamomile, sage, sassafras, nutmeg, boneset, mullein, and horsemint.[23] These teas tasted horrible. Many of the previously enslaved complained about how awful it was to drink them. But the teas often worked. Some of these herbs, like boneset and horsemint, would hasten a fever's passage. And some of these teas would simply support a patient's immune system—like chamomile, which creates a mild sedative effect and could relax the patient, encouraging the much-needed sleep for recovery.

Sometimes teas were used as a component of homemade cough syrups made by Negro Mammies. For instance, Negro Mammies would take pine tree bark and boil it as a tea to extract turpentine, which soothes congestion. To the turpentine, they would add onions and honey as a rudimentary cough syrup. If pine tree bark was unavailable, vinegar was substituted. One person previously enslaved remarked that this cough syrup was *one of the best cough remedies that [they] know of.*[24] Another ex-slave remarked that this cough syrup *was real good—better than anything these here doctors can give these days.*[25]

Negro Mammies were especially fond of horsemint and mullein. As a member of the mint family, horsemint contains menthol, which not only cools your nasal passageways, providing soothing relief, but also causes you to produce more saliva, flushing out the bacteria or viruses that made you ill.[26] Mullein is an expectorant. It contains an element that loosens up mucus clogging the airways, which makes coughs more productive in expelling bacteria and viruses from the body.

Mullein is also a demulcent, which reduces inflammation or relieves irritation by forming a smooth coating over our mucus membranes. With these chemical properties, mullein was especially useful for coughs and colds. It could assist what your body was *already* doing: coughing and sneezing and dripping all that nasty stuff out of your nose. And perhaps most important, the administration of these herbs by teas restored the vital fluids the body also needed for recovery.

Negro Mammies also used inhalation to prevent catching colds or to ease a patient's suffering. Among the enslaved, the most common method for keeping off chills and fevers, flus and colds in the nineteenth century was to tie a little bag of asafetida around the neck.[27] Asafetida, an expectorant, is a gum extracted from plants in the celery family. It had a smell so pungent that it is seared into the memory of African Americans of my grandparents' generation. My great-uncle, Daniel Perkins Jr., still talks about how much this herb stank when my great-grandmother, Margaret "Booie" Lindsey Perkins, strung it around his neck every winter.

I suspect the theory was that, as the person moved, the asafetida would rub against their neck, sending up fumes that they would then inhale.[28] (The smell was also so bad it kept people away—perhaps the proverbial six feet we've all come to know through COVID.) Sometimes the enslaved would also add camphor or mothballs (which incorporated camphor) to these small bags as well.

It was also common to rely on salves that use both inhalation and stimulation as an external treatment for sore throats and chest pain caused by colds. These were created using teas of herbs mixed with a carrying component, like lard or grease. One ex-slave, whose parents were directly from Africa, remembers a *green salve* for sore throats that *a black woman told [her] how to make*, using *camphor gum and fresh lard*. Another former slave remembers how their mother, a Negro Mammy, *used roots, herbs, and grease, and medicine the overseer got in town. When [her] mother got through rubbin' you, you would soon* be well. And yet another ex-slave remembers *some of de ole folks used "life everlasting," now called rabbit tobacco, for cure of bad colds or pneumonia. Dey boiled it and make a plaster and put it on sore places [of the] chest.*[29]

One recipe for such a salve includes jimsonweed, lamp oil, quinine, turpentine, and camphor.[30] The turpentine and camphor in this recipe are especially noteworthy. The turpentine not only creates a warm sensation when rubbed onto the skin, but it also, when inhaled, can relieve chest congestion. The camphor induces a cold feeling in the nose, which makes it feel easier to breathe when you are clogged up. Turpentine and camphor are not just inhaled when they are rubbed upon the chest during a cold; the massage itself stimulates the turpentine and camphor to produce hot and cold sensations upon the body, which also provides much-needed breathing relief.

This is exactly how Vicks VapoRub works. According to the oral histories of Lunsford Richardson's family, included in the self-published book, *The Annals of an American Family*, the salve's ingredients and mode of application set it apart from other cures for common colds at this time. The source of innovation, according to the family, is the mixture of stimulation and inhalation in the mode of treatment. The salve *rubbed on over the throat and chest... had the stimulative action of a poultice or plaster. At the same time, its medicinal ingredients were volatilized by body heat and inhaled directly to areas of the upper breathing passages.*[31] To be sure, Richardson's "innovation" had already been in use by Negro Mammies for centuries.

CHAPTER FOUR

A Doctor's Visit in the Nineteenth Century

THE GENTLE MEDICAL TECHNIQUES EMULATED IN VICK'S SALVE—inhalation and stimulation—were strikingly different from the methods nineteenth-century doctors preferred to use when treating colds. While Negro Mammies focused on methods that were non-invasive and boosted the immune system, nineteenth-century doctors prioritized methods that depleted the body of fluids, especially blood.[1]

Harriet Jacobs provides insight into the training Lunsford Richardson's father, a medical doctor, would have received and passed onto his son. Her slave master, Dr. Flint, was a medical doctor. Her brother, William, served as an apprentice to Dr. Flint and so was taught the common methods of the day: such as *to put up medicines, to leech, cup, and bleed*. The most popular method during this time, cupping and bleeding, was a form of bloodletting, the process by which doctors withdrew blood from the sick, in hopes of curing them. Over the nineteenth century, this process had evolved from leeches on the skin to cupping and bleeding: scraping the skin with several tiny knives attached to a small wooden box to draw blood, then cupping the skin to capture the flow. They might also apply poultices of mustard to irritate the skin and cause it to blister, so that blood would ooze from the body.²

It is likely that Dr. Flint also taught William the use of emetics, which make you vomit, and purgatives, which make you defecate. Emetics and purgatives were regularly used by doctors in the nineteenth century to make excess or bad humors exit the body of the sick. Dr. Flint likely taught William how to use calomel as well. Calomel, which contained mercury, was believed to aid removal of bad bile from the body by making you puke. Many of the previously enslaved remembered and complained about the administration of "blue mass pills," which were also mercury based.

These methods, especially bloodletting, were often ineffective. Sometimes they worked, but more often they drained the sick of the fluids they most needed for recovery. The experience of blood being taken or substances being forcefully wrenched from your body would also drain you of the physical (and mental) energy needed for recovery. So why did nineteenth-century doctors insist upon these methods?

During Dr. Flint's practice as a physician, the theory of germs, which holds that disease is caused by germs invading the body, was only beginning to gain ground in the medical community. Viruses had also yet to be discovered (that came rather late, in 1898). The main model of health and medicine instead came from Hippocrates, a Greek physician of the fifth century BCE. Hippocrates held that the human body is composed of four basic substances or humors: black bile, yellow bile, blood, and phlegm. To Hippocrates, health is the perfect balance of these humors. Disease is the imbalance caused by an excess or deficiency of one of these humors.

Hippocrates's four humors model was a radical shift in thinking about health for Greek society. He was claiming that the source of disease was not found in the divine, as many fellow Greeks thought, but in the pathology of the body's humors. Sickness, to him, was something that could be mechanically observed and measured. With this system, Hippocrates offered physicians a way of diagnosing, cataloging, and curing sickness without reference to gods and spirits. And doctors like Dr. Flint, centuries later, still held firmly to Hippocrates's insight.

Although Hippocrates named four humors, Galen of Pergamum, a later Greek Roman physician, designated blood as the dominant humor and, thus, the primary cause of disease. So removing blood from the sick was thought to remove the bad or defiled humor that was causing the disease. This is why bloodletting became the dominant method for treatment. And it remained one of the most popular treatments among doctors well into the nineteenth century.

Although both Negro Mammies and nineteenth-century doctors shared the belief that illness is caused by imbalance, their methods to restore balance in the patient drastically differed. While Negro Mammies had a model of healing that stressed cooperation and partnership between the healer and the ailing, dominion came to define nineteenth-century doctors' approach to patients.

For example, the model of health provided by Hippocrates meshed well with the Christianity that many doctors observed during the nineteenth century—including Dr. Flint, who was a devout member of the Episcopal Church. For many Christian doctors, medical healing was seen as the natural outworking of God's command to "subdue the earth." Not only must the Earth be subdued for them to summon medicine from its raw materials, but the symptoms of the patient, too, must be subdued for effective medical treatment: Their pain must be mollified by opium, their bodies forced to expel disease through vomit and defecation. The symptoms of disease, such as coughing and fevers and chills, had to be forcefully overcome.

These symptoms were not seen as the body's attempt to heal itself but as obstacles to healing. Bloodletting and large doses of harsh drugs, as such, became "heroic" methods of medicine.

These methods of medical treatment were widely despised. During the nineteenth century, many people, both Black and white, preferred the gentler methods of administering medicine, such as baths and teas that were plant based. This made Negro Mammies, who reached for plants more often than bloodletting knives, more popular to the American public.

When more influential Americans like Thomas Jefferson began to publicly challenge these heroic methods of medicine, nineteenth-century doctors doubled down.[3] They became dogmatic about defending their harsh methods and the ancient model of diagnosis that supported them. They began to increase bloodletting and their doses of powerful drugs.[4] And if their patients failed to respond to these measures, well, it simply wasn't the will of God that they recover.[5]

American doctors did not begin to change their views until the middle of the nineteenth century. In the 1830s–1850s, a new generation of American doctors trained in Paris. By focusing on human anatomy, incorporating autopsies in the study of disease, and closely observing masses of patients in hospitals, doctors in Paris shed Galen's antiquated model for a clinical approach to treatment. American doctors who had trained in Paris returned to the United States with new tools, and the Civil War that soon broke out gave them a chance to test these methods on a wide scale.

In the South, American doctors had an extra incentive to abandon their old methods—the Union blockade cut off their access to many of the commercial medicines they typically used.[6] So chemists and botanists who had been raised on plantations, like Francis Peyre Porcher, turned to "negro remedies."[7] Porcher began to research the herbs and roots that Negro Mammies used. He soon found that many of these herbs and roots worked, and then he reported his findings in books and medical journals as if these ideas had been his own. Porcher did what slaveholders had been doing for generations before him—passing off the cooking and medicinal recipes of the enslaved as their own in "domestic receipt" books and cookbooks.[8]

Lunsford Richardson grew up in this context of grand medical shifts and intellectual theft. Unlike what he was taught by his father in medicine, Negro Mammies enlisted techniques that made Vicks VapoRub unique on the market of commercial medicines in the late nineteenth century—inhalation and stimulation through massages. And due to their conjure, Negro Mammies also had a superior knowledge of local herbs and roots in the woods than their white medical counterparts. That local knowledge, such as the use of pine trees and mint, was a source of innovation in the development of American medicines like Richardson's Vicks VapoRub.

Given all these factors, along with his close relationship with a Negro Mammy on his family plantation, I'm convinced that the Stancil-Shepherd family's claim that Richardson based the patented Vick's formula on their enslaved ancestor's recipe is due more merit than recorded history has afforded. In fact, their story might be similar to a number of descendants of the enslaved on the Richardson's plantation. During this time, there was often more than one Negro Mammy on plantations who cared for the sick, so it's possible that the salve recipe the Stancil-Shepherd family used was in circulation across the enslaved community. If this were the case on the Richardson's plantation, there's good reason to suggest that the Vicks VapoRub formula had existed in some form in many enslaved families for generations before it was patented by Lunsford Richardson.

CHAPTER FIVE

What History Will We Choose to Remember?

GENERATIONS AFTER SLAVERY, EDWARD SHEPHERD, A GRANDSON OF Miley Stancil, "went to his grave" proclaiming that it was the Stancil-Shepherd family who had actually created Vicks VapoRub. The family claims that he even wrote letters to Oprah Winfrey to bring attention to his family's role in the creation of the beloved American staple. But his family never received the national acclaim he pursued.

The Stancil-Shepherd family shared with me a bit of Miley's healing methods that were passed down through generations from mother to daughter. Juliet (Shepherd) Davis and Velvaline (Shepherd) Sanders remember being taught lessons about the woods and healing by their mother, Victoria (Stancil) Shepherd, who in turn had learned these lessons from her mother, Miley Stancil, who had learned from Wiley.

Juliet learned how important the woods were for healing because her mother "always made us go into the woods—she would say 'go get this or that herb,' and you know what, we knew what it was." Juliet also seems to have inherited the kind of knowledge of plants and herbs that is encapsulated in the Yoruba's concept of *ashe*. She "knew what worked for what, what weeds in the fields and woods." And so, when "[her] mother said go away and get that," both she and her siblings "knew what it was—we just knew what to get. And never one time we went and came back with the wrong thing."

What Juliet learned about the forest was crucial to her family's survival. She explained to me that they "didn't have any money [so they] depend[ed] on stuff from the earth." They had to "rely on what [they] could." When I asked her if she recalls specific herbs and weeds picked from the woods, she told me they often picked up "rabbit tobacco," also called "life everlasting." She also remembers "some kind of mint used for head [colds] and [other] stuff used for colds."

Turpentine was central in their remedies. For colds, they would "take young pine trees—they were reachable, [you] don't see those anymore—[take] the pine top leaves and boil, add honey, and give it by teaspoonfuls." This remedy is a variation on the cough syrup consistent among Negro Mammies across the Coastal Plain, such as a mixture of turpentine, honey or vinegar, and onions.

For aches and pains and coughs that just won't let up, they used salves that "had a little smell to it" along with "a little sting to it when you put [it] on a sore [that] eventually would stop." The salves they described included inhalation (the smell) and stimulation (a precise method of rubbing) and were sometimes used for congestion in the chest, much like Vicks VapoRub. Velvaline remembers that "when they used a salve, they would rub it on the chest with a warm towel that they ironed (no dryers or things like that), and then you couldn't get it wet or go out—you had to wash it off before exposing [your chest] to the air." Juliet also said that they would "rub linoment [or salve] on [their] chests to break up colds." Camphor oil was likely used in this salve. Their brother, Wesley Shepherd, remembered that their mother, Victoria, would rub camphor oil on their chests for colds.

It is said among the family that Juliet was selected to be the guardian of private remedies passed down from Wiley to Miley to Victoria to her, like a West African *griot*. Her remedies incorporate a variety of herbs and roots—from sage to High John de Conquer, the root of the Ipomoea plant, beloved by conjure women for centuries. One of her tonic recipes used "white liquor, rock candy (sold in old 'country stores'), honey, and peppermint." To this day, when anyone is sick in the family, they receive a call from Juliet asking if she should bring this concoction, affectionately dubbed "the stuff."

Peppermint, which the Stancil-Shepherd family had used in this way for generations, is also crucial to this story. In the nineteenth century, peppermint oil was the main source that chemists like Richardson used to derive menthol.[1] The Vicks VapoRub lore is that Lunsford was *the first in this country to experiment with the then new drug, menthol*, which was the principal ingredient of Vicks VapoRub that set it apart from other cold remedies on the market.[2]

The Stancil-Shepherd family told me how the effect of Richardson's alleged theft has reverberated throughout generations of their family. The outcome of this encounter between Miley Stancil and Lunsford Richardson conveys a profoundly dark American story. Richardson and Stancil both came of age in a world of massive social change, when the country ended slavery and segued into Reconstruction. The advent of Reconstruction promised equal opportunity to all entrepreneurs to pursue their dreams. But Richardson and Stancil had very different outcomes.

Richardson saw the gap that Negro Mammies left in the wake of slavery's demise. He saw a large section of the population could no longer rely on the Negro Mammy, for she was no longer enslaved and thus no longer bound to their care. Richardson also knew many in this population still fondly preferred the care offered by Negro Mammies over the expensive and often unpleasant and inefficient treatment of white doctors. He stepped into this gap with Vicks VapoRub, an over-the-counter medicine that not only made dreaded doctor visits unnecessary but also made the Negro Mammy obsolete.

In the development of his salve, Richardson erased the medical contributions—the conjure—of Negro Mammies. Later in life, Richardson, for over twenty years, gave up every Sunday afternoon to teach Bible classes in the Black community in Selma to advance their education.[3] Perhaps he did so out of guilt for how his Vicks VapoRub had cheated Negro Mammies of their due.

While Richardson was amassing wealth off his salve, Miley Stancil managed to make enough money to help maintain the plot of land that her husband's family had given to her and her husband. What Juliet remembers most about her grandmother Miley is that she was an entrepreneur. According to Juliet, Miley was "always trying to do something" and "put[ing] things [together] to make things." She had multiple streams of income, from making candy to sewing clothes to canning fruits. She instilled in her children such values as "work, work, work," "sticking to the guns," and, a personal favorite of her grandchildren, "cash today, credit tomorrow."

Miley was driven and incredibly hardworking, earning enough money to convince her husband, Alexander Stancil, to approach a white man for a loan, in hopes of expanding their property even farther. The white man agreed, and Alexander Stancil worked off his debt. But then the white man said, "No, I don't remember you paying off your debt," and the land was seized and stolen, leaving a harsh lesson to be repeated throughout generations in the family:

"never get anything without a receipt" because white people, during this time, could not be trusted—they had suffered the deep corruption of slavery.

The drama of Miley's family—their generations of grit and hard lessons and incredible contributions to America—is also the story of Negro Mammies as a whole. It is a story of the Black conjure women who cared for and treated and saved us during slavery when we were ill. It was conjure women who made possible the remedy for colds that now sits in your medicine cabinet. And its high past time to give them their due. So when you can't get relief from your incessant coughs, remember them. When your child is sick, late in the night, remember them. When you reach way into your cabinet to grab that little blue bottle to soothe what ails you, remember them.

PART TWO

The Voodoo Queen's Mermaid

CHAPTER SIX

Why Can't Disney's Ariel Be Black?

As a child of the 1980s, the first film I ever saw in a theater was Disney's 1989 *The Little Mermaid*. I could not get enough of Ariel's defiant spirit. Even as a child, I knew what it was like to feel boxed in, to hear the world constantly tell you, "no, you can't do that." I admired that Ariel was courageous enough to disobey the rules she'd been given and travel to a completely different world.

I loved the movie so much that my parents got me a mermaid doll. Representation was important to them, so my parents always got me Black dolls when they could: a Black Kid Sister doll, a Black Cabbage Patch Kid, a slew of Black Barbies. Upon *The Little Mermaid*'s release, my mother spent precious hours after working as a cashier at a small southern grocery store in search of a Black mermaid doll for her daughter, who could think of nothing else but these water women. She finally found one—with a bejeweled fish tail that changed colors under the water. Once I had my Black mermaid, as far as I was concerned, no other doll would do. I spent hours in the bath with her, enthralled by the ever-changing hues. Even though it took me decades to learn Oshun's name, from a young age, it was never a question to me whether mermaids could be Black.

So, I took particular interest in the controversy that arose when director Rob Marshall cast Halle Bailey, a young Black woman, as Ariel in the 2023 remake of *The Little Mermaid*.

I knew to expect the racist backlash. Many white Americans opposed the choice to cast Ariel as Black. They complained loudly on social media, putting forth a gamut of reasons for their outrage: mermaids are underwater, so they can't have black skin; the mermaid in the original story is Danish, so she can't be Black; the 1989 Ariel had red hair, which doesn't occur among Black people naturally; casting Ariel as Black inserts adult political issues into a film for children.

Many African Americans responded with their own social media posts, articles, and media appearances, asserting that representation matters in a world where Black children see so little of themselves reflected in TV and film. Some also pointed out that Danish people (and Europeans, more broadly) do not have a monopoly on mermaid stories. Mermaids appear in mythology all over the world, including the continent of Africa. And there is an incredible story to be told about how Black mermaids came to be a powerful image of rebellion, revenge, and empowerment for millions of enslaved Africans.

Disney missed out on the chance to engage that story in their original release. Instead, their 1989 film is based upon the fairy tale *The Little Mermaid* by Danish author Hans Christian Andersen. Written in 1837, Andersen's tale makes no reference to the slavery that largely shaped his world. Denmark did not abolish the slavery practiced on its Caribbean islands, then called the Danish West Indies, until 1848. Despite its absence from *The Little Mermaid*, Andersen's literary imagination was shaped by the reality of slavery. Andersen not only wrote against slavery in his other work, such as his play *The Mulatto*, but also spent a considerable amount of time throughout his career researching and traveling to the continent of Africa. When Andersen sat down to pen his tale of a little Danish mermaid, enslaved Africans in the New World were busy swapping very different stories about Black mermaids among one another. Largely based upon the 1811 German novella *Undine* by Friedrich de la Motte Fouqué, Andersen's *The Little Mermaid* conveys what mermaids meant to Europeans of the nineteenth century. But what did mermaids mean to the countless Africans who were enslaved in the New World by these very same Europeans?

I want to tell you a story about the mermaids who show up in conjure, and two women who worshipped them in nineteenth-century New Orleans. One woman is the famed Marie Laveau (1801–1881). She was a nineteenth-century Creole of African, European, and Indigenous descent. An illiterate free woman of color, she was dubbed by anthropologist Zora Neale Hurston (1891–1960) as the "queen of conjure."[1] Laveau was a historical figure (who may have, in fact, been not one but two women) who reigned as the leader of Voodoo under the same name during the nineteenth century.[2] In her lifetime, she was believed to be *the most powerful woman there is*.[3] Her death in 1881 was national news, even earning lengthy coverage in the *New York Times*. The other woman is Juliette, an enslaved woman who was drawn into Laveau's inner circle in the middle of the nineteenth century, well into Laveau's reign over New Orleans. In our present-day attempts to justify slipping a Black mermaid into Andersen's Danish tale, we must take a closer look at the water women who laid the foundation of our conjure during the antebellum and Reconstruction periods.

CHAPTER SEVEN

Juliette and the Voodoo Queen

JULIETTE DID NOT FIT OUR CONVENTIONAL STORIES OF SLAVERY. Unlike many of her enslaved counterparts in the United States, in New Orleans Juliette held the special designation of *statu liber*, a legal status dictating that she was to be freed at a later date (when she turned twenty-five). Under Spanish law, this provided a legal pathway to the enslaved to pursue their freedom. Along with the noteworthy *statu liber* status, Spanish law allowed the enslaved to bypass their slave masters and directly negotiate the price and payment for their freedom through the courts in a process called *coartación*.[1] These practices became part of New Orleans's legal code while the Spanish held ownership of the city (1769–1802). Juliette followed the status of her mother, who was also denoted *statu liber*. When the Americans took over New Orleans in 1803, they put an end to *coartación*, but they still, in theory, recognized the legal standing of *statu liber*.

Juliette's best legal pathway to freedom was to await her twenty-fifth birthday. But Juliette also understood that the law could be fickle when it came to the enslaved. She knew it was folly to wait for this law to be honored in a society whose economy thrived on her stolen labor. So, by the time she was a teenager, she had a reputation of being prone to *marronage*, or running away. One slave owner disclosed to another in his sale of Juliette that *[she] absented herself while in his possession.*[2]

Upon entering her twenties, Juliette was brought into a tight-knit network of powerful conjure women in New Orleans. These conjure women practiced Voodoo, a distinctive tradition of conjure that combines Roman Catholicism with many spiritual traditions: Islamic magical charms (*gris-gris*) in Senegambia, spirit-filled amulets (*minkisi*) in the Congo, worship of spiritual deities called *loas* from the Vodou of both Haitians and the Fon people of Benin and Togo, and veneration of spiritual deities called *orishas* by the Yoruba. These conjure women were often called Voodoo Queens. Reminiscent of the *iyami aje*, Yoruba witches who wielded Oshun's power and were known for turning into birds at night, another nickname for Voodoo Queens was *reine des zozos*—"queen of the birds."[3]

Like Negro Mammies, Voodoo Queens in New Orleans drew upon the herbalism in conjure to heal. A nineteenth-century journalist who spent time in New Orleans remarked the *skill of [Voodoo] women in natural medicine is extraordinary and of the highest importance.* He marveled at their *herb-decoctions, tisanes [medicinal teas], vegetable teas, vegetable sudorifics and aperients, vegetable nerve medicines and vegetable cures for the skin*. He was so moved by the efficacy of their herbal remedies that he *tried to induce one [of the women] to give [him] a recipe*. But she turned him away. *It was her secret, she said, which she would only impart to her children.*

There was some overlap in the herbs and plants used by Negro Mammies and Voodoo Queens, but the context of their conjure practices varied greatly. Negro Mammies were often tucked away on rural plantations, while Voodoo Queens were in the heart of a bustling cosmopolitan city. Negro Mammies were enslaved, while

Voodoo Queens were often free Black women. Across the South, over several generations, slave masters tried to make Negro Mammies forget the gods of their ancestors. But Voodoo Queens remembered their African gods—especially the vengeful ones—and called upon them frequently in worship. So, in nineteenth-century New Orleans, slaveholding whites saw Voodoo Queens as a threat—especially when they freely associated with the enslaved, like Juliette.

When Juliette turned twenty-three in 1847, she was sold to Marie Laveau. It may come as a shock to find that there were Black women who owned enslaved people in New Orleans. But as historians note, when a Black person owned a small number of enslaved people—as many of these conjure women did—they were often motivated by a desire to offer protection from a harsh system rather than a desire to greedily benefit from unpaid labor.[4]

This seems to be Marie Laveau's intention with Juliette. From 1847 to 1849, Juliette changed hands with key players of the Voodoo community of the time: not only Marie Laveau, the famed Queen of the Voodoos, but also Sanité Couvreure, a congregant of Betsy Toledano, a notorious high priestess of Voodoo.

By the time Juliette came to these free women of color, it was clear that they were not purchasing a "slave" in any normal sense of the term. Given how often Juliette ran away, she could not be relied upon to perform her assigned duties as a *nounoute* or nanny. In fact, she was "missing" most of the time she was "owned" by Marie Laveau.[5]

Juliette barely lived with Marie Laveau. Instead, she moved in with another woman of color in town, Charlotte Miles. During this time, Juliette "represented herself as free" rather than as Laveau's slave. At Miles's house, she openly hatched plots *with a white Frenchman named Jean who walked arm and arm with her in the street.*[6] Juliette did not appear to be afraid of capture, even though she was an enslaved runaway.

She should have been afraid. The punishments for running away were extreme. First offense: your ears were cut off, and they branded you with a fleur-de-lis on one shoulder. Second offense: your hamstring muscles, imperative to your ability to run with ease, were cut, and your other shoulder was branded. Third offense: you were executed.[7]

A habitual runaway like Juliette should have long been dead before her twenty-fifth birthday under such harsh governance. Perhaps her loose "ownership" by these free women of color, which granted her some protection from these cruel punishments, emboldened her. The behavior of Juliette—an enslaved woman who seemed to do as she pleased—was precisely what most slaveholders in New Orleans feared came from an association with the free women of color who were conjurers.

But Voodoo was too widely practiced for it to be stomped out at the beginning of the nineteenth century. Instead, the Americans tried to regulate it. In 1817, a law was passed restricting gatherings between the enslaved and free people of color in the heavily policed Congo Square, a public square behind what we now call the French Quarter.[8] All other meetings were deemed illegal unless they had been granted permission by city officials. So Voodoo Queens carried on their worship services in secret.

The *Times-Picayune*, a popular newspaper in nineteenth-century New Orleans, reports that the secret Voodoo meetings led by these conjure women brought *the slaves into direct contact with disorderly free negroes and mischievous whites ... to promote discontent, inflame passions, teach them vicious practices, and indispose them to the performance of their duties to their masters.*[9] Such meetings between enslaved and free Blacks were strictly outlawed and subject to frequent raids by the police.

One of these raids holds particular interest for our story. On July 2, 1850, the police raided a Voodoo ceremony held at Lake Pontchartrain, an estuary that lets into the Gulf of Mexico. At that raid, they arrested Sanité Couvreure and three enslaved people she owned on the charge of "unlawful assemblage." In the records, one of those enslaved persons was called Julia. As historian Carolyn Morrow Long suggests, it is likely that this enslaved woman Julia was our Juliette, who had been sold to Couvreure in 1848.

What kinds of things could these conjure women have been teaching the enslaved to make the city so fearful of these meetings? How did their Voodoo make the enslaved "indisposed" to a life of slavery?

Consider a popular Voodoo dance at the time called the Calinda. This dance struck fear into the hearts of slaveholding whites. When performed by enslaved Black men, it became warlike, with sticks brandished in mock fights. When performed by enslaved Black women, the lyrics of the song that accompanied the dance carried veiled threats: *I was a negress / More beautiful than my mistress / I used to steal pretty things / From Mam'zelle's armoir / Dansé Calinda, Bou-doum, Bou-doum / Dansé Calinda, Bou-doum, Bou-doum.*

These play scenes of challenge, from combat to theft, left an eighteenth-century French historian to exclaim that *nothing is to be more dreaded than to see the [negroes] assemble together on Sundays under pretence of Calinda or the dance.* This historian understood that at these meetings where they danced the Calinda, *[the enslaved] sell what they have stolen to one another and commit many crimes. Likewise, they plot rebellions.*[10]

Perhaps the most threatening thing these conjure women taught the enslaved were the *feminine mysteries* they contemplated at their women-only meetings.[11] One of these mysteries was the worship of mermaids. Newspapers at the time report that the police often confiscated mermaid figurines during their Voodoo raids.

Take an earlier raid, on June 27, 1850. The newspapers reported that during this raid, police confiscated a figurine dubbed the Virgin of the Vodous—*a quaintly carved figure resembling something between a centaur and an Egyptian mummy.*[12] The top half of the Virgin of the Vodous was human, like a centaur; the legs of the bottom half were sewn together, like a mummy. Or like a mermaid's tail. The Virgin of the Vodous was remarkably similar to a figurine that had been confiscated during another police raid just a few decades earlier, on August 16, 1820, which newspapers described as *a woman with the lower extremities of a snake.*[13] In both cases, these confiscated figurines were half women, half aquatic animal (a water snake or fish), like mermaids.[14]

Shortly before the Civil War, the police and conjure women in New Orleans were embroiled in a decades-long fight over the possession of these figurines. You may wonder why the police even bothered to take these mermaid statuettes at raids when they had much bigger issues to attend to, such as enslaved and free people of color plotting to overthrow slavery. But this decades-long altercation holds the key to understanding how conjure came to lie at the heart of racial and gender dynamics in New Orleans. This mermaid figurine, a symbol of nineteenth-century New Orleans Voodoo, is the culmination of a very long relationship between conjure and slave rebellions across centuries in the United States.

CHAPTER EIGHT

Mermaid History

IN THE NINETEENTH CENTURY, THE WORSHIP OF MERMAIDS IN BLACK communities spanned the Gulf and (lower) East Coasts, from New Orleans all the way to South Carolina. Mermaids were especially venerated by the Gullah Geechee people. They were descendants of the Yoruba, Ibo, Senegambian, and Ovimbundu, who had been kidnapped for their labor and expert knowledge of rice and indigo production.[1] Their isolation on the southeastern coast and islands gave rise to tight-knit communities that preserved much of their West African and Central African heritage. A key part of their heritage was the *simbi*, water spirits of the Congo who took the form of mermaids, sowing messages of freedom and rebellion among their worshippers.[2]

There's an old folktale passed among the Gullah Geechee about a mermaid who caused a rebellion in the 1850s, about the same time that Voodoo raids were increasing in New Orleans. At the turn of the twentieth century, Arminta Tucker, a Black nurse in Charleston, South Carolina, relayed this story to folklorist and writer John Bennett, who popularized the tale as "The Apothecary and the Mermaid." In a 1907 *New York Times* article, Tucker confirms that this story had been passed down through generations in the Black community in

Charleston, so [a]ll them old people can tell you about [the mermaid]. Yes, Sir; that is the mermaid history.[3]

During the summer of 1853 in Charleston, South Carolina, a white male doctor by the name of Dr. William Trott set up a new apothecary shop. Dr. Trott rose early, hung an open sign upon his door, and waited all day for the bell above the door to ring. He was anxious for customers. As soon as he had a few people try his medicines, he knew word of mouth would spread through the community. Perhaps rumors of his exceptional products would reach the ear of a wealthy slaveholder in need of his services.

His disappointment grew day by day as he watched townsfolk walk up and down the street without ever sparing a glance toward his shop. For a week, there were no customers. On the eighth day, when his first customer, a white woman, finally entered his shop, he leaned across his pharmacy counter and asked why more of the town had yet to stop by.

She raised her eyebrows at him. "Bless your heart—you don't know?"

He shook his head. She looked over her shoulder and told him that most of the people in town went to a Gullah Geechee conjure woman, an old *calabash-colored woman from Cow Alley*.

It wasn't just enslaved Blacks and their slaveholders who relied upon this conjure woman. Charleston had a large population of free Blacks, and they also went to her. And even the poorer whites in town preferred her. During the yellow fever outbreaks, she had built up an impeccable reputation for her healing methods. Those who had survived the outbreaks reported how helpful this conjure woman had been during those trying times of incessant bells ringing the dead, muddy carriages carrying bodies festering under family quilts to mass graves, the stench of sulfur and sweat and bloody vomit, ever rising from the streets. And those who survived the epidemic could tell you how people who saw doctors, more likely than not, fared much worse than people who saw this woman who gave them teas and massages to help them get through the worst of the fever. She did not bloodlet or leech her patients as the doctors in those days typically did. And she was more affordable to boot.

When Dr. Trott heard that this conjure woman serviced most of his potential customers, he grew incensed. A Black woman who had never been to medical school—whose medical practice, to his mind, was built on superstition and magic rather than science—was stealing his business right out from under him. So he decided to try to beat her at her own game. He began to advertise a free magic show at his shop, which would feature a live mermaid, among other aquatic specimens.

Even without the mermaid, the sight of colorful tropical fish would have delighted his customers—aquariums were uncommon at this time. But with the mermaid, he hoped to persuade the townsfolk that he, too, had access to the same divine power that this conjure woman claimed to have. Sure enough, guests began to trickle into the shop on the third day of the show. In Charleston, they were surrounded by water from the coast, but those who lived there had never interacted with the inhabitants of the sea in such an intimate way. On that day, they stepped right up to frogs and seahorses and fish in glass cages, privy to their once secret watery underworld.

Those who were bravest wandered to the back of the shop, into the dark room that housed the mermaid. Dr. Trott lifted a sheet covering the largest aquarium in the shop. Potential customers squealed as they saw a huge tail dart quickly among the tall plants in the tank. Dr. Trott grinned and quickly covered the tank back up, assuring them that they had just glimpsed a live mermaid. The visitors left the shop in a whirl of excitement, spreading the word about the mermaid throughout town.

That evening, it began to storm. But it was not like other storms that the townsfolk were used to. Sturdy roofs teetered upon their house hinges. Oak trees that had stood proudly for centuries relinquished their roots in the blink of an eye. Folks in town leaned out their windows and saw their neighbors' prized keepsakes floating side by side with cockroaches and drowned rats down the street. At this sight, a *[w]izened old wom[a]n began to shriek inarticulate prophecies of vague but terrible disaster.*

The Gullah Geechee conjure woman *professed knowledge* about what was behind the storm; she knew she had to forewarn the community. All evening, she *walked down streets prophesying that the city would continue to drown until the mermaid [from Dr. Trott's shop] was returned to the sea.* She told anyone who would listen that the storm had arisen because *the mermaid had a baby in the sea,* and that, *until she was released to go back to nurse her child, the rain would continue to fall.*

If the townsfolk had bothered to ask her, she could have told them something bad was coming the moment Dr. Trott began to advertise the free magic show. That day, she went to the marsh to gather sweetgrass to make decorative baskets to sell in town at the market. And she'd seen signs of the coming storm. The rising buzz of mosquitos in anticipation of rain. The cattails that rattled in violent wind. The cypress trees that rocked on their knees as they whispered to their neighbors of the coming waters.

She knew all about the fragile balance of land and sea and the mermaids who dwelled in the murky in-between. She gained this knowledge from the *wizened old women* who had taught her how to weave baskets of sweetgrass, in the tradition of their West African ancestors.[4]

When she was a child, the conjure woman had helped the old women in their basket-weaving tasks. As she passed pieces of sweetgrass to the old women, she likely heard stories about mermaids who were as beautiful as they were vengeful. In South Carolina folklore, there are stories of mermaids who dwell in many of the rivers like the Saluda, Congaree, and Edisto.[5] These mermaids bring good luck to those who are good to them and drown towns that offend them. In these tales, some of the mermaids even fall in love with humans and have children with them.

These mermaids also have a special love for children, and sometimes they snatched them from the world of the living, bringing them to their own watery depths for company. Down Rainbow Row, just a few short blocks from Cow Alley where the conjure woman lived, there was talk of a mermaid who took a young girl named Sarah for her own. Every night, the mermaid would take on legs and sit out on a porch with a golden comb, like that of Oshun. The comb, glinting in the moonlight, caught Sarah's attention. Tired of seeing the mermaid disappear every evening, Sarah decided to follow her to the river one night. Sarah never came back home.

Given how fond these mermaids were of children, the conjure woman understood that the mermaid held captive in Dr. Trott's shop would raise hell because she was separated from her baby. So she took care to continue spreading the rumor about Dr. Trott's captive mermaid among the women she treated both near and far in the area as the storm raged on. Many enslaved Black women could relate to the forceful separation of mother and child. Some of them had had babies ripped from their arms by their slave owners. These women, in turn, told their families about the captive mermaid. Soon the whole town was in an uproar.

Folks in town began to drop into Dr. Trott's shop, sopping wet, to complain about the mermaid and urge him to return it to sea. Annoyed by the complaints, Dr. Trott turned to the authorities. He blamed the conjure woman for causing a panic in the town. So the police collected the conjure woman from the streets.

But the rain continued. The police could not help but be rattled by the conjure woman who thundered her warnings to them from the cell. A strange wind shook the bars of the jail as she looked the police dead in the eye and *vowed that the city would sink beneath the sea unless she herself was immediately released from the jail and the mermaid returned to the deep.*

The police released her from the jail.

Dr. Trott continued to brag about the mermaid in his shop. So, just as the conjure woman forewarned, the rain continued. The wind battered buildings that had been erected upon the city's founding. Children drowned in the water surges while their parents lost precious heirlooms in the flood. The smell of rotting fish remained upon the air day and night.

The Black population knew all too well the dangers posed by *a mermaid ashore*, a mermaid who had been displaced from her home and her family in the sea. They began to despair for the mermaid's fate. They knew all too well that, in the Carolinas, the law gave slave masters *absolute power and authority over [their] negro slaves.*

Many enslaved women, like Harriet Jacobs, knew firsthand that slave masters meant to exert that power and authority over the most intimate parts of their bodies as well. Slave masters saw Black women's wombs as property: Our wombs were theirs to meddle with, and the fruit our wombs bore was theirs to sell. And in the first few decades of the 1800s, Black communities had witnessed the rise in ghastly fascination that slave owners and doctors exhibited toward Black women's wombs.

When the United States banned the transatlantic slave trade in 1808, slave owners could no longer rely upon a steady stream of enslaved people from Africa to increase their "property." So slaveholders began to greatly increase their efforts to force enslaved women to bear more children. And they often enlisted doctors in their endeavors to shore up their "investment" in Black women's wombs. Doctors were brought in to verify that a woman was physically fit enough to bear children, to handle complications that arose during labor, and to find cures for infertility.[6] In the course of their treatment, these doctors performed dangerous, and often deadly, surgeries on enslaved women, like C-sections.[7]

Facing such callous carelessness from doctors, perhaps it is no surprise that the Black population believed, as the rain continued on, that the mermaid was dead, never to be reunited with her baby. They supposed that Dr. Trott had, like so many other doctors, experimented on her and killed her.

But the conjure woman insisted that the mermaid was alive. Instead of despairing, she began to organize the Black people in town for a protest. On the thirtieth day of the storm, the Black people in town stormed Dr. Trott's shop. The conjure woman, along with two other community leaders, Old Man Rutter and William Holmes, led the charge. They pounded on the doors to the apothecary shop and demanded that Dr. Trott come out. And he did, trembling as he swore to the crowd that there was no mermaid in his shop.

This outraged the crowd more. They began to yell *Bring out the mermaid!* and pressed toward the shop as if to go in and free the mermaid themselves. Dr. Trott kept insisting that there was no mermaid to be found. The crowd yelled louder, *There is a mermaid! Bring her out. Send her back to sea.*

Perhaps fear of escalation of the crowd is why the city capitulated to the demands of the free and enslaved Black population, agreeing to send people into the shop to search for the mermaid. Some of the city officials may have had a living memory of Denmark Vesey's revolt in 1822. Vesey bought his freedom and then won the lottery. Inspired by the Haitian Revolution in 1791, Vesey decided to use his income to fuel a rebellion and free the enslaved in Charleston.[8] Although they successfully tamped down the revolt, whites in Charleston were still afraid of another racial uprising. And they had good reason to be. Blacks were nearly half the population of the city—and many of those Blacks were free, like Denmark Vesey.

Two white city leaders pressed toward the front of the crowd. They, along with Old Man Rutter and William Holmes, went in to search the shop. It was an easy enough request for the city to grant. The city did not believe in mermaids. It was easy, so easy, to focus on the literal request of the people rather than hear the political message that seemed to be at its heart: stop separating enslaved Black women from their children.

Hours later, the men emerged from their search of the shop and told the crowd that they did not find a mermaid. But some claimed that if the men had only *more closely scrutinized the top shelf in the apothecary's back room they might have seen the mermaid there, shrunk to about a span long, swimming in a jar.* Those who whispered this explained that the mermaid, *having been so long out of her native sea water,* had simply *shrunk to a creature of no greater bigness than the size of a frog; that she had been there all the time in a bottle on the shelf.*

This is in keeping with how many West African religious

traditions conceptualized mermaids. According to the Yoruba, Oshun can take many forms, from an old woman to a beautiful mermaid. The Congolese also believe that the *simbi*, powerful water spirits, can take the form of mermaids, as well as many aquatic creatures, including frogs, snakes, and water beetles.

This might explain why many in the Black population claimed that the mermaid had, in fact, been released on the day of the protest. When the searchers came out of the shop, a strong wind came through and ripped the roof off Dr. Trott's apothecary. The wind continued to howl as it turned over the aquariums. Out came snakes and frogs who slithered and hopped back to the river. Shortly after Dr. Trott's roof blew off, the rain stopped. For those who recognized the many forms these water spirits can take, the mermaid had indeed been released back to the sea—as one of those creatures making their way back to the river. So the storm finally ceased.

In this story, the mermaid calls attention to the harms Black women experienced under slavery.

And across the South, mermaids play a similar role: They arise to avenge the social imbalances that slavery caused—the terrible things Black women endured, like being separated from their children. The conjure woman's knowledge of herbs and roots gave her a position of authority in her community that she galvanized for social protest. And in the 1850s, this is how conjure women who worshipped mermaids became figures of rebellion and vengeance, unifying Black communities across the country, strengthening us in our fight against oppression.

CHAPTER NINE

Conjure Fuels Rebellions

SLAVE OWNERS KNEW THERE WAS AN INTIMATE CONNECTION BETWEEN the practice of conjure and the rebelliousness of the enslaved. Frederick Douglass, the most famous ex-slave who led the abolitionist struggle, was carrying a conjure root when he successfully fought off a slave overseer who tried to whip him. Harriet Tubman, who helped hundreds of slaves escape along the Underground Railroad, was widely known for her healing knowledge of herbs and roots, as well as her spiritual visions. And many of the large-scale slave revolts in the United States were fueled by conjure. From the 1712 slave revolt in New York and the 1742 slave revolt on the slave ship the *Jolly Batchelor* to the ones led by Denmark Vesey and Nat Turner in 1822 and 1831, those who led these rebellions drew inspiration from practices steeped in conjure: visions and prophecy, plants and rootwork, oaths and spells.[1]

The fears of American slaveholders regarding conjure and rebellion were most fully realized in a revolt that took place off United States soil: the Haitian Revolution (1791–1804), which still stands as the greatest and most successful slave revolt in the Western Hemisphere. It was widely known that a Vodou ceremony sparked the revolt of the enslaved in Haiti, then French-owned Saint-Domingue.

Under the cover of night, men led by Priest Boukman swore a blood oath to one another to "overthrow the French."[2] This blood oath nourished the courage of the enslaved, for it moved the enslaved to believe that "their deities [had] made them invulnerable." For the enslaved, the veneration of their gods was key to their fight. One particular deity, the Haitian Vodou *loa* Erzulie, who sometimes takes the form of a mermaid in Haitian lore, was believed to have *fought in the ranks with the soldiers of the war for the Independence of Haiti against Napoleon's armies as artillerymen and as prostitutes who instructed the insurgent slaves.*[3]

The success of the Haitian Revolution at the turn of the nineteenth century sent shock waves through Western civilization that still reverberate today. In the United States, many whites still view Haitian Vodou as a political threat. These whites fear that, should this religion gain a foothold in America, Black people will seize power and bring chaos. I suspect this is why, in the 2024 presidential debate, Donald Trump invoked the baseless rumor that Haitian immigrants in Springfield were stealing people's cats and dogs and eating them.[4] He was insinuating that Haitian immigrants were performing animal sacrifices as part of secret Vodou meetings.[5] Making these claims in the middle of a debate opposite our first Black and South Asian woman presidential candidate, Kamala Harris, sends a warning signal to white Americans: If this Black woman gets elected to office, chaos will ensue—just like in the Haitian Revolution. Given the history of Haitian Vodou and African American conjure women, it's not a surprise to me that white people of the far right have said that Kamala Harris's career-long success is due to "witchcraft."[6]

THOSE WHO FLED HAITI DURING the revolution brought their gods with them to New Orleans in 1809. No wonder the largest slave revolt in the United States occurred just outside New Orleans only a few years later, in 1811. Charles Deslondes led hundreds of enslaved people in revolt along the stretch of plantations that hugged the Mississippi River near New Orleans, nicknamed the German Coast of Louisiana.

The sudden influx of Haitians in New Orleans at the beginning of the nineteenth century had strengthened the legacy of insurrection that was already present in the area. For along the German Coast were maroon camps—settlements established by runaway enslaved people—where the inhabitants still remembered San Malo, their fearless leader who'd led a string of slave rebellions in 1784. San Malo's memory was preserved through New Orleans Voodoo in the following century, where he was worshipped as St. Maroon, the patron of enslaved runaways.[7]

It is against this backdrop of slave rebellions that the Negro Mammy, the enslaved conjure woman of the South, transforms into the "evil" Voodoo Queen of New Orleans during the antebellum and Reconstruction periods. The conjure that the Negro Mammy worked—nursing the sick and assisting births—was considered valuable when it contributed to the economy of the plantation. This is why, in proslavery literature, you find the authors taking such pains to paint the Negro Mammy as a loyal figure, whose life and desires and aims are all tied to the plantation, the master, and his family. Those in favor of slavery desperately wanted to believe that the Negro Mammy was *actually part of the household, enjoying the glory of the family when it came or suffering its hardships and disappointments*. Such writers insist that the *Mammy of the Old South was not a voodoo character*.[8]

But the reality is that Negro Mammies had an extensive knowledge of plants that could be used to harm their masters, from temporary paralysis to poisonous deaths. They knew exactly how much of these roots, barks, and flowers to administer to achieve the results they wanted. Slaveholders knew this as well. Throughout the eighteenth and nineteenth centuries, there was a flurry of court cases where enslaved conjurers were accused of poisoning their masters. Subsequent laws were introduced to restrict when and where it was appropriate for the enslaved to practice conjure. This meant that the practice of conjure by Negro Mammies was only considered legitimate when they "practiced under the knowledge, direction, and order of whites."⁹

The brewing tension between conjure women and slaveholders was brought to a head in the city of New Orleans in the decades before the Civil War, where there was a sizable population of free women of color who had regular interactions with the enslaved. Unlike Negro Mammies in other parts of the South, the free women of color who practiced conjure by way of Voodoo were not tied to the plantation. There was no slaveholder to curb their magic, no slaveholding family to hem in their wishes. These free women of color could use their conjure as they pleased. So they posed a significant threat to slaveholders. Imagination abounded among the white people; slaveholders wondered: Would these women equip the enslaved with poison, so they could turn on their masters? Would these free women of color encourage the enslaved to escape? Would they harbor runaways, like Juliette? Regardless, something must be done.

On the eve of the Civil War, the city of New Orleans largely discharged the task of containing these conjure women to the police force, the Third Municipality Guards. But by then, the police were far too late to rein in the threat of social rebellion. The incredible social unrest in New Orleans had begun long ago.

The Third Municipality Guards were responsible for policing a city that had seen government turnover multiple times between the seventeenth and nineteenth centuries. New Orleans was ruled intermittently by the French (1682–1762, 1801–1803) and the Spanish (1763–1801). And when the Americans arrived in 1803, having bought the territory from Napoleon in the famous Louisiana Purchase, New Orleans, then the capital of Louisiana, was wildly out of step with other American cities in terms of racial dynamics, gender relations, and religious traditions.

In New Orleans, Americans were confronted with a Black population that was more autonomous than its counterpart in many other slaveholding states. Much of this was due to the differences in slavery practices observed by the French, Spanish, and Americans.[10] Under French rule, the Code Noir largely established the rules regarding how the enslaved were to be treated. As you might expect, there were some harsh restrictions in the Code Noir. Enslaved people could not carry weapons or gather in large groups on their own or trade products or make money or testify against a white person in court.

But enslaved people also had some small measures of autonomy, such as time off on Sundays and holidays. And, under French rule, it was prohibited to sell children under the age of fourteen away from their parents.[11] Keeping families together and allotting them time off gave the enslaved the space to uphold and further pass down their own cultural (especially religious) traditions.

These aspects of French slaveholding practices greatly contrasted with how slavery proceeded in the British colonies. In the Constitution of the Carolinas in 1669, it was stated that *[e]very freeman of*

Carolina shall have absolute power and authority over his negro slaves, of what opinion or religion whatsoever. This "absolute power and authority" meant that there were no limitations or guidelines that outlawed mistreatment of the enslaved by their masters. Infants could be sold away from their mothers; enslaved men and women could be put to death at merely the whim of the master.

Spanish rule was by far the most liberal.[12] Under the Spanish Codigo Negro, many legal paths of manumission, the release from slavery, were provided. And unlike the Code Noir, the Codigo Negro also granted enslaved people the right to conduct business and hold property. Under Spanish rule in New Orleans, many of the enslaved managed to amass quite a bit of wealth—enough, even, to free themselves. The number of free people of color quadrupled under the Spanish, from 7.1 percent of the New Orleans population under French rule to 33.5 percent under the Spanish thirty-eight-year rule.

With the large amount of social mobility among Blacks in New Orleans, a tripartite racial class system emerged: enslaved Blacks, free Blacks and Creoles known as *gens de couleur libre* (or free people of color), and whites. In contrast, the rest of the United States informally followed what we now call the "one-drop rule" of racial classification, where any African ancestry designated you as Black. Under the one-drop rule, race is binary: You are either Black or white. And if you were Black in a slaveholding state, you were most likely enslaved.

But in New Orleans, there was flexibility. Free women of color, who greatly outnumbered free men of color, largely benefited from this tripartite system. And under the civil law of the French and the Spanish, these free women of color were able to not only keep their maiden names but also their property when they chose to marry—unlike the majority of white women in the United States at the time, where common law was still practiced.[13] (Common law, unlike civil law, gives all authority and property to the male head of household.) Many of these free women of color were also largely successful business owners, and their positions of esteem in the Catholic Church lent them a robust network of clients. They attained a position of such high esteem in New Orleans society that whites sought to curtail them.[14]

In 1786, the Spanish introduced a law specifically designed to mark free women of color as inferior to whites.[15] This law required that free women of color "dress in a manner befitting their subordinate status." Specifically, free women of color were ordered to comb their hair *flat, [covered] with a tignon*; they were strictly forbidden to *wear feathers, [or] curls in their hair*. A tignon was the headscarf enslaved women were also required to wear at this time. Even though these women of color were free, they were required to wear it to mark their "inferior" African origins, creating social distance between them and their white women counterparts.

While their public lives were systematically shrunken, these free women of color were at the heart of New Orleans Voodoo. Unlike the patriarchal structure of Haitian Vodou, the Voodoo in New Orleans was matriarchal. These free women of color were spiritual leaders of their community, and the secret Voodoo meetings they led were the worst nightmare of the Americans, who feared that the mixture of racial classes would especially foment revolt.[16] The Americans did not understand the gods these women worshipped, but they knew well enough that where Black mermaids went, so, too, came rebellion.

CHAPTER TEN

Oshun, Mami Wata, and a Pantheon of African Water Deities

On the evening of June 27, 1850, Captain Mazaret of the Third Municipality Guard raided a secret Voodoo meeting at a house tucked deep into the woods. He arrested eighteen women on the charge of the "unlawful assemblage" of white women, free women of color, and enslaved women. But he was unable to arrest Marie Laveau, the Queen of the Voodoos, that night.

Captain Mazaret was probably disappointed that the Queen of the Voodoos escaped his grasp, but the mermaid figurine he confiscated instead was no mere consolation prize. It was highly valued by the women in the New Orleans Voodoo community. Scholar Denise Alvarado has argued that this mermaid figurine, the Virgin of the Vodous, was important because it was a representation of Mami Wata, a powerful water deity worshipped among enslaved people across the African diaspora.

Mami Wata arose within the context of the transatlantic slave trade, where she served a very specific purpose for the enslaved: rising to avenge the horrific injustice of slavery. She was able to take on this role for the enslaved due to her origins, which are much, much older than the slave trade. In fact, Mami Wata is intimately connected with the Yoruba *orisha* Oshun.

When the *orisha* Oshun touched down in the Caribbean in the sixteenth century, she settled into the form that her followers needed most. Over previous centuries in West Africa, Oshun appeared in myths and images as a peacock and a vulture, a sensuous young lady and a stately old woman. Occasionally, she appeared as a beautiful woman in a river with a mysterious fish tail. And this is how Oshun became known to the millions of enslaved Africans who landed in Cuba, Haiti, Jamaica, and even New Orleans, often considered the northernmost point of the Caribbean.[1]

During the sixteenth century, Oshun merged with other water spirits that Africans brought with them to the Caribbean. There was the *simbi* from the Congo, who support, protect, and preserve social order in communities that honor them.[2] *Simbi* were believed to live in "watery domains such as streams, rivers, lagoons, springs, waterfalls, marshes and whirlpools."[3] In Congolese mythology they took the form of persons, mermaids, pythons, calabashes, aquatic plants, parrots, and insects that live in or near water, such as mosquitoes. Most often, though, they were depicted as snakes.

Among the Fon of Dahomey, there were the duo water spirits Damballah and Ayida Wedo, who helped the supreme god, Mawu-Lisa, create the world. Both Damballah and Ayida Wedo take the form of water serpents. It's said that when Damballah, a male snake, shed his skin, he caused the first rain to fall upon the Earth. With the first rain came the rainbow that represents Ayida Wedo, the goddess of fertility, water, and serpents.[4]

Between the sixteenth and nineteenth centuries, over generations of cultural exchange among these various West and Central

African groups, the Indigenous of the Caribbean Islands, and their European counterparts, Mami Wata was born. Mami Wata shares many of Oshun's traits, especially her beauty, ferocity, and love. She is a comforting mother and a fierce warrior. She is a tide of good fortune and has the wits needed to ride those waves of wealth from grace to glory. She wields a mirror that reflects her seductive beauty. But that beauty, too, can be a weapon; it is said to disarm her foes as she drags them down to her watery depths, never to be seen again. She is a fantastic lover who will end you if you cross her. She is the waters that heal the sick and bring comfort to those troubled in spirit. Mami Wata carries lessons of love and vengeance in her tail, which winds from Africa all the way to the Caribbean. And from the start of the transatlantic slave trade, she has offered that tail to Black women in need of power. Like Oshun's *iyami aje*, the conjure women who invoked Mami Wata were considered powerful healers in both the physical and social realms of their communities.

Mami Wata strongly resonates with Oshun. But Mami Wata also represents more than Oshun. In depictions of Mami Wata, she not only carries Oshun's mirror, she also carries the water serpents who were worshipped by the Congolese and the Fon of Dahomey.

Haitian Vodou, which was developed over the sixteenth to nineteenth centuries, especially carries all the traces of this merging of Yoruba, Congolese, and Fon mythology. Mami Wata was syncretized with Erzulie, a family of *loas* who bear a striking resemblance to Oshun. Many of the *loas* of Haitian Vodou were not only derived from the Congolese but also from the Fon of Benin (ancient Dahomey). The Fon people were neighbors to the Yoruba, and as a result, the gods of the Fon (the *rada* in Haitian Vodou) merged with the gods of the Yoruba (*orishas*).⁵ So the *loa* family Erzulie has traits of Congolese gods as well as Oshun.

Erzulie is the goddess of love, and her various manifestations as Erzulie Freda, Erzulie Danto, and La Siréne embody different aspects of that emotion.⁶ Erzulie Freda is beautiful, sexy, and flirtatious. She can "grant you favors when she loves you but can quickly be enraged when she feels offended, spurned, or neglected." Erzulie Danto is the darker side of love, a warrior, and vengeful, preferring a dagger to the sweet thrills and trifles of Erzulie Freda. La Siréne is the mermaid form that the *loa* Erzulie takes when she abides in water. As La Siréne, Erzulie is both loving and cruel. She can bring you good luck just as easily as she can drown you. Like Oshun, La Siréne "carries a mirror in one hand and a comb in the other," and in the Caribbean, she is also known as Mami Wata.

Erzulie is also associated with snakes, which may be where the serpent coiled on Mami Wata's arm comes from. Snakes hold a central place among Haitian *loas*, representing their supreme god, Damballah, who not only absorbed the Fon god of the same name but also the Bantu-Congo's most high god, Nzambi.⁷

It was possible to merge these various African water deities into the figure of Mami Wata because they all share an important function in Yoruba, Fon, and Congo cosmologies: guarding and maintaining social harmony. When the balance of social harmony was upset, such as a community member committing an offense, it was thought these water spirits would send devastating waters to right that imbalance. This is why water spirits were considered as dangerous as they were alluring. The waters that nurture us, the streams and rivers and lakes, can also become the water that kills us—the rain that drowns, the hurricane that destroys. Accordingly, in these mythologies, water deities were known for their hunger for vengeance just as much as for their seductive comfort.

There is, of course, a long tradition of mermaid imagery in European lore, as in Andersen's *The Little Mermaid* and the Greek sirens of old. European mermaids also tended to be vengeful, like these West African water deities. But the context of the transatlantic slave trade provides an important political dynamic to this cross-cultural lore about mermaids. Mami Wata encompassed all the water deities that the enslaved brought with them on the ships, which means that the mermaid Mami Wata was a pantheon of African water deities, condensed into the single plea of millions of kidnapped Africans tossed upon the sea: "Mother of the Water. Please. Help me."

The fact that kidnapped Africans turned to this mermaid figure when they crossed the Atlantic attests to their protest of the disruption of their communities, the ripping apart of families and kin networks as they were sold across the waters.[8] Mami Wata embodied their protest because, like the other water goddesses the enslaved knew from their home in Africa, she could be called upon to avenge these horrific social wrongs.

This vengeance was sometimes quite physical. Some estimate that open rebellions by the enslaved occurred on at least one in ten slave ships that journeyed across the Atlantic.[9] Perhaps, in the sixteenth century, enslaved Yoruba women saw Oshun in the knife that gleamed as a mirror when they fought off sailors who tried to rape them. Maybe, toward the end of the sixteenth century, the enslaved from the Congo believed that it was the *simbi* who sent the stormy fogs that sank slave ships, sending African captives into the arms of a loving Mother, waiting beneath the waves. But by the nineteenth century, somewhere along the numerous journeys across the Atlantic, the water deities that enslaved Africans called upon to avenge the horrors of slavery became Mami Wata.

Many of the enslaved who endured this journey landed in or traveled through New Orleans, one of the most essential port cities during the transatlantic slave trade. And during the antebellum period, New Orleans contributed its own deity to the Mami Wata pantheon. The mixture of African religious traditions present in New Orleans Voodoo reflects the vast array of groups brought to Louisiana during French and Spanish rule: the Bambara people from Senegambia; the Fon and Yoruba people from Benin, Togo, and Nigeria; the Congolese and Angolans from the Democratic Republic of Congo; and, of course, the Haitians.[10] New Orleans took in all the water deities of these groups—the *simbi* from the Congo, Oshun from the Yoruba, Erzulie from the Haitians—and birthed its own Voodoo *loa*: Marie Laveau.

Within the nineteenth century, stories about Marie Laveau took on some of the imagery of Mami Wata. As the Queen of the Voodoos, Laveau was largely associated with snakes; she even had a special snake dance that she performed during Voodoo ceremonies. An ex-slave reported to the Federal Writers' Project in the 1930s that *Marie Laveau had a dance she did all by herself. She would wrap a snake around her shoulders and shake and twist herself like she was a snake. Her feet would never move.*[11] Other times, Laveau would *hold a big red fish behind her head and do her snake dance*. In these dances, she became one with the snake or the fish, like a mermaid.

Marie Laveau was also associated with the sea. On St. John's Eve, Laveau would hold grand Voodoo celebrations on the shore of Lake Pontchartrain. Zora Neale Hurston tells us one story of a ritual that has striking resemblances to mermaids.[12] For nine days before the feast on St. John's Eve, nobody would lay eyes upon Laveau. On the day of the feast, *when the great crowd of people at the feast call[ed] upon [Marie Laveau], she would rise out of the waters of the lake with a great communion candle burning upon her head and another in each one of her hands.* Then, *[s]he walked upon the waters to the shore.* When the feast ended, Laveau simply *went back into the lake, and nobody saw her for nine days again.* These stories suggest that Laveau had become an instantiation of Mami Wata in her own right. And according to Voodoo practitioners in New Orleans, Laveau is currently "elevat[ing] to the status of *loa*," or goddess in Voodoo.[13]

MARIE LAVEAU'S PROFOUND CONNECTION TO Mami Wata may be why she caused a grand public stir when the police confiscated her mermaid figurine during the raid of June 27, 1850. Laveau was so incensed by the behavior of the police during the raid that she and one of her colleagues, Rosine Dominique, sued the Third Municipality Guard the month following the raid.[14] In court, Marie Laveau accused the guard of "harassing" the women and stealing from her. The trial over the release of the mermaid figurine took place a month later, on August 10, 1850. The court decided that the figurine would be given to whomever paid the court fine of $8.50 (about $200 today).

The figurine was seen as a token of leadership among Voodoo worshippers. So, every Black conjure woman in the city showed up at the August 10 trial to lay claim to it. To these conjure women, its confiscation by the police provided a chance for them to challenge Marie Laveau's reign. The June 27 raid had put the figurine and, thus, the throne of the Voodoo women, into play.

According to the oral history, a Voodoo Queen by the name of Rosalie, a known rival of Marie Laveau, managed to secure the mermaid figurine at the August trial.[15] Perhaps she had simply been the first to pay the fine that day. But this did not phase Laveau, who just walked into Rosalie's house sometime afterward and took the figurine back, true queen that she was. When Rosalie took Laveau to court later for "stealing" it, Laveau was somehow able to prove in court that the mermaid—and the title of Queen of the Voodoos—was, and forever would be, hers alone to hold.

CHAPTER ELEVEN

The *Gris-Gris* of the Downtrodden

Over the course of Marie Laveau's life, the association of conjure with rebellion and vengeance transformed how the public viewed her. At the beginning of her career, she was beloved for her successful efforts to heal the sick, much like the Negro Mammy. Her use of conjure—methods of prayers, baths, and teas that Creole women used to treat fevers—was lauded by the public in New Orleans at large. But by the end of her career, Laveau was denounced as a devil just as often as she was celebrated as a saint. This was because of her use of conjure as *gris-gris*, which in nineteenth-century New Orleans referred to anything used to harm or heal someone through spiritual means, especially charms and amulets.[1] Her *gris-gris* was associated with social rebellion, which greatly upset those in power. Healing the sick was one thing; accruing power to challenge the prevailing social order was quite another.

It was yellow fever that first brought Marie Laveau to the public's attention. Between 1825 and 1905, an epidemic arose in New Orleans nearly every summer. Named yellow fever because of the golden tinge of eyes and skin at its onset, this virus was highly feared as the *worst sickness that ever was* during this time.² Over a span of a few short days, victims would go from fever to aches and pains to vomiting black bile to gripping hallucinations that made them *jump from their bed with death on 'em an' grab other folks*. Death was swift and certain. With people *dying like flies,* these outbreaks seemed hopeless. When yellow fever reared its ugly head up and down the Mississippi River in 1878, doctors in Memphis were so devastated they simply gave up. And yet, when Laveau, an illiterate Black woman with no professional medical training, treated these victims, they survived.

She healed these victims by rituals she'd learned from her mother, who in turn had learned them from *her* mother. Methods that were mystifying, for they were kept as a secret and passed down among the women in Marie Laveau's family line. A mixture of prayers and herbs, baths and teas, they were commonly employed by Creole women and, thus, often referred to as "Creole medicinal arts."³ These practices were of a piece with the methods Negro Mammies were using across the South—all were based in the spiritual traditions of conjure.

Like the conjure women before her, Marie Laveau primarily turned to the healing waters of Mami Wata when she administered her plant-based medicines. Many of the traditions that flow into Mami Wata—such as Yoruba, Congolese, and Haitian beliefs—held that water and plants were divine and that the combination of water and plants was particularly effective when it comes to remedying disease.⁴ Yoruba healers, for example, often paired the herbs found in the forest (the *orisha* Osanyin's lair) with Oshun's fresh water for healing. In Haitian Vodou, both Loko, the *loa* of plants and herbs, and Simbi, the water snake and *loa* of springs, rain, and magic, are associated with physical healing. And in the Congo, people often bathed in the waters of the *simbi* spirits "in the hopes of restoring vitality or to ease the disabilities caused by birth defects, paralysis, and rheumatism."[5]

Conjure women like Marie Laveau turned to these plant-infused waters instead of the more common methods of dealing with fevers at this time, such as bloodletting, purgatives, and emetics. Nineteenth-century doctors especially favored bloodletting, believing that illness was caused by an imbalance of bodily humors or fluid. However, when doctors took out the blood, the body lost too much of the vital fluid it needed to recover from disease. Replacing the vital fluid in the course of a fever was much more effective.[6] It was vital fluid that these conjure women replenished in their patients by infusing their medicines with the waters of Mami Wata.

By the end of the 1820s, Marie Laveau's name was on the tongues of many New Orleanians because of her incredible success as a yellow fever nurse. But that was just a taste of her power. In the following decades, she became, to those under her care, *the most powerful woman there [was]*. During her nearly fifty-year reign as Voodoo Queen, the tales of power that made this woman a legend were highly threatening to the prevailing social order: young girls who went to her house pregnant and came out no longer so, their futures curiously unfettered; police whom she hypnotized when they tried to get in her way; witnesses who failed to show up when they were supposed to testify against a client of hers in court; and judges who, at the last minute, unexpectedly ruled in her client's favor when they had been poised to hang them.[7] These tales grew and grew so that, by the end of her life in 1881, Laveau was believed to be a powerful woman who could make your troubles go away, whether it be illness or heartbreak, conflict with the police or peril with your employer.

The source of her power? *Gris-gris*. It was believed by many New Orleanians that Marie Laveau's *gris-gris* gave her power over the police, favor in the courts, and success in managing love affairs. Her *gris-gris* is what made *lawyers, legislators, planters, merchants all pay their respects to her and seek her offices* such that she *possessed a larger* clientele *than the most astute and far-seeing legal counselor*.[8] It was even rumored that the queen of England requested Marie Laveau's *gris-gris* and that she sent Laveau a cashmere shawl as payment for services rendered.[9]

Like the figure of Mami Wata, the phrase *gris-gris* absorbed multiple African traditions brought over by the enslaved in Louisiana.[10] *Gris-gris* included the *ashe* of the Yoruba, the divine energy or power that makes change and transformation possible. *Ashe* was a portion of Olodumare, the supreme god of Yoruba, that flows through all things, including the water, plants, and minerals that the Yoruba used for medicines.[11] *Gris-gris* included the *nkisi* of the Congolese, magical bundles believed to be possessed by spirits that could heal or harm. In the Congo, these bundles were often large nuts or wooden figures or jars with openings that practitioners could fill with objects symbolizing the spiritual request being made, alongside plants and minerals. And *gris-gris* was the *ouangas* of Haitian Vodouists, small talismans of power that were similar in function to the *gbo* of their Fon ancestors. During the antebellum period, *gris-gris* became synonymous with the Voodoo practiced by Marie Laveau and her followers—a conjure tradition.

Most strongly, however, the *gris-gris* conjure women used in slaveholding New Orleans was associated with the rebellion of the enslaved. This association had begun years before Marie Laveau was even born, for slaveholders long associated conjure with slave rebellion. And due to a court case of 1773, the amulets of *gris-gris* especially struck fear into the heart of slaveholders. In this case, enslaved Africans were tried for conspiracy to kill their masters. The enslaved Africans were accused of trying to accomplish the murder through *gris-gris*.[12] The use of *gris-gris* in this way by the enslaved rendered these charms (and, by extension, the Voodoo from which they came) not only dangerous to slaveholders but also evil in the eyes of the ruling class of the time.

Many of the stories about Marie Laveau drew upon the association of *gris-gris* with slave rebellion. For example, upon Laveau's death, Doctor J. B. Bass, a New York Voodoo priest, told the *New York Sun* that *[Marie Laveau] made a powerful sight of money selling charms to protect runaway slaves while they followed the North Star*.[13] The *gris-gris* Marie Laveau gave enslaved runaways was *to prevent them from being captured*. Robert Tallant, a writer for the 1930s Federal Writers' Project, also adds that Marie Laveau taught the enslaved to use *gris-gris* to enact revenge on their masters. *[Marie Laveau] trained many of her people to prepare gris-gris*, Tallant informs us, *and it was not unusual for white persons who were unpopular with their servants to find their pillows very uncomfortable*, stuffed with *gris-gris*.

Along with Marie Laveau's consistent invocation of St. Maroon, the patron saint of enslaved runaways in Voodoo, these factors have led some scholars to suggest that Laveau's house was a secret stop in the Underground Railroad.[14] (During slavery, enslaved people not only escaped north to Canada but also southwest to Mexico.) Laveau's participation in buying and selling the enslaved could be seen as a helpful ruse to hide her work in antislavery activities. This view cannot be supported by the archival record alone; instead, it draws upon the wider historical context of Laveau's life. In the 1850s, the slaveholding society of New Orleans would have considered any free woman of color using *gris-gris* to be inciting rebellion among the enslaved. How much more so the famed Queen of the Voodoos?

CHAPTER TWELVE

"She Was Hard on the Men"

DURING THE ANTEBELLUM AND RECONSTRUCTION PERIODS, THE majority of VOODOO worshippers were women. As the spiritual leader of Voodoo, Marie Laveau held sway over women in multiple sectors of the New Orleans population: free women of color, enslaved Black women, and even white women. And the message she delivered to them was often one of empowerment in their romantic relationships. It was said that Laveau was *hard on the men*.[1] I suspect that this was behind the accusations that Voodoo, and especially Laveau as the queen, was "corrupting" the young women in New Orleans. Some newspapers even claimed that Laveau was running a sex work ring during her secret Voodoo ceremonies![2]

Enslaved Black women were an especially vulnerable population among the Voodoo worshippers. Slave masters could (and often did) sexually abuse enslaved women. Even after slavery, Black women continued to be vulnerable to sexual abuse, for the law did not protect them. The men in their lives could rape, beat, and abandon them with impunity.

So, it is perhaps no surprise that most of the stories about Marie Laveau focus on romantic autonomy—especially in response to domestic abuse. There are stories of women whose husbands all of a sudden stopped beating them once Laveau's services had been sought. There are even stories of Laveau's ghost appearing to abusive husbands and scaring them into treating their wives better. In this way, she encouraged social rebellion across several domains. She not only encouraged rebellion along lines of racial conflict, such as slavery, but also along lines of gendered conflict, such as domestic abuse.

We can see the latter kind of rebellion in one of my favorite stories about Marie Laveau's *gris-gris*, a tale that was often swapped over porch railings by Creoles in New Orleans at the turn of the twentieth century.[3]

An old Creole man was smitten with a Creole woman young enough to be his granddaughter. She was like a thousand others: beautiful cream-colored women whose fathers' fortunes had mysteriously vanished during the Civil War. Perhaps he'd spotted her in Congo Square, where Black people gathered freely on Sundays for dancing, singing, selling, and all manners of revelry. Beneath the eye of Marie Laveau, the presiding queen over these meetings, the women would do a dance called the Bamboula. You would think that the man's part in the dance—leaping, twirling, and jumping higher than young trees—would gather all the attention. But the women understood yearning and just how far a little could go. They danced without ever moving their feet. All the action was in the slow undulation of their hips and the madras handkerchiefs flapping from their hands. They'd stand at opposite corners with the cloth between them, pull the handkerchief tight, tight, tight, and when they finally released the cloth, you'd realize you'd been holding your breath all that time. If the old man had spotted the young woman at one of these gatherings, he would have seen enough to be taken with her. Break-into-a-cold-sweat-at-night taken.

Although arrangements like these were common in those days, the young woman refused. She was already in love with a soldier in the West Indies. She tucked tales of fights and narrow escapes from her soldier's letters beneath her pillow each night. The old man didn't have a chance. How could he compete with a soldier who was handsome, daring, and much younger? So, he turned to the girl's father.

The father was thrilled at the chance to get his long-lost fortune back. When his daughter made it clear that she would not give up her soldier, the father turned to threats; he even began to physically beat the girl in front of the old man. Still, the young woman told her father that she did not even want to hear the old man's name, much less lay eyes on him.

The father decided upon still more devious tactics. He locked the young woman into a cabin on the shores of Lake Pontchartrain. The cabin was close enough to the city that he and the old man could check on her every day, but also far enough away that their dirty work would go unnoticed. For weeks, the father and the old man would go to the cabin in the middle of the night to "persuade" the young woman into the marriage arrangement. But she would not relent, saying, *I will become a nun; I will never marry.*

It was a mistake to lock the girl up at the lake because the lake probably strengthened her resolve and brought her hope. During the day, she would have been reminded of her West Indies lover if, just outside of her cabin, she saw couples laughing as they chased each other through a thicket of palmettos or nestled in between the knees of cypress trees along the shore. At night, the young woman would have seen Marie Laveau, the Queen of the Voodoos, hold ceremonies under the full moon. She would have seen the Queen of the Voodoos walk straight into the water, head held high, as wave after wave after wave washed away all the worries of the world until she disappeared into the lake. For nine whole days, she would have seen people search for and perhaps even presume the death of the Queen of the Voodoos, for who could survive under the water for that long? And then she would have seen the Queen of the Voodoos come forth from that same water, reborn as if a mermaid, alight with candles and glorious as a goddess. The Queen of the Voodoos was powerful and belonged to no man. Perhaps the young woman could be, too, if she just held out a little longer.

In desperation, the old man sought the use of Marie Laveau's *gris-gris*. He had heard enough rumors to believe that she could help. It was said that Laveau could make people *fall in love* just as easily as she could make *wives turn on their husbands*. And so, like many a savvy businessman, aspiring politician, or wealthy wife, personal troubles brought the old man to the modest, two-room wooden shack of a Black woman who was said to be *the most powerful woman there is*.

Though she did not live far from his mansion, the old man would never have been able to find Marie Laveau's cottage on his own. Most of the houses nearby were near the front of the yard, making them visible from the street. Laveau's cottage was set in the back of her yard, a high wooden fence shielding her life from curious onlookers.

Once inside the gate, the old man was greeted by a garden teeming with life. Tall banana trees with leaves that gave shade to fig and pomegranate trees. Grass as high as his knees. Watermelon vines that could easily ensnare him if he didn't watch his step. Herb and vegetable and flower patches. He even had to negotiate a pathway through a group of Choctaw women whom Marie Laveau let camp in her garden—they lived on the other side of Lake Pontchartrain and crossed it often to sell herbs, vegetables, baskets, and other wares in the French market downtown.

Once the old man made it past the Choctaw women, he waited for a bit by the front door. Laveau's statue of St. Anthony, just outside of the door, was turned upside down, a signal that she was already working with a client. When the door finally opened, he heard a group of young Black girls behind him dare each other to get a peek at the woman their mothers called a hellcat and who their fathers blamed for their bouts of infidelity.

The old man stepped into a room full of light. Candles overflowed from every crevice of the room, so many that others would wonder *how that house never caught on fire*. There were altars with pictures of saints, flowers, and statues of animals (a bear, a lion, a tiger, and a wolf). In the middle of the mantle was a box that held a big black snake in honor of the duo water serpents, Damballah and Ayida Wedo. The old man's eyes were particularly drawn to the statue of two saints that stood beside Laveau: St. Peter, who opened spiritual pathways, and St. Maroon, the patron saint of enslaved runaways.

Marie Laveau's beauty up close took his breath away. All the accounts we have of her state that she was exceedingly beautiful. But beauty is indeed in the eye of the beholder. To some, she was *banana-color*, to others *a brown skin woman*, and to a few she *looked just like a Indian*. We do not know definitively what she looked like, but we do know that she wore a big full skirt that swished powerfully when she walked and large gold hoops that winked in the sunlight. The winking disarmed the old man as he sat down to tell her about his heartache.

She was used to the desperation that brought the old man to her door. After all her years of treating yellow fever, she knew when someone was coming down with something. When the old man leaned into her face, saying he "must have" that young woman, she saw the goose bumps along his arms. When he whispered the young woman's name, Laveau saw the small shivers that wracked his spine. He didn't need to tell her about the night sweats. She was already aware that this young woman was the worst fever of his life.

Marie Laveau did indeed come to the old man's aid. She persuaded the young woman to return home. Laveau also gave the young woman's father powders made from ground-up roots and herbs to be put in the young woman's food. Then she advised the old man not to bother the young woman with another proposal for two weeks.

So, the old man took to bothering Marie Laveau instead. *Do not be impatient*, she told him, *I tell you she will marry you. I can't say more than that.* At the end of the two-week period, the young woman agreed to marry the old man, though she looked pale and her voice trembled as she said it.

The marriage took place, just as Laveau had promised. But a rather strange thing happened at the reception. The old man took his young bride into his arms to dance. Guests looked on in admiration at the couple, the father busying himself at a fountain from which champagne flowed, chuckling at his luck. And then, the old man became flushed. Some of the guests thought it was just excitement at his old age. But he turned from red to crimson to purple as he fell from his new bride's arms. He died right there on the dance floor. The young woman, as a result, inherited his fortune. It was enough money to send for her soldier, whom she promptly married.

It was rumored that Marie Laveau's *gris-gris* was actually responsible for the old man's death. When people asked her about the wedding, Laveau would stare back at them with a twinkle in her eye, gold hoops winking. And then she would say, with the ghost of a smile, *I promised only that the wedding would take place.*

The social rebellion of Marie Laveau's *gris-gris* continues to outlive her. In New Orleans, and all over the Caribbean, people often say, with the same twinkle in their eye, that men ought to beware when eating any red sauce dish prepared by women who fancy them. When I was a child, I even overheard my mother joking with my father about the dangers of men eating spaghetti prepared by women. This is because of an old trick of Laveau. It was believed during her time that a woman could "hold a man" by *tak[ing] some of the blood from her menstrual flow and mix[ing it] in her man's food. Once the man ate this, he was hers forever and she had him completely under her dominion.*[4] Many Black men at this time *live[d] in fear of it being done to them* because it was well known that Laveau taught many women this trick.

Today, these things are said in jest. But if you listen closely, you can pick up the threat that lingers beneath the joke, as one lover reminds another of this old ritual. The power of this ritual did not lie in menstrual blood per se. The power of this ritual was that it turned one of the very things that supposedly marked women as frail and weak in the eyes of men—our reproductive system—into a source of power and strength. The ritual reminds us that in a situation of oppression, the tables can be turned when you least expect it. A tool of oppression can be transformed into a weapon of rebellion. This is what Oshun did for the *iyami aje*, when she persuaded

Olodumare, the supreme creator, to give the women a special power over the men. This is the lesson of Mami Wata, who lures men to their deaths with their desire for her beauty. And this is what Marie Laveau, our own Mami Wata in New Orleans, taught many of the Black women who came to see her.

When I think of Black mermaids of New Orleans Voodoo, this is what they mean to me: the knowledge that radical change is possible. I see the fish tail, which so easily becomes legs in mermaid lore, as a symbol of the social metamorphosis that often occurs in these stories, where those that are oppressed gain the upper hand in vengeance (such as the young Creole girl forced into a marriage she absolutely did not want). When we tell these stories, we are not only sharing cultural myths; we are also passing down knowledge of the transformative power of Black women. As Toni Morrison describes it: "our canny ability to shape an untenable reality, mold it, sing it, reduce it to its manageable, transforming essence."[5] This knowledge informs us that even in the bleakest of times, power never lies solely in the hands of those who would oppress us.

CHAPTER THIRTEEN

Our Mermaids, Our Stories

WHEN DISNEY REMADE HANS CHRISTIAN ANDERSON'S *THE LITTLE Mermaid* in 1989, they added many of the African (by way of Caribbean) elements that were sorely missing from the original tale. True, Ariel is a white woman in this classic film. But Sebastian the sea crab's Jamaican accent—not to mention the calypso style of his signature song "Under the Sea"—signals Blackness to his American audience, Blackness that has been historically shaped by the conflicts of slavery in the Caribbean, from Haiti to New Orleans. Although Ursula the sea witch is based on the white drag queen Divine (Harris Glenn Milstead), the accoutrements of this character speak volumes when you consider the larger impact of conjure women, the Caribbean, and the transatlantic slave trade upon American culture. Ursula's snakelike eels, her wily magic, her ornate mirror, her shrewd business sense, and her bold embrace of sexuality are shared with another fantastical water figure to which so many black people around the world relate: Mami Wata.

Ursula is an independent woman with a passion for revenge who uses her magic to get over on a white-looking male power figure (King Triton). So, it's easy for African Americans to see her as one of us, so much so that we clamored for her character to be played by a full-bodied Black actress when the film was first announced. She reminds us of the Black conjure women who have dotted our history for centuries. And like many conjure women, Ursula is read as evil for trying to (rightfully) usurp the man who rendered her an outcast from her *own* kingdom. But what would it mean to retell Ursula's story from the juncture of African, Caribbean, and European mermaid lore that arose in the nineteenth century?

Journalist Evie Muir seems to be wrestling with a similar question in her piece, "Actually, Black Mermaid Folklore Has Been Around Long Before Disney's *The Little Mermaid*." In response to the 2023 Disney remake of *The Little Mermaid*, when we are finally given a Black mermaid through Ariel, Muir urges us to consider the powerful alternative mermaid tales that have been shared throughout the African diaspora for centuries. Indeed, in the 1830s, when Andersen gave us his beloved story of a little Danish mermaid, New Orleans gave us Marie Laveau, a powerful Mami Wata figure. Telling Laveau's story provides an occasion to not only recenter Black water spirits in these mermaid tales but also a chance to think about why, even now, Laveau still resonates with us.

After all, Marie Laveau was just one of countless Voodoo Queens who arose in New Orleans. Consider her rival, Rosalie, who faded into the background, and *[n]othing more was ever heard of [her]*.[1] It's conceivable that Laveau, too, could have faded into the background. But we still remember her.

In addition to oral stories preserved by the Federal Writers' Program in the 1930s, there are several novels and biographies about this shadowy nineteenth-century figure. Her grave is the second-most visited site in the United States.[2] People from all over the world take pilgrimages to New Orleans to sit by this Black woman's tomb to ask her to grant the deepest desires of their hearts.

Marie Laveau even appears in the popular television series *American Horror Story*. Over a hundred years after her death, we are still telling Marie Laveau's story.

I think we rehearse Laveau's story over and over, not only because she was considered a powerful woman, but also because, regardless of who she actually was, she represents to *us* justice and vengeance and the incredible help needed to make our world right. This is why scholar Denise Alvarado claims that "if Marie Laveau were alive today... she would be at the forefront of the #MeToo and #BlackLives Matter movements," just as she advocated for Juliette, the young, enslaved woman who was tossed into a horribly unjust system.

Out on the shores of Lake Pontchartrain on July 2, 1850, Juliette would have seen a woman become one with a fish in dance, just like a mermaid. And at that precise moment, she would have heard that woman sing: *L'appé vini, Li Grand Zombi / L'appé vini, Li Grande Zombi, pour fair gris-gris / L'appé vini, Le Grand Zombi, pou fair mourir.* Translation: "The Grand Zombi, the Supreme God of Voodoo, is coming. They [for the supreme god is not gendered] are coming to make *gris-gris*. They, the Supreme God, are coming to kill."[3] The *gris-gris* Marie Laveau brought, the power she wielded to strike down her enemies, even to kill, would have brought much needed hope to a young, enslaved girl facing a monstrous system that had withstood centuries, a seemingly insurmountable barrier to freedom. *This* is the power Black mermaids wield in the culture, lore, and imagination of African Americans, a power far beyond what Andersen's little Danish mermaid could ever dream.

PART THREE

The Mojo of Aunt Jemima

CHAPTER FOURTEEN

Aunt Jemima's Grand Debut, the Chicago World's Fair of 1893

WHILE MOST AMERICANS TODAY WOULD LIKELY BE HARD PUT TO name a modern-day conjure woman if asked, a caricature of one has smiled warily at them from their kitchen cupboards for over a century: Aunt Jemima, Pearl Milling Company's cherished pancake mix mascot. Introduced in 1889, Aunt Jemima is a fictious character based on Negro Mammies, enslaved women who held a central place on plantations. They were women like Harriet Collins and Harriet Jacobs, women who played a major role in the development of American food traditions and medicine (like Vicks VapoRub). Negro Mammies were conjure women who used local flora to heal minor ailments; nursed all the children on the grounds, both Black and white; cooked and organized food in the Big House; provided advice to younger enslaved women; and offered spiritual comfort, often by way of mojos, sacred amulets, to the enslaved.

Mojos were a staple of hoodoo, a conjure tradition that developed in the Deep South and lower East Coast. Like the *gris-gris* (magical charms and spells) of nineteenth-century Voodoo Queen Marie Laveau, mojos often gave the oppressed confidence to rebel against their oppressors—slave against master, wife against husband. This use of mojos would live on well into the twentieth century, becoming one of the defining aspects of African American culture, especially our music.

While newly freed African Americans were busy telling stories about the mojos of Negro Mammies in their early blues songs, the American public began to wax nostalgic over plantation life. In the eyes of the American public, the Negro Mammy was a docile slave who championed the institution of slavery. The national worship of Negro Mammies reached a fever pitch in 1923. At the start of that year, a bill was put forward in the Senate to erect a million-dollar marble and granite statue of their beloved Negro Mammy in Washington, DC.

Most white Americans never even had slaves, much less been raised by a Negro Mammy. So how did the Negro Mammy, a figure who was tucked away on rural southern plantations, a figure who was relatively obscure in the nation before the Civil War, become a wildly popular national icon and lightning rod of racial conflict?

It began with a party.

In 1893, the United States government decided to throw a grand party in Chicago: the World's Columbian Exposition, an international fair to celebrate the four hundredth anniversary of the "discovery" of America by Christopher Columbus in 1492. (The complications in setting up the fair, a daunting task in the then largely industrial and hardly picturesque Chicago, made the fair a year late for the anniversary.) At the World's Fair, several countries, from neighboring countries like Mexico to countries in the Far East, like Japan, were invited to set up an exhibit. The World's Fair organizers wanted to display to the nations—especially Europe—how far the United States of America had come in four hundred years; they wanted to stress that our wild democratic experiment had been a success. The evidence of that success was our rapid technological innovation at the turn of the twentieth century.

And if you were one of the twenty-seven million people who purchased a ticket to the fair for fifty cents between May and October, you would have indeed been privy to grand feats of innovation that showcased American ingenuity: the world's first Ferris wheel, a 264-foot-tall wheel that spun on a seventy-one ton axle, carried thirty-six cars that could fit sixty people at a time, and whose heights rivaled the Eiffel Tower, which was featured in the 1889 World's Fair in Paris; electric lights whose colors danced to music and whirled in fountains at a time when most Americans were still using oil lamps to light their homes; one of the first electric train lines, ferrying visitors on a loop in the air over the fair's 663 acres; and Thomas Edison's kinetoscope, which displayed a mesmerizing precursor to movies.[1]

The contributions of African Americans were noticeably missing from this grand celebration. The World's Fair organizers refused to include African Americans in the fair's planning, actively barring our proposals for booths that showcased our extraordinary cultural and economic progress achieved merely thirty years after enslavement. The proposed booths would have been astounding to an American public who believed we would never rise above the status of lowly, ignorant servants. By the 1890s, we had doubled our literacy rate, providing a robust education to thousands of Black people who, under slavery, had been violently prohibited from learning to read or write. We had tripled the number of books written by African Americans. And there was a significant increase of African

Americans who took up the professions of teaching, ministry, medicine, and law.

In the end, it was Haiti, not America, that gave African Americans a place at the Chicago World's Fair. Haiti, like many other countries, was represented at the World's Fair with its own dedicated building. The Haitians opened their doors to African Americans to voice their complaints about and their contributions to the nation. Ida B. Wells, at the time an investigative journalist, partnered with other leading Black intellectuals—Irvine Garland Penn, Ferdinand Lee Barnett, and Frederick Douglass—to produce a pamphlet called "The Reason Why the Colored American Is Not in the World's Columbian Exposition." Wells stood on the steps of the building dedicated to Haiti at the World's Fair, passing out copies of this pamphlet to the visitors from all over the globe who stopped to gaze upon and consider the first and only free Black republic in the New World.

In the pamphlet, Wells pointed out that *the wealth created by [African Americans'] industry has afforded to the white people of this country the leisure essential to their great progress in education, art, science, industry and invention.*[2] Wells understood that to try to tell the story of America without African Americans is as foolish as building a house upon shifting sands—which was exactly the physical construction of the fair.

At the center of the fair was a gleaming "White City" that swayed on stilts. Workers had cleared forlorn-looking oak and gum trees in the large muddy swamp of Jackson Park, which sat on the shore of Lake Michigan. They drove large stilts deep into the sandy marsh to support six large buildings of stucco—a low-cost plaster. They painted these cheap buildings bright white to look as if they were marble. Styled after Greek and Roman architecture, these six buildings formed a square called the Court of Honor, showcasing the major areas of innovation in America: liberal arts, agriculture, anthropology, electricity, machinery, and mining.[3] These hastily built, faux marbled buildings on shoddy foundations were to be the symbols of American progress. And so, the Court of Honor, a make-believe city, held all the tensions of the American dream: buildings with a gleam so white, so bright, they detracted from the muck below that upheld them.

It was in the Court of Honor's agriculture building that you would find the exhibit of Aunt Jemima's pancakes. Many of the products that were sampled in this building are still found in our grocery stores today, over a hundred years later, such as Quaker Oats, Cracker Jacks, and Wrigley's Chewing Gum.

In 1890, R. T. Davis, the president of Davis Milling Company, bought Aunt Jemima's pancake mix from Chris Rutt and Charles Underwood, who first developed the product in 1889. The first self-rising flour mix on the market, Aunt Jemima's pancake mix was made of wheat, rice, and corn. This was a striking departure from the pancakes of the South—called hoecakes, ashcakes, johnnycakes, or pone—which were typically made from cornmeal.[4] To market this unfamiliar product to the American public, Chris Rutt decided to draw upon the preeminent form of entertainment in the late nineteenth and early twentieth century: minstrel shows, where white men darkened their skin with burnt cork to imitate the songs and dances of the enslaved.

Fairgoers who visited Aunt Jemima's pancake exhibit would have recognized her name from "Old Aunt Jemima," a staple song and skit of the minstrel circuit. When Rutt heard the song performed in an 1889 minstrel show and saw how popular it was among the crowd, it struck him that Aunt Jemima would be the perfect "face" for his product. After the show, Rutt plastered a grotesque painting of Aunt Jemima on every newspaper, magazine, and paper box advertising their new pancake mix. R. T. Davis took the branding further by casting Nancy Green, a formerly enslaved Black woman, to play the role of Aunt Jemima at the World's Fair.

At the pancake exhibit, an enormous barrel of pancake flour loomed behind Green. At sixteen feet high, twelve feet wide, and twenty-four feet long, this barrel was bigger than the average SUV. Draped in an apron and donning the Negro Mammy's customary red bandanna, Green flipped over one million pancakes over the six months the fair was in operation. While she made pancakes, she sang spirituals and relayed stories about the "good old days" of slavery. It was said that the exhibit drew a crowd so large the police had to step in to keep the walkways clear. The live advertisement was an incredible success, fetching over fifty thousand orders of Aunt Jemima's pancake mix from fair visitors hailing from all over the country. Due to her laudatory reception, the officials at the fair named Aunt Jemima "Queen of the Pancakes."[5]

AS MUCH AS THE WORLD'S Fair organizers wanted to stress that America was a peaceful democracy, the fair took place during profound racial strife due to Jim Crow. In the South, African Americans strove to exercise their newfound freedom by voting, negotiating better work contracts, securing housing, or protesting the segregation they faced while riding trains, dining in restaurants, and perusing shops. White communities often responded with acts of terror—from whippings to rapes to lynchings. During the Jim Crow period, nearly four thousand African Americans were murdered by lynch mobs.[6]

At the turn of the twentieth century, African Americans began to flee the South to escape these harsh conditions. The mass relocation in the 1890s precipitated the Great Migration (1910–1970), which resulted in over six million African Americans fleeing the South, of which half a million landed in Chicago alone. Both southern and northern white Americans were unhappy about this migration.

Ida B. Wells, who also migrated to Chicago from Memphis shortly before the World's Fair, remarked that white southerners were dismayed that this migration of African Americans resulted in *a dearth of servants to cook their meals and wash their clothes and keep their homes in order, to nurse their babies and wait on their tables*—all things a Negro Mammy would do in the old order of slavery.

Meanwhile, white northerners were not willing to welcome the newly freed wholeheartedly into their communities. White northerners worried that our presence would upset a social hierarchy that placed whites on top: not only would we compete for jobs, but also our ties to Africa would cause social degeneration, or worse, racial mixing. Many of these white northerners had never even met African Americans before, but they believed what minstrel shows told them about us: that we were lazy, childlike (African) savages who were unable to govern ourselves and likely to cause chaos if left to our own devices. Never mind that it was our own devices—our conjure—that had nursed America's children for generations, given Americans powerful salves to soothe their aches and pains, and informed the cooking that kept their bellies full.

The 1893 World Fair's pancake exhibit was so successful because it tapped into the very real fears and anxieties that white northerners had, especially in cities like Chicago, where the fair was held. And Pearl Milling Company banked on the comfort that the Aunt Jemima figure would bring to white southerners who had lived through the Civil War. Whites in America had seen a nation torn apart, and they thought the only way to restore that national peace was to put African Americans "in their place." Consider the souvenir gift of the exhibit: a button pin featuring a smiling Aunt Jemima with the phrase "I'se in town, honey!" scrawled across the top. Aunt Jemima's successful move from the rural, southern plantation to the bustling, urban "town" of the North (like Chicago) is predicated upon her willingness to remain a servant, a Negro Mammy to whites. This sentiment captures the attitudes of both northern whites who were agitated by the influx of African Americans and southern whites who were dismayed at the loss of their workforce during the mass migration. Through Aunt Jemima's pancake mix, the longed-for Negro Mammy could return to white kitchens once again. "I'se in town, honey," the button declared, "so there's no need to worry or fret, I know my job is to take care of you."

But while white Americans saw in Aunt Jemima the docility and domesticity of the Old South, African Americans took something entirely different from the exhibit. African Americans, too, were familiar with the song "Old Aunt Jemima"—but it held a radically different meaning. African American minstrel performer and former slave Billy Kersands originally came up with the "Old Aunt Jemima" song and dance routine in 1875. And when African Americans came onto the minstrel stage, they often added layers of nuance to the routine that whites did not pick up on. After all, it was an incredibly ironic performance: African Americans were mocking white Americans, who had built a career out of mocking their castmates' days of enslavement.

As scholar M. M. Manring observes, Kersands's "Old Aunt Jemima," which impersonates a Negro Mammy, is based upon a slave song called "Promises of Freedom." This song added a great irony to his act, subtly making fun of the very whites who enjoyed minstrel shows. In the song, the enslaved ridicule slave masters who made vacuous pledges of future manumission. One verse features a mistress who promised to free the enslaved upon her death. Rather than fulfill her promise, she simply refuses to die, going plumb bald in her old age.

Whites in America did not realize that by welcoming Aunt Jemima into their homes, they were not only gaining access to her delicious pancakes; they were also partaking of the conjure African American women have been wielding for centuries. Beneath the light melody and playful dance that accompanied the song "Old Aunt Jemima," the lyrics issued a deadly serious threat: a mojo used by the enslaved to get back at their masters who failed to uphold past promises of freedom.

When Rutt's Aunt Jemima and Kersands's "Old Aunt Jemima" are laid side by side, they tell a story of two different Americas. At the 1893 Chicago World's Fair, Aunt Jemima's pancakes gave whites the America they longed for—one where newly freed African Americans embraced the docility and domesticity posed by an imaginary Negro Mammy. But "Old Aunt Jemima" describes an America that has fallen short of providing the freedom it guarantees to all its citizens—an America that newly freed Blacks wanted to hold accountable for such failings. In Black America, Aunt Jemima rises like a ghost from kitchens across the nation, wielding the mojos of past Negro Mammies. Behind this popular pancake mix stands a secret history where Aunt Jemima is no longer a slave but a Black revolutionary.

CHAPTER FIFTEEN

From Negro Mammy's Hoecake to Aunt Jemima's Pancake Mix

*M*AMMY'S LITTLE BABY LOVES SHORTNIN', SHORTNIN', MAMMY'S LITTLE *baby loves shortnin' bread.*[1]

In the Big House kitchen and in the slave quarters, the enslaved would sing this song while they made an assortment of quick breads like hoecakes. (It's a testament to the long life of this song that I, too, grew up with it, more than a century after slavery's demise.) In this song, the Negro Mammy is tasked with taking care of three gravely ill enslaved children.

Three little children lying in bed, two were sick and the other almost dead. The doctor's treatment is sought, but he does not give it. Instead, the doctor commits the children to the Negro Mammy's care. *Sent for the doctor and the doctor said, "Give those children some shortnin' bread."* The mere mention of the Negro Mammy's quick bread is enough to revive the nearly dead children. *When those children sick in bed, heard the talk about shortnin' bread, popped up well to dance and sing. Skipped around and cut the pigeon wing*, a dance that was comprised of rhythmic foot shuffling and occasionally lifting one foot in the air as you flailed your arms like a bird in flight.[2]

Although this song is a nursery rhyme, it captures two aspects of the Negro Mammy's role on the plantation. We know that Negro Mammies were skilled herbalists with a wide range of botanical knowledge. Their conjure provided methods of healing—such as teas for fevers and salves for aches and pains—that put them a step ahead of doctors who were still primarily relying on leeching and bloodletting in the nineteenth century. But healing wasn't their only role on the plantation; often, they were nannies to the children on the plantation, both Black and white.

Gus Feaster, an ex-slave interviewed by the Federal Writers' Project in 1937, provides valuable information on these women who were vital to both the operation of the plantation and the enslaved community.³ He tells us that *[o]n all de plantations dar was old womons, too old to do any [field] work and dey would take and study what to do fer de ailments of grown folks and lil' chilluns.*

A central part of their care included setting the diet for the children. Gus tells us that a Negro Mammy called *[o]le lady Abbie looked out fer [their] rations.* Enslaved children were fed a diet that usually included milk or buttermilk, pot likker or some type of vegetable mush that might include a small piece of meat, occasionally yams, and almost always some variation of corn bread: corn pone, ashcakes, or hoecakes.⁴ The difference between the hoecake and ashcake (or corn pone) lies in the method of preparation. The hoecake was cooked on an iron griddle on the hearth, while the ashcake was prepared in the manner of many Indigenous Americans: cornmeal batter wrapped in oak or poplar leaves, buried under smoldering ashes, and baked to a golden brown by a skillful cook.⁵

As Gus Feaster reports, the enslaved saw these quick breads of corn as essential to a child's diet because they could provide nutrients that would *make you fat and strong*. In their interviews with the Federal Writers' Project, many ex-slaves go further to compare the flour-based breads that were available in grocery stores after slavery to the hoecakes they used to receive from Negro Mammies. They insisted that the hoecakes under slavery made them healthier and less likely to get sick. Formerly enslaved Willis Cofer claimed that we'd be more hardy if we *let all dis wheat bread and sto[re]-bought, ready-made bread alone 'cept on Sunday*.[6]

Health, of course, was not the only reason the enslaved preferred hoecakes. Taste was also a huge factor. The Negro Mammy's skill at hoecakes was especially revered among the enslaved, whose interviews with the Federal Writers' Project are filled with nostalgia and longing. They report that there was *[n]othin' like* the Negro Mammy's hoecakes after slavery's demise.[7] They were so good *[y]ou could knock you mammy in the head, eatin' that ash cake bread*.[8]

The Negro Mammy's botanical knowledge, gained from her conjure traditions, also played a definitive part in the flavor profile of these cakes. Gus tells us that the Negro Mammies on his plantation used poplar leaves. They would lay cornmeal batter onto poplar leaves *over coals* while they *bake[d] in de ashes*. And there was a special trick for making sure the flavor of the poplar leaves infused the cake as it baked. Gus asks, *does you know dat de poplar leaves was wet [before] de meal pone was put in it?* Once the cake was done, you would eagerly blow off the ashes in anticipation. The leaves would *fold back from de cooked pone* under your breath, like flower petals falling away to reveal their alluring pistil. You would be rewarded with a crisp sweetness on your tongue, as *[d]e poplar leaves give de ash cake a nice fresh taste*.

After slavery, African Americans began to migrate away from plantations, and the Negro Mammy's hoecake began to vanish.

Many of the formerly enslaved lamented that people didn't cook like Negro Mammies anymore and that their hoecakes could no longer be found. Their expression of this loss is of a piece with how, upon emancipation, African American conjure traditions, which had a largely herbal base, were displaced. When they migrated away from plantations, thousands of African Americans lost access to the fields and woods from which Negro Mammies harvested vital medicines and cooking essentials. From gardening techniques to knowledge of which parts of the plant to administer and which parts to avoid in treating illness, the botanical and medicinal expertise passed down through conjure was soon replaced with mass-produced conjure oils, powders, and dried herbs targeted toward the influx of African Americans in new cities.[9]

Some aspects of our conjure also went underground as the newly freed came into more direct contact with broader (white) American culture. In several states, there was a rise in laws that outlawed various aspects of conjure at the turn of the twentieth century, from practicing medicine without a license to fortune-telling.[10] There was also a large group of African Americans who believed our best bet to equality in America was to assimilate to white American culture and jettison some of our more "African" practices. So conjurers began to live double lives, concealing their practices and making it harder to identify for sure who dabbled in conjure. Some conjurers, like Voodoo Queens, became spiritual advisors who could be cajoled into folk doctoring; some specialized in women's problems, like midwives; and some channeled their conjure into preaching.[11]

During the onset of Jim Crow, conjure became fragmented as it adapted to these pressures and migrated to new locales. Conjure continued, but it was less centralized. And it was precisely in this moment of destabilization that savvy white businessmen made their move to culturally appropriate conjure—like Chris Rutt, co-developer of Aunt Jemima's pancake mix. Rutt's advertising campaign effectively transformed the Negro Mammy's conjure into vapid culinary magic.[12]

One powerful example of this transformation can be found in "Life of Aunt Jemima: The Most Famous Colored Woman in the World," a pamphlet by Purd Wright in 1895. The Chicago World's Fair brought explosive sales that only went up and up in the following years. Aunt Jemima was so popular that Pearl Milling Company commissioned Wright to produce a pamphlet that told Aunt Jemima's "story" for a national audience.

In 1895, two years after the Chicago World's Fair, Wright sat down with Nancy Green, the fair's real-life Aunt Jemima, to compile stories from her life as a Negro Mammy during slavery, when she served as a nurse, cook, and nanny to a prominent family in Kentucky.[13] These stories form the spine of his pamphlet, where a major myth is sold to the American public about the origins of the pancake mix. Although the pancake mix was made by two white men, Rutt and Underwood, in the pamphlet, Wright tells us that the recipe comes from Aunt Jemima, a Negro Mammy of slavery.

According to Wright, Aunt Jemima grew up spending much of her time in the woods, which made her *wise in the laws and limitations of knowledge*. Because of her nursing duties, *health was [Aunt Jemima's] guide. No one knew its value better. To her, happiness meant perfect health*. Aunt Jemima was also an incredible *cook, unsurpassed in the preparation of certain dishes which she prepared in a manner that showed a surprising knowledge of the properties and possibilities of their wholesome ingredients*. And so, Aunt Jemima is credited with the invention of the pancake mix: she *discovered that the great cereals—wheat, corn, and rice—could be so combined in pancakes that the beneficial properties and flavor of each could be retained.*

This fictious character draws upon the Negro Mammy's real reputation of herbalism and cooking in the South, making her the perfect person to convince the American public to try an untested and largely unfamiliar product. The nostalgia of the Negro Mammy's hoecakes would grant Rutt's new product an air of familiarity and authenticity. Rutt hoped that the American public would simply see Aunt Jemima's pancakes as an improvement on the Negro Mammy's daily servings of hoecakes, *the griddle cakes so common in the South.*

This is striking, considering that real Negro Mammies did not want anything to do with the white flour in Aunt Jemima's pancakes and certainly didn't consider it healthy. In Federal Writers' Project interviews, many of the formerly enslaved asserted that the Negro Mammy's diet of hoecakes kept us hale during slavery and that replacing it with *all dis wheat bread and sto[re]-bought, ready-made bread* after emancipation was making us ill. This is perhaps why one former Negro Mammy, Aunt Clara Walker, exclaimed in her Federal Writers' Project interview, *Yes ma'am, I likes cornbread. I eats it every meal. I wouldn't trade just a little cornbread for all de flour dat is.*

All the same, Rutt whitewashed the Negro Mammy's hoecake with white flour, just as Wright whitewashed the Negro Mammy's conjure in his story of Aunt Jemima. In the pamphlet, Aunt Jemima *knew nothing of artificial flavoring extracts, or chemical solutions calculated to tempt the palate.* Wright insists that Aunt Jemima did not have a formal education that would have provided *a rudimentary knowledge of chemistry.* It is framed as sheer luck and coincidence that she is the originator of the sensational pancakes that made her a *celebrated colored cook, whose fame has since extended to the very bound of civilization.*

It is not ancestral knowledge of plants and medicine, passed down through generations of conjuring, that puts Aunt Jemima on par with world-famous chefs. It is simply due to an innate gift, a magical essence that is tied to her race and makes her fit to be a slave. And this magic is put to a very specific purpose in the pamphlet to lock in a million-dollar business idea and make Aunt Jemima a national sensation: unity and compromise between the South and the North after the Civil War.

Wright tells us that one day, long after the Civil War, a famous ex-Confederate general was on a south-bound train with a group of northern and southern men. As they reclined into their seats and watched the oak trees and palmettos and bald cypress go by, they drifted *into a discussion of famous dinners, how they could best enjoy them, and what the courses should comprise.* The ex-Confederate general grew tired of the northerners' boasting and weighed in. *You may talk about your big dinners, but the best meal I ever ate in my life was at a negro cabin not far from where we are now. It was prepared by a slave, called Aunt Jemima. The meal consisted solely of pancakes, but I tell you, gentlemen, that no banquet ever spread tasted half as good as that "one-course" repast did.*

He remembered that hoecakes were sometimes the only source of sustenance to be found in the South during the Civil War when they were *surrounded on all sides by the Union troops* and *deprived of almost [all] the necessities of life.* During those bleak times, a life-giving meal was to be found in Aunt Jemima's cabin, even with scant resources. The art of Black cooking, after all, is making a feast out of scraps.[14] The ex-Confederate general remembered that Aunt Jemima's cooking turned these meager cakes into *home cooking to the tired and weary generals, to whom her pancakes alone made up for the loss of luxuries.*

The ex-Confederate general convinced his companions to detrain early and see for themselves. This group of northern and southern men traipsed side by side through the forest, where perhaps they had fought as enemies merely decades before during the Civil War. When they reached her door, Aunt Jemima welcomed them, even those who had fought to keep her enslaved, *with all the courtesy of the ante-bellum darkey.* The meal was a success and *without a dissenting voice the party declared the cakes the most delicious they had ever tasted.* Some of the men were so impressed with the meal, they clamored over Aunt Jemima, making *tempting offers for her recipe.* Among the group was a representative of R. T. Davis Milling Company, who convinced R. T. Davis to later buy the pancake mix from Aunt Jemima.

What makes it possible for white southerners and northerners to bond in the myth of Aunt Jemima? In this story, the happy slave is crucial to the promotion of unity and peace in a nation that had just been ravaged by civil war. A pancake dinner, where a formerly enslaved Black woman serves white northern and southern men just like she did before the Civil War. An implicit bargain is made at this dinner. In return for the white northerners' compliance with slavery in its new form, Jim Crow, the South will give them the plantation pleasures that had once been forbidden, such as pancakes with that "old-time Southern flavor."[15]

This fictional story exposes the very real resentments of white southerners over the demise of slavery at the turn of the twentieth century. Ida B. Wells writes that *the Southerner had never gotten over his resentment that the Negro was no longer his plaything, his servant, and his source of income.*[16] Long after the 1895 pamphlet, ads explicitly cast

Aunt Jemima's delicious pancakes as "magic" to be reproduced by white housewives over and over again. Aunt Jemima's magic pancakes make Black women, once again, a servant of whites.

The advertising campaign also gave white southerners their plaything, literally. Soon after the World's Fair, Aunt Jemima's pancake mix came with a paper doll of Aunt Jemima in the box. In 1895, Pearl Milling Company also offered its customers an Aunt Jemima rag doll as a special gift.[17] These rag dolls remained popular throughout many decades. White parents clamored for *a delightful southern mammy that could be cuddled, dropped, thrown and sat upon, and would still turn up, good as new.*[18]

But you can only make the Negro Mammy a plaything of whites if you ignore the threat her spiritual traditions bore toward the system of slavery itself. It's these very traditions that Billy Kersands hearkens to in his "Old Aunt Jemima." When white folks kicked back to enjoy Kersands's show, when white folks made pancakes for breakfast and gave their children Aunt Jemima dolls to cuddle, they had no idea that a new form of conjure was emerging, right under their noses.

CHAPTER SIXTEEN

Sarah Byrd's Cakewalk

IN 1875, BILLY KERSANDS PERFORMED THE MOST POPULAR SEGMENT OF his minstrel show, "Old Aunt Jemima." Before he stepped onto the stage, he wrapped his head in the same kind of scarf Negro Mammies often wore—a red bandanna. As he sang, he danced a cakewalk. It was an easy enough dance for his white audience to join: you just puff your torso and kick your legs as high as you can.[1] By the time Chris Rutt, the codeveloper of the Aunt Jemima's pancake mix, stumbled upon "Old Aunt Jemima" during a minstrel show decades later in 1889 (then performed by whites in blackface), the minstrel show was the preeminent form of national entertainment in the United States and its cakewalk, the national dance.[2]

But the cakewalk that America loved is not what it seems. While whites donned blackface to mock the cakewalk that the enslaved performed on the plantation, the enslaved cakewalked, in part, to mock their slave owners.

It was easy for America to miss. To understand the true intent of this dance, white Americans would have had to entertain the viewpoints of those they held in bondage, who often did the cakewalk at "frolics" on the plantation. These frolics, fondly remembered by the enslaved, varied in frequency from plantation to plantation. Although these frolics were largely secular occasions, conjure was embedded into the songs and dances performed, marking the plantation yard as a powerful liminal space where the enslaved understood that anything could happen, if only for one night.

These frolics were highly anticipated nights, as formerly enslaved Sarah Byrd recalls in her 1936 interview for the Federal Writers' Project: *I use ter be so glad when Saturday night came cause I knowed us wuz go have a frolic and I wouldn't have a bit'uv appetite I would tell my ma we gwine dance ter night I don't want nothin [to eat].* [3]

At these frolics, you could fall in love or steel yourself to run away or get into a brawl or meet nearby Indigenous folks who joined the fun or run into a relative from a nearby plantation who you feared was dead or catch up with a lover who'd been sold away or plot an insurrection or simply make fun of the master and be rewarded not with punishment but with the rare generosity of food.

Sarah saved her appetite especially for the ashcakes. Only the best dancer would receive the beloved prize of the ashcake, from which the famous cakewalk dance of the enslaved gets its name. To be given this culinary prize not only meant Sarah was a highly skilled dancer but also that she would be treated much better than she usually was during the week. Her mistress never gave the enslaved *anything but the coarsest of foods*. Sarah tells us that her mistress was a *mean un*, for the mistress would often give them food only once it was rotten. Sarah recalled many a day the mistress would leave butter to sit out in the pans. Only once that butter had spoiled *would [she] call some uv [them] and give it ter [them]. The mistress would also give [them] bread that had been cooked a week.*

Sarah often met her mistress's meanness with the defiance of sneaking away. There was one time she snuck off to enjoy some plums. *I nebber forget once [mistress] sent me after some brush broom and told me ter hurry back. Well plums wuz jest gitting ripe so I just took my time and et all the plums I wanted after that I come on back ter the house.* Sarah savored those plums as she strolled, keeping the mistress waiting.

Enraged that Sarah went off and ate plums instead of hurrying back, the mistress called Sarah up the stairs promptly upon her return to the house, meeting Sarah with *that old cow hide. She struck me three licks and I lost my balance and tumbled backward down the stairs. I don't know how come I didn't hurt myself but the Lord wuz wid me and I got up and flew.*

On Saturday nights, enslaved pairs would take to the center of a ring of dancers as they competed for the cakewalk's prize. The ring dancers would perform the juba, a dance derived from the Congo thigh-slapping dance called *nzuba*.[4] Banned by slave owners for fear it would incite rebellion, the drum was replaced by rhythmic stomps and claps of the enslaved, bringing the juba to life. Against this steady pulse, Sarah would hear bits and pieces of songs she encountered throughout the week—field hollers, spirituals, work songs—in the melodies musicians played *on the banjo, by knocking bones, and [by] blowing quills.*

The juba dance also came from the religious practices of the enslaved. Sarah tells us about one night when two Negro Mammies from a nearby plantation, Aunt Patsy and Aunt Prudence, slipped into her cabin for a prayer meeting, where they could *sing pray and shout as much as they wished.* While they prayed, they joined in the sacred counterclockwise dancing that was prevalent in many West African societies. In the North American context, that sacred counterclockwise dancing evolved into the Ring Shout.⁵ The shout here refers to not only the style of singing—what anthropologist Zora Neale Hurston calls *an emotional explosion, responsive to rhythm*—but also many of the dance moves of the sacred counterclockwise circle, like juba.⁶

The *shout* that Aunt Patsy and Aunt Prudence performed struck fear into the heart of slave masters, for this spiritual practice challenged their authority. In one story relayed by previously enslaved Andrew Moss, a slave master gets enraged when he spots his slave shouting *in de field or by the side of the road*. When the slave master *come 'long and see a slave on his knees,* he asks his slave, *What you prayin' bout?* The slave says, *Oh, Marster I'se jes prayin' to Jesus cause I wants to go to Heaven when I dies.* The slave master at once orders the slave off his knees and reasserts his authority as the slave's master in the here and now. *Youse my negro. I git ye to Heaven. Git up off'n your knees.* The slave's contemplation of a realm where he might be free threatened the slave master so much that even mention of the slave master's own god, Jesus, did not spare the slave from his master's wrath.

Through the slave's shout, a spiritual realm of freedom showed itself to be immanent in this earthly one. For the enslaved, the shout was a form of spirit possession, conveyed not just by sound, but also by dance in the enslaved community. In North America, when the enslaved were lost in the shout, they often *cut the pigeon wing* as they sang. In Haiti, Hurston observed that *when a man or woman is "mounted" by a loa, or spirit,* they also *danc[ed] mostly on one foot and stumbl[ed] about to a loose rhythm.* This led her to conclude that the shout is *a survival of the African "possession" by the gods.* And so, in the throes of the shout, heaven was brought down to Earth, and just for a moment, the divine resided in the enslaved. The message of the shout was this: in communion with the spirit, we could receive the help we need in an insurmountable situation, making a way out of what seems like no way.[7]

Sarah seemed to grasp the shout's connection to freedom as well as the threat it bore to slave masters. She tells us that during their prayer meeting, Aunt Patsy and Aunt Prudence's *old master came there and whipped 'em and made 'em go home*. Sarah surmises as to why their slave master punished them for it: *I reckin[s] [their slave master] thought us wuz praying ter git free*. The defiance that Sarah may have felt as she shouted with Aunt Patsy and Aunt Prudence would have carried into her dancing at Saturday night frolics on the plantation when she was "patting" juba, waiting for her turn to take to the center.

During the cakewalk, daring feats would be undertaken by the dancing pairs who took to the circle's center in competition. Upon her turn, Sarah might have pantomimed various tasks of labor she undertook on the plantation, such as shucking corn or shelling peas or pitching hay. Or she might have simply *danced jigs, too, in a circle, jumping up and down* as she shouted in song with the others: *sugar in de gourd / sugar in de gourd / iffen you wanter git / de sugar out— / [r]-o-o-l-l de gourd over*. Perhaps she winked at her partner in the dance as she sang, wishing he would put his "sugar" in her "gourd" that very night. As a proficient dancer—for only the best would attempt this—she might have danced with a jug of water on her head *without spilling a drop*.

As she cakewalked, mocking her master and mistress, she might have also sung a highly popular song, "Promises of Freedom," that previously enslaved John Moore remembers being sung at these frolics: *My ole Mistus promise me / [w]'en she died, she'd set me free / [s]he lived so long d'at her head got bald / [a]n' she give out'n de notion of dying*

/ [a]t all. Not to worry, though, because the slave master's renege on his promise of freedom isn't the end of the story in this song: *[y]es, my ole Masser promise me / [b]ut "his papers" didn' leave me free / [a] dose of pizen (poison) he'ped him along / [m]ay de Devil preach his funer'l song.*[8]

"A dose of poison." Zora Neale Hurston explains that, for the enslaved and newly freed, the word *poison* usually did not mean a toxic substance that could be ingested. Rather, it meant *something has been put down* or strategically placed for the victim to come across, such as a magical bundle or amulet that delivered a potent death threat.[9] These amulets were derived from West African spiritual traditions, like the *nkisi* of the Congolese. The enslaved called these bundles mojos, charms, tobys, jacks, goopher packs, hands, or the *gris-gris* of our Voodoo Queens. Mojos were small bags constructed out of several objects: plant elements like roots and herbs; body parts and secretions like fingernails, hair, or urine; powders made of corn, snake venom, or even dirt from graveyards, often called "goopher dust."[10] Throughout slavery, mojos were used for a wide range of purposes: protection, healing, love, revenge, poison.

Sarah knew all too well about this type of poisoning. In her interview, Sarah tells us about a woman on the plantation who scared her to death with her use of poisons: *all I know I wuz fraid 'uv her 'ez I could be. They [said] she put snakes and scorpions in you.* This type of "poisoning" was often done through mojos constructed with the dried powder of snakeskin or venom.

The mojos Sarah encountered on the plantation were intimately tied to the Ring Shout, the sacred version of her cakewalk. Mojos were believed to be alive. Like the enslaved in the throes of the shout, mojos were believed to be spirit possessed. Much like the Holy Spirit in the shout, it was the spirits that came from the world of the dead who inhabited mojos. Because mojos were believed to be alive, these amulets had to be ritually "tied" through enclosure in cloth, jugs, clay bowls, even brown parchment paper. Red flannel, which Negro Mammies usually wore around their heads as a bandanna, was the most common material used to tie mojos. For the Congolese, a *nkisi* wrapped in red cloth was considered one of the most powerful charms.[11]

The enslaved passed these beliefs down throughout generations. By the nineteenth century, mojos wrapped in red cloth were used by the enslaved so that nobody could put evil on them—if someone did, it would turn on that person.[12] This poison, the mojo, was a vital aspect of conjure that survived the migration of thousands of African Americans at the turn of the twentieth century.[13] African Americans carried mojos on them as they made their perilous escape from the South; they swapped stories about mojos in their newfound communities up North; and they made mojos central to their new music, the blues, which also registered the profound disappointment of African Americans with the nation's promises of freedom.

Consider a common mojo's ingredients: One Negro Mammy tells us *[a] good charm bag [is made] of red flannel with frog bones and a piece of snakeskin and some horse hairs and a spoonful of ashes. Dat bag [protect] you from you enemy.* The red flannel of a Negro Mammy's headscarf. The horse that carried your loved ones away from the plantation when they were sold. The bones of a frog who, over the course of its life, comes to master the lessons of change, as the tadpole who once breathed with gills like a fish makes a new life on land as an adult. The skin of a snake. The ashes layered on top of delicate corn cakes.

The conjure of Negro Mammies turned such commonplace objects into a weapon the enslaved could wield against their masters.

Although some masters chalked this up to superstition, they were also afraid. For through these conjure rituals, the enslaved created a liminal social space where the stringent rules of slavery lapsed. And in such spaces, anything could happen. For a moment, a mojo could embolden a slave to turn a whip upon his master, as in the case of Frederick Douglass. A secret prayer meeting of Voodoo Queens could foster plots of escape. A silly plantation dance could be used to mock the slave master and deliver a death threat.

When the enslaved sang "Promises of Freedom," they exposed not only the hypocrisy of their slave masters, but also that of the nation. Both promised freedom if only Black people would do what's asked of them. The bite of this song, which makes fun of the master's baseless promises, is sweetened by an exaggerated dance that the master sees as amusement rather than mockery. The slave master laughs at the spectacle the enslaved make in the cakewalk and indeed misses the point: the slave's moral judgment of the master; the pressure for freedom exerted by the slave; and the veiled threat if that freedom is not granted.

In 1875, Billy Kersands took this song about the bald mistress and poisoned slave master, sung by the enslaved on plantations across the nation, and interjected the shout of Aunt Jemima: *[m]y old missus promise me / [o]ld Aunt Jemima, oh! Oh! Oh! / [w]hen she died she-d set me free / [o]ld Aunt Jemima, oh! Oh! Oh! / [s]he lived so long her head got bald / [o]ld Aunt Jemima, oh! Oh! Oh! / [s]he swore she would not die at all / Old Aunt Jemima, oh! Oh! Oh!*[14]

As a former slave, Kersands knew intimately what it was like to have his freedom denied, legally restored, and then taken away every day under Jim Crow. In his performance, Kersands takes elements from his life as a slave—the cakewalk and mojos—onto a national stage. Doing so not only tapped into the collective mood of many other African Americans who were also former slaves, but it also gave migrating African Americans tangible roots, traditions that could help Blacks across the nation identify with one another.

"Old Aunt Jemima" was beloved among African Americans because they deeply agreed with the notice Billy Kersands was trying to serve to America. With his remake of "Promises of Freedom" as "Old Aunt Jemima," Kersands sends a powerful message, veiled in popular entertainment, to a nation that reneged on its promises of freedom to Black folks through its observance of Jim Crow. And it is Aunt Jemima, the Negro Mammy of slavery, who delivers the implicit threat in the song. Should America continue to fail to keep its promises to the newly freed, a *dose of poison* might hurry the nation along to its demise.

CHAPTER SEVENTEEN

Aunt Caroline Dye's Mojo

IN THE 1910S AND 1920S, MOJOS BECAME A LIGHTNING ROD FOR RACIAL politics in America due to an important event that occurred overseas: the United States' invasion and occupation of Haiti, which lasted from 1915 to 1934. At the turn of the twentieth century, Haiti went through a period of political instability: A Haitian president was assassinated, and the people of Haiti took to the streets in violent protest of his murder. In 1915, the United States sent in troops to "restore" order and democracy to Haiti. A large part of that restoration involved eliminating the presence of their Vodou practices, which the US government took to be a source of social degeneracy and barbarity. Americans saw Haitian charms and amulets, their dolls stuck through with shiny pins, as evidence of their secret pacts with the devil.[1]

The West has long feared the Vodou of the Haitians, for it was intimately linked to Black struggles for freedom. It was rumored that a Vodou ceremony incited the Haitian Revolution over a century earlier in 1794. On one fateful night, the enslaved Haitians gathered to worship the *loas* or spirits. During the ceremony, a worshipper danced with a foot in the air as she flailed her arms, like her counterparts in the United States did when they were overtaken by the shout. She was "mounted" by the *loa* Ogun, the god of war, who encouraged the enslaved to join in a blood oath to fight their oppressors and overthrow the French government.[2]

Decades earlier, in 1757, Francois Makandal, an enslaved fugitive, used the botanical knowledge common in Vodou to poison the French colonial water supply, killing over six thousand people.[3] Shortly after this incident, the French colony outlawed making any amulets or charms of Vodou. These charms, often called *paquet Congo*, were also derived from the Congolese *minkisi*.[4] They were sometimes bundles like the mojo of African Americans. *Paquet Congo* also took the form of cloth dolls. Haitians brought these dolls with them to New Orleans at the turn of the nineteenth century, where they evolved into the infamous voodoo doll. Like their Congolese ancestors, the Haitians often drove metal pins or nails into these objects to awaken the spirits within.[5]

For the United States, part of what it meant to gain control over Haiti was to suppress the Vodou practices of Haitians. So during the United States' occupation of Haiti, soldiers were sent with instructions to rid the island of these objects and religious practices.[6] In memoirs and travel reports, these soldiers relayed stories that vilified Vodou practices to the American public: rituals that involved cannibalism of children; voodoo dolls that cursed unsuspecting neighbors; spells that turned people into zombies or the living dead. These soldiers reported that Haitians worshipped a god of Vodou that *is a big negro with supreme power, no morals, and an unlimited appetite for rum, women, whoopee, and blood*.[7] Newspapers widely circulated these images to everyday Americans. As African American studies scholar Kameelah Martin observes, the emerging movie industry seized these stories in the 1920s, making the zombie figure an American staple that is still with us today in popular television shows like *The Walking Dead*.[8]

These manufactured images of savage Haitians gripped the American imagination. White Americans began to link the state of Blacks in Haiti with the state of Blacks in their own country. White Americans believed that if Blacks were left to govern themselves, like in Haiti, they would lapse into the "barbarity" of Vodou. In the minds of white Americans, inherent African savagery justified US occupation of Haiti, just as it justified the system of Jim Crow in their own country. The mojo of African Americans, to the broader American public, was a reminder of what happens when Blacks take control. Haitian zombies and voodoo dolls came to represent what white Americans feared would happen if Blacks were truly free—that we would turn around and enslave them.

Anything that threatened white supremacy, anything that represented Black freedom and independence, was seen as evil by our oppressors. But this devaluation of our conjure by the broader American public did not deter us. Rather, as Zora Neale Hurston notes, we just went on in our conjure, *unknowingly influencing American music and enjoying [our]selves hugely while doing so, in spite of the derision from the outside.*[9]

So while America was busy ridiculing conjure, African Americans were placing mojos at the heart of their blues. We can see this in the work of W. C. Handy (1873–1958), who is called the father of the blues for his hand in bringing the delta blues of the South to bear on ragtime, the music that accompanied the cakewalk of minstrel shows. In his verses and chords, Handy prominently features conjure, especially the mojo, in his musical revolution.

THE CONJURING OF AMERICA

RAGTIME CAUGHT ITS BIG BREAK at the Chicago World's Fair of 1893. Black pianists like Handy were not formally invited to the fair. So they played in booths and tents just outside the Midway Plaisance, a roughly mile-long stretch on the eastern side of the fair that housed the Ferris wheel. According to Will Cook, a preeminent African American composer of the late nineteenth century, before the Chicago World's Fair, ragtime was largely on the fringes of American culture. You could only hear it if you traveled to questionable "resorts" along the Mississippi, like brothels and jook (juke) joints.[10]

Hurston describes the jook as *a Negro pleasure house. It may mean a bawdy house. It may mean a house set apart on public works where men and woman dance, drink and gamble.*[11] As African Americans moved away from the rural plantation, they lost the space where their Saturday night frolics were once held. The jook became a replacement. These *pleasure house[s]* arose on the outskirts of cities, as dive bars on the side of the road or tiny shacks that squat in bayous.

Although jooks were unglamorous (they were often *smelly, shoddy*, and *seedy*), they were the birthplace of much of American culture. Hurston tells us that the *Negro dances [that] circulated over the world were also conceived inside the Jooks*, like the Black Bottom, the Twist, and the Lindy Hop.[12] And in terms of music, the jook has *born the secular music known as the blues, and on blues has been founded jazz.* The blues has also founded what came long after it: not just jazz, but rock and roll, soul, funk, rhythm and blues, and hip-hop.

At the turn of the twentieth century, pianos soon began to appear in jooks, replacing the guitars of the early delta blues. Black pianists like W. C. Handy, barely a generation out from slavery, drew upon all the music they heard at plantations as they crafted ragtime tunes. With their left hand, these pianists "pat" juba upon the keys, as the enslaved had once done upon their bodies in the absence of drums.[13] With their right hand, these pianists provided the syncopation that plantation fiddlers supplied at dances, drawing upon melodies from Saturday night frolics and hollers across cotton fields and spirituals sung in secret prayer meetings. The music these pianists played summoned scenes of rebellion: plantation dances where the enslaved mocked their owners or ran away; field hollers that encoded secret messages of escape; mojos tucked into apron and pants pockets so that the enslaved could tap into help from beyond; and spirituals that protested slavery.

The Chicago World's Fair made secluded jook music mainstream. Handy likely enjoyed this exposure to a national audience. When people stopped to gaze in his tent, tapping their foot as they were carried away by a jolting beat, he probably thought about his father, who had discouraged him from becoming a musician.[14] Taking in the streams of people coming in and out of his tent, he must have felt like he was doing something that would have a massive impact for years to come—even if his father thought he was *selling [his] soul to the devil*.

But twenty years after the Chicago World's Fair, Handy felt that ragtime was beginning to run out of steam. Handy had grown dissatisfied with the path that ragtime had taken, where meaningful depth had been traded for technical artistry. He now found ragtime trite, and he understood that this popular music form would soon be passing out of fashion. So, he decided he would use ragtime's passing to create a musical *number that would go beyond its predecessor and break new ground*. His approach for this new number, "St. Louis

Blues," was to *use all that is characteristic of the Negro from Africa to Alabama* in the melody and plot of the song.[15]

Handy chose *to combine ragtime syncopation with a real melody in the spiritual tradition*. He did this by building the melody around the "blue notes" of the Negro spirituals and the shout, where we were *sure to bear down on the third and seventh tones of the scale, slurring between major and minor*. The song's plot *centered around the wail of a lovesick woman for her lost man*. Wrapped in musical motifs of slavery—the blue notes in the melody along with the *plagal chords* that would *give spiritual effects in the harmony*—the song would encourage those who heard it to draw parallels between the woman's desolation at the abandonment of her lover and the desolation African Americans felt at the abandonment of their nation at this time, when Jim Crow was raging.[16]

The lovesick woman's troubles are resolved by a visit to the conjure woman, referred to euphemistically as a "gypsy": *[b]een to the Gypsy to get my fortune told. Cause I'm most wile about my Jelly roll*. During her visit, the lovesick woman is given a powerful mojo by the gypsy to get her man back. The gypsy in this song was a real conjure woman of the time, Aunt Caroline Dye, who Handy refers to by name in his 1923 "Sundown Blues": *I'm going to Newport, Arkansas. I'm going there to see Aunt Car'line Dye*.[17]

IF YOU WERE IN TROUBLE in the 1910s, you might take a trip on the "Carolyn Dye Special," a train line that would take you near the house of Aunt Caroline Dye in Newport News, Arkansas, a mere hundred miles from Memphis. Once you deboarded the train, you might ask others at the station, "Do you know where Aunt Caroline Dye lives?" A little Black girl off to the side would overhear and flag your attention. She would offer to take you there for a quarter. As you followed the little girl along to the *big house, with a small house to one side and a lot in the back* where cows and chickens grazed, your heart might sink at the buggies and cars that lined the road. The sheer volume of people milling about Aunt Caroline Dye's yard meant that your wait for a consulting session would be mighty long. Perhaps the little girl would smile and point to the *long table[s] with white cloths* a few paces away where you could get a good meal for just thirty-five cents as you wait—*fried chicken, bisquits, buttermilk if you wanted it or sweet milk, all you could eat or drink*. There was not much else to do as you waited your turn to visit with the woman who newspapers called *the worst woman in the world*.

Aunt Caroline Dye was one of the most famous conjure women in the Mid-South during the twentieth century. She was born into slavery around 1843. Though she never charged for her services, people still gave her money for a job well done. By the end of her life, she had acquired a *tidy fortune amounting probably to $100,000 upon her death, about $1.5 million today*. This she had done *as a wealthy landowner [and] rental property entrepreneur* even though she was *unable to read or write*.

Among African Americans, Aunt Caroline Dye was considered a powerful spiritual leader. It was said that African Americans held *great reverence* for her and considered her *word [as] law*. Her spiritual leadership, in part, was granted because of the real problems she helped them face. Due to the herbal base of her conjure, she had incredible skills as a lay nurse. Due to her special knack at finding lost things, they turned to her to reunite families often forcibly separated during slavery. And due to her mojos, she gave African Americans the hope and strength they needed to endure and protest Jim Crow.

Even white men went to consult with her. It was said that *men high up in business affairs laid great store by her alleged remarkable power to foretell occurrences, and that before making a financial move involving any considerable amount of capital they would first consult Aunt Caroline Dye.* Shuffling a deck of cards to help her focus, Aunt Caroline Dye would offer these men advice on their business affairs, much like a money manager on Wall Street. She was so successful that men from *as far as Chicago and other cities of the north and east [came] for a "sitting" with the old woman* in her Arkansas home.

During Jim Crow, any Black woman who possessed Aunt Caroline Dye's amount of wealth and authority would draw unwanted attention from neighboring whites in the community. In 1909, newspapers report that Aunt Caroline Dye was *visited by a deputation of citizens in an endeavor to ascertain whether a cowering wretch [Albert Turner] being guarded by a mob was the right man to hang, following an assault upon a young woman [Bertie Warren] of a distant town.* Similar scenes occurred frequently across the South during Jim Crow: a Black man accused of assaulting a white woman as pretense for lynching. But there was a twist in this story. The deputies who appeared at Aunt Caroline's doorstep wanted her to use her conjure to confirm that Turner was indeed responsible for the crime.

Aunt Caroline was powerful, but even she was not in the position to outright refuse her services to law enforcement. Instead, she simply strung the white citizens along without naming who was responsible for the assault. At first, she told the deputies that Turner was not guilty, but that she could name the guilty party at a later date. So the deputies set a mass meeting where she could name the assailant in front of a mob of four hundred people. When the meeting came, she *gave them much general information but did not specify who is guilty.*

Her conjure put her in a precarious position, which is probably why she was *always surrounded by a veritable bodyguard of negroes who live with her and are always near her.* She understood that whites wanted to use her social position as a conjure woman to enforce white supremacy, much like Rutt's Aunt Jemima character. And when she failed to comply, whites maligned her conjure as superstition and a danger to the broader community. Newspapers associated her with Haitians and their revolution to stoke fear in the general white public, stating that Dye *claimed to be gifted with powers of foresight and other mysterious capabilities approaching the famed voodoo powers of the Haytion [Haitian] negroes.* Like the Haitians, her confounding talents, ancestral knowledge, and especially her penchant for mojos foreshadowed the threat of Black independence.

Blues musician Will Shade tells us that Aunt Caroline could make a mojo or "hand" so powerful you could win anybody's money. *Take her "hand" wit' ya, win everybody's money wit' that spell. Had that much brains—smart lady. She break up all kinds of spells you had.* In his 1923 song "Aunt Caroline Dyer Blues," Shade tells us of a time that Aunt Caroline Dye gave him one of these mojos during a personal consultation. He went to Newport News just to see Aunt Caroline Dye. Once he sat down with her, she said to him, *Son, you don't have to feel so rough. I'm gonna fix you up a mojo, Lord, so you can strut your stuff.* Aunt Caroline Dye likely gave Will Shade a mojo made with what was called High John de Conquer root, the most common type of mojo at this time.[18]

Zora Neale Hurston provides a typical ritual used to make mojos with High John de Conquer root: *Take a piece of fig leaf, sycamore bark, John de Conquer root, John de Conquer vine, three Paradise seeds. Then take a blank piece of paper and draw a square. Write down your heart's desire in that square. Put the square in the "hand" [mojo] and sew all up* in red flannel. *Sew with a strong thread and when the seams are closed, pass the thread back and forth through the bag til all the thread is used up.* Like the nails of the Haitians, the sewing needle is driven through the mojo, over and over again as you use up the leftover thread, to awaken the spirit within.[19]

ZORA NEALE HURSTON TELLS US that High John de Conquer informed many aspects of African American culture during the late nineteenth and early twentieth century.[20] In African American culture, High John appears in stories as an enslaved man who "gets over on the master" (like Bre'r Rabbit, upon whom the Warner Brothers cartoon character Bugs Bunny was based). High John de Conquer also refers to the root of the jalap plant (related to the sweet potato), which African Americans tucked into mojos. Hurston also places High John de Conquer at the center of rituals, like the Ring Shout.[21]

High John de Conquer comes from Africa and is present across the African diaspora. He is analogous to the Yoruba *orisha* Elegua (also known as Eshu) and the Voodoo *loa* Legba, both gods of the crossroads who prepare the way for us to connect with the other *orishas* or *loas*. As the trickster god, High John de Conquer controls the pathways of communication, and he must be approached first when we make our way to the gods for requests. We can see High John de Conquer take up this role in blues music, where he is depicted as the devil you meet at the crossroads and with whom you must strike a bargain for power or success or help out of a bad situation. Due to the primary place his analogs occupy in West African religious traditions, High John de Conquer also enjoys an elevated status in African American conjure.[22]

For African Americans, High John de Conquer is a symbol of our struggle for freedom and our source of hope. He is our laughter, our dance, our mischief, our *drum tune*, our song, our secret pleasure amid terrible oppression. He taught the enslaved his tricks, how to *hit a straight lick with a crooked stick*. He helped the enslaved *kn[o]w that something better was coming. So they [could] laugh in the face of things and s[i]ng, "I'm so glad! Trouble don't last always."* High John reminded the enslaved that *no matter how bad things look now, it will be worse for those who seek to oppress [them]*. That is what Hurston finds when she interviews two conjure women who worked with the root of High John de Conquer: Aunt Shady Anne Sutton and Aunt Diskie.

Aunt Shady Anne Sutton, born two years after the Civil War, was the daughter of an enslaved woman. It was through her mother that Aunt Sutton learned about conjure, including how to use the root of High John de Conquer for mojos. *My mother told me, and I knew she wouldn't mislead me, how High John de Conquer helped us out.* Her mother's participation in these practices led her to believe that her freedom from bondage was inevitable, that freedom just *had* to come. High John de Conquer *done teached the black folks so they knowed a hundred years ahead of time that freedom was coming. Long before the white folks knowed anything about it at all.* Aunt Sutton knew: if you watched the signs and saw the defiance that thrummed through our conjure, you'd know that slavery was unsustainable, that the master couldn't be on top forever.

This belief—that freedom just *had* to come—altered the power dynamics on American plantations. Consider what a newly freed conjure women, Aunt Diskie, reports learning from her work with High John de Conquer. Aunt Diskie tells Hurston she learned that she should *pay what [the slave master] say no mind*. This is because, when her master tried to degrade her, High John de Conquer reminded her of her own self-worth, the place inside herself *where [she] got something finer than this plantation and anything it's got on it.* The master may think that he has broken her soul with his oppression, but he knows nothing about *where [she] gets [her] pleasure from.*

And as we know from the secret pleasures of Sarah Byrd's stolen plums and sly cakewalk, as well as Aunt Patsy and Aunt Prudence's secret prayer meetings, these covert expressions of freedom can greatly threaten the slave master's authority. These acts of joyful defiance helped Aunt Diskie understand how power dynamics can shift, even when they seem intractable. *Ain't that funny?* Aunt Diskie quips. *Us got all the advantage, and Old Massa think he got us tied!*

These lessons about freedom and defiance were passed down through the conjure rituals the newly freed maintained during Jim Crow, like the mojo that W. C. Handy incorporated into his blues. Conjure gave women like Aunt Caroline Dye the psychic strength to *mak[e] a way out of no-way* during a horrible situation that was all too similar to the slavery they had left behind. As scholar-activist Angela Davis writes of the period when the blues emerged, "High John de Conquer, the root incorporating the spirit of hope—the hope of a woman whose man has abandoned her, the hope of a people still striving to be free—metaphorically captures the soul of Black America."[23]

This is why Aunt Caroline Dye, the most powerful wielder of mojos, is so prominent in the blues, even though she was not a musician herself.[24] Blueswomen like Bessie Smith, some of the first musicians to record the blues, would carry on Aunt Caroline Dye's legacy by singing about the power of mojos, especially High John de Conquer.[25] Bessie, too, *went to the gypsy to get my fortune told.* She tells Aunt Caroline Dye, *I've come to see you, gypsy, beggin' on my bended knee. That man put something on me, oh take it off me, please.*

Mojos like High John de Conquer would not only reverse the spell Bessie's man put on her, but bring him under her control, as she sings in "Red Mountain Blues": *[g]ot myself some snakeroot, John the Conquer, too / [c]hewed them both together, I know what they will do / [t]ook some in my pocket, put some in my boot / [t]hat don't make him love me, I'll start right in to shoot.* Conjure is what enables Bessie to remain defiant amid the racism and sexism she faced during Jim Crow. Like a mojo, she's *got the world in a jug, the stopper's in [her] hand. [She's] gonna hold it until you men come under [her] command.*

If the wayward lover here is taken to be America itself, then a thundering message resounds in her blues. With the mojo, Bessie carries forward the threat delivered by Negro Mammies of the previous generation, urging America to deliver on its promise of freedom.

This message was carried on through the next generation of African American singers in the 1960s. Nina Simone, the high priestess of soul, frequently took up a leaf from Bessie Smith's songbook. And the conjure Bessie Smith invoked in her blues had a profound influence on Simone's development of soul music. Just three years after the Ku Klux Klan's murder of four Black girls in the 1963 Birmingham, Alabama, church bombing, Simone penned her much beloved song "Four Women." This song channels the rage of four generations of Black women—a Negro Mammy, Aunt Sarah; Saffronia, the offspring of a slave master's rape of Sarah; Sweet Thing, the daughter of Saffronia, who makes a living as a sex worker; and Peaches, the daughter of Sweet Thing, who exacts revenge for all the pain of her ancestors.

In a 1977 live performance of "Four Women," Simone invokes Aunt Jemima: "Aunt Sarah, she wears a rag on her head. And dig it, head rags are in fashion these days; they're all the fashion these days.

They're all in vogue. Aunt Jemima is in style. Aunt Sarah has lived long enough to see the full circle come round."[26] At her mention of Aunt Jemima, I hear the implicit threat in Billy Kersands's "Old Aunt Jemima." It takes four generations for Kersands's deadly warning to come to fruition in Simone's "Four Women"—in the form of Peaches. Simone sings of Peaches, *I'll kill the first mother[fucker] I see.* Peaches will do so because *[her] life has been rough* so *[she's] awfully bitter these days, because [her] parents were slaves.*

In the nineteenth century, Peaches's enslaved ancestors might have given their slave masters *a dose of poison.* In the 1920s, Bessie Smith would chew snakeroot and High John de Conquer to bring her oppressors *under [her] command.* In the 1970s, Black women were sure to turn Aunt Jemima herself into a mojo to deliver their ancestors' dire warning to America.

CHAPTER EIGHTEEN

Aunt Jemima, the Black Power Revolutionary

On June 15, 2020, Aunt Jemima's legacy entered cyberspace and landed in the infamous TikTok "For You Page." African American singer and songwriter Kirby Lauryen took on the racist history of America's favorite pancake mix mascot with a TikTok video, "How to Make a Nonracist Breakfast." In the video, Lauryen wanders about her modern kitchen, looking for something quick that she can feed her family for breakfast. Peeking into the fridge, she finds a box of Aunt Jemima's pancake mix. A smiling Black woman peers at her from the left corner of the bright red box, the same Black woman who is a staple of all our childhoods. Lauryen takes the familiar box and, instead of pouring the mix into a bowl, holds it to her face as she pummels us with questions that expose the racism behind this national icon:

"Did you know the name Aunt Jemima means slave mammy on the plantation South?"

"Did you know the founder, Chris Rutt, a white man, got the name after attending a minstrel show? Think blackface."

"Did you also know that he hired former slave Nancy Green to be his very own Aunt Jemima, where she went around cooking pancakes and telling people stories of the good old South and afterwards, they could take home a box of Aunt Jemima and the feeling of having their very own mammy?"

Kirby shakes her head at these questions, then smirks as she exclaims, "Not today." She then unceremoniously dumps Aunt Jemima's pancake mix down the drain as she states, "Black Lives Matter, people. Even over breakfast."

This viral video, which garnered millions of views, changed the course of Aunt Jemima's history in the United States. The current owners of the Aunt Jemima franchise, PepsiCo, could not ignore the public discussion and demands of its consumers. Two days after the video launched on TikTok, PepsiCo relented. They decided to "update its image over the years in a manner intended to remove racial stereotypes that dated back to the brand's origins" in slavery. The pancake mix and its associated products were renamed to Pearl Millings Company. And the iconic Negro Mammy was discretely erased from the label as if she had no part to play in the pancake mix's popularity and accrual of cultural cache for nearly a hundred years.

While Kirby's line of questioning brought awareness to Aunt Jemima's hidden origin, I take issue with the initial question she poses: *Did you know the name Aunt Jemima means slave mammy on the plantation South?* She asks it as if we should be ashamed of Negro Mammies. As if Black Americans should not be proud of what we were able to accomplish in such dire constraints as US chattel slavery. They certainly were proud, and they certainly wanted their legacy to live on.

I can't help but think of Negro Mammies like Mariah Robinson who said as much in her 1937 interview with the Federal Writers' Project. She looks back over her ninety-plus years in this world and says *I have ever lived a useful life.* She *served a number [of] years helpin' Doctors on baby cases, nursed an' cared foh de sick both white an' colored.* There seems to be no shame when she says, *I am de Mammy "Black Mammy" of a number of white an' black young men an' women.*[1]

Given the racist history of the Pearl Milling Company, I understand why there has been widespread celebration that Aunt Jemima, the mythic Negro Mammy, was erased from its iconic red box. But the real history of Aunt Jemima, captured in the mojos of the Negro Mammy and the blues of the newly freed, begs to be told. I do not want *that* version of Aunt Jemima erased. So what are we to do with this unwieldy national icon?

I suggest we follow the model of African American artist Betye Saar. Angela Davis credits Saar's iconic 1972 piece, *The Liberation of Aunt Jemima*, with launching a Black feminist wave in the 1970s.[2] *The Liberation of Aunt Jemima* is an assemblage, a piece of art that is constructed from found objects—items that are already used in our culture for another purpose—rather than drawn or painted or sculpted from original materials.

In the tradition of conjure women before her, Saar attempts to hex America in order to free Aunt Jemima. Her ancestors would take toenails, bits of hair, or something the victim had recently worn when they tried to gain power over someone. So Saar gathers the objects that represent some of the worst aspects of our country's history. A Negro Mammy figurine, where she remains frozen in time, forever sweeping plantation porches. A nostalgic scene of a Negro Mammy, lovingly tending a white child. Postage stamps of Aunt Jemima, selling the lie that we were happy as slaves. A tuft of cotton—what America would kidnap, brutalize, and break the backs of our ancestors over for hundreds of years.

To make a mojo, Saar's ancestors would also add objects that signaled the task they wanted the indwelling spirit to complete. So Saar places a fist of Black power in the middle of the display. Finally, she places a gun in the hand of the Negro Mammy figurine. Because the America that created Aunt Jemima's pancake mix—an America that believes Black people were meant to be the docile slaves of whites—must be blown to bits for the real Aunt Jemima to break free.

Like Nina Simone in "Four Women," Saar channels the rage hidden beneath Aunt Jemima's wary smile—the same rage that fueled Billy Kersands's high kicks in his "Old Aunt Jemima" cakewalk, the same rage that first provoked enslaved women like Sarah Byrd to sing about *a dose of poison*. And like other Black women who called the divine down to Earth through spirit possession—those who summoned the Holy Spirit in their shouts during their secret worship meetings, those who called down the *loas* Erzulie and Ogun in their Voodoo ceremonies at the dawn of the Haitian Revolution, those who entreated the spirit of High John de Conquer to reside in their mojos as they migrated from rural plantations to busy cities—Saar calls upon the true spirit of Negro Mammies to inhabit the box. Possessed by the spirit of all the anonymous Negro Mammies who toiled on America's plantations, Aunt Jemima is transfigured as a powerful mojo.

When I look at the gun in Aunt Jemima's hand, I can't help but hear an echo of Bessie Smith's warning in "Red Mountain Blues": *if [this mojo] don't make [America] love me, I'll start right in to shoot.*

Regarding *The Liberation of Aunt Jemima*, Saar explains that "the idea of the work, the accumulation of the materials, the putting them together, the sharing of a work are all part of a ritual."[3] The ritual is one that the descendants of the enslaved made central to African American culture at the turn of the twentieth century: mojos. *The Liberation of Aunt Jemima* was an outcome of this ritual, revamping the docile Negro Mammy found on Aunt Jemima's pancake mix to the rebellious warrior of Saar's enslaved ancestors. By doing this, Saar taps into Aunt Jemima's true legacy: covert resistance, strength in the face of nearly insurmountable adversity, and joyful defiance. Saar's *Liberation of Aunt Jemima* is one model of how we can not only recover that legacy but also participate in the mojo tradition of African Americans to fashion a message of liberation and hope that is still sorely needed today.

PART FOUR
The Quilts of Granny Midwives

CHAPTER NINETEEN

Our Ancient Textile Tradition

I BET YOU HAVE AT LEAST ONE PAIR OF JEANS IN YOUR CLOSET. These pants have had an epic journey that spans two centuries. They've been worn by enslaved African Americans and predestined queens; celebrities and movie stars; presidents, hippies, and punks; civil rights protesters, rebellious youth, and civic-minded soldiers; beauty models and factory workers; rappers and pop icons. They've gone from the humble overalls of the late nineteenth century to the bell bottoms and bootcuts of the 1960s and 1970s, from the ripped jeans of the 1980s to the edgy low-rise pants of the late 1990s—and who hasn't tried at least once to get into those skinny jeans of the 2010s? Today, jeans are still evolving—with the baggy, wide-legged style taking precedence in the 2020s. Their expansive versatility has helped these denim pants maintain their dominance in fashion, both in America and worldwide.

Even today, Americans still love their blue jeans. Three in four Americans claim that jeans are their favorite pants to wear.[1] Over half of Americans report that they wear jeans regularly.[2] And there is no fabric that better captures the myths and identity of America.[3] When Christopher Columbus traveled to the Americas, his ships had sails made of jean fabric.[4] Jeans were sold among the Pilgrims who settled Plymouth Rock.[5] And in the nineteenth century, jeans became the fabric of the American dream.

Jeans were worn by the men who rushed out West to search for gold in the 1840s and 1850s. These miners were a cultural cross-section of the America that would come to be—white, African American, Chinese, Mexican, South American, European. They mucked about in the mud in their denim jeans, bootstraps pulled up tight, eyes wide open for that flash of gold that would, in an instant, turn a pauper into a king.[6]

Manifest destiny, the belief that America had a right to expand and settle the continent from the Atlantic coast to the Pacific, was woven into the seams of these iconic pants. When Chinese miners were forced to give up their search for gold in the 1860s, they were hired to lay the railroad tracks that connected the coast of California to the rest of the nation.[7] Jeans were worn by the white, African American, Mexican, and Indigenous cattle herders, called cowboys, who later shipped the meat and hides from these animals across the nation on those railroads in the 1870s and 1880s.[8]

It was at this time that Levi Strauss patented the blue jeans that we now wear. In 1873, he improved upon the blue jeans worn by miners and cowboys by adding rivets, small metal buttons, that reinforced the areas where the pants were likely to tear.[9] The rivets, created by his business partner, Jacob Davis, made jeans all the sturdier for workwear, skyrocketing the demand. Over the twentieth century, Levi's jeans made waves in American culture, becoming the "American uniform," worn by people of all genders, races, and classes in the country.[10] And over 150 years later, most Americans are still donning jeans based upon Levi Strauss's design.

But while most Americans wear jeans for utility and fashion, the darker history of their jeans remain in the shadows. In this country, jeans were first worn and made by the enslaved.[11] Called "negro cloth," jeans were made using a twill pattern that wove together cotton and indigo-dyed threads (often wool) in a diagonal pattern that made them heavy and sturdy for work in the fields.[12] These two materials, cotton and indigo, were not only essential for the construction of the iconic jeans we all love but also for the economy of slavery. They were major crops that founded America's wealth. And before the cotton boom in the Deep South at the turn of the nineteenth century, indigo was the nation's leading crop. It was considered so valuable that blocks of indigo dye were used as currency to purchase the enslaved.[13]

Although white slave owner and botanist Eliza Lucas is credited with introducing the indigo plant to the American economy in the 1740s, it was her West African slaves who possessed the knowledge of how to cultivate this delicate and demanding plant and how to master a complex and tricky process of extracting dye from its shiny leaves.[14]

Indigo dye production was only one part of a rich textile tradition that the enslaved inherited from their West African ancestors. Among the Yoruba, women were expert dyers of indigo, and they protected this knowledge, passing down their techniques of pigment production from mother to daughter.[15] Intimately linked with religion, it was believed that women in the community originally received the tradition of making indigo dye from the gods. In Yoruba folklore, three *orishas* are considered the patrons and creators of indigo dye: Yemaya, goddess of the ocean and mother-sister of Oshun; Iya Mapo, the patron goddess of women's crafts; and Oshun herself.[16] The women who made indigo dye were part of the *iyami aje*, the secret witches, led by Oshun. As they stood over their dye pots, steadily turning, these sorcerers summoned forth the same *aje* that was used to create the world and, like alchemists, transformed bright green leaves into blue gold.[17]

The entire process of textile production, from dyeing to weaving cloth, held spiritual significance for the West African ancestors of the enslaved. For the Ashanti people of Ghana, the trickster spider god Anansi taught people how to weave the colorful and vibrant kente cloth.[18] In Dogon cosmology, the god and goddess pair Nummo taught humans how to weave.[19] In fact, among the Dogon, the practice of weaving was equivalent to the act of speaking. The connection of weaving to speech in West African culture highlights the spiritual power of textiles, for many believed that speech itself had the power to transform realities, to curse or to bless.[20]

While women took up the mantle of producing indigo and dyeing cloth in West Africa, it was mostly men who were given the sacred task of weaving.[21] In the fifteenth century, many societies in West Africa—like the Mande, Yoruba, Fon, and Congolese—primarily made thin rectangular strips of cloth on looms that could be used as currency or patched into larger textiles like clothes or quilts.[22] In these groups, the men primarily wove the textiles designated for commercial and ceremonial use.[23] They used small portable looms, hence the long vertical strips. But in some groups, like the Yoruba, the women wove too. They wove on large looms that were stationary, so their rectangular strips were a little wider and shorter than the men's textiles.

The women who wove cloth were often overshadowed by the men. With their lightweight looms, the men were able to gain more exposure for their crafts, often weaving on the spot in market squares. But there is one form of textile art for which Yoruba women are especially renown: hairdressing. Some Black women artists, like Sonya Clark, have argued that hairdressing should be considered the first textile art, since it is "the earliest manipulation of fiber [hair] toward an aesthetic and functional purpose."[24] And in fifteenth-century West Africa, women's hair was but another fiber among the raffia (straw made from palm leaves) and cotton and silk woven into textile art that spoke to their neighbors and their gods. In Yoruba women's hairstyles, geometric designs were woven onto the scalp through intricate braids, like cornrows. Cowries and beads, threads and cloth were sewn into plaits that were then styled into elegant coiffures.

In the art of hairdressing, the crafts of weaving and midwifery merged in Yoruba culture. The hair on your head was an extension of your *ori*, your soul and the path it was destined to take in this world.[25] This is partly because your hair is closest to the heavens, making it the first point of contact between you and the gods.[26] And it was by the hair that Yoruba midwives interpreted your *ori* upon birth. Children born with thick, tight curls prone to dread locks were considered a gift from the *orishas*, a child who would bring good fortune to their parents.[27] This is because their curls resembled cowries, a symbol of wealth. Children born with soft, fine curls that spiraled like seashells were believed to be associated with water spirits.[28]

In Yoruba lore, Oshun was the ultimate hairdresser. Oshun's role as a hairdresser overlaps with the role of a midwife in that she assisted and guided the process of birth, which the Yoruba believed was the transition of spirits (ancestors or *orishas*) from the heavens, *orun*, down to Earth.[29] When we were in the womb, Oshun decided which ancestor or *orisha* will return to the Earth through our birth. Oshun's judgment in births was the basis for her praise name, Oshun Seegesi, which roughly translates to "the owner of the flawless, perfectly carved beaded comb."[30] Before we were born, we were simply spirits in the heavenly realm, our existence undefined like loose hair on the scalp. With her comb, Oshun parted the "pathways of existence," setting the course of human lives, much like a hairdresser sculpts loose hair into braids.[31] Upon our birth, Oshun wove the essence of our ancestors or the *orishas* into our *ori* in a never-ending braid of past, present, and future, where spirits cycle from the heavens to the Earth, again and again.

So it may be no surprise that when the enslaved came to the Americas, Oshun became both a midwife and weaver in the lore of the African diaspora. For example, among those who practice Santería in the Caribbean, the *orishas* had many "paths" called *caminos*. On the path of Oshun Ibu Yumu, you would find Oshun depicted as an old woman who weaves without ceasing, dispensing wisdom to the community.[32]

It's said that long after the many times that Oshun saved the world from destruction—after she taught her brother *orishas* the importance of her precious waters when the Earth was created; after her perilous flight into the sun to beg the supreme god, Olodumare, not to destroy the world when her siblings attempted to overthrow the god's rule, burning her bright peacock feathers to the crisp black of a vulture's; after she prevented the men from carrying out their secret pact to gain power over the women—she grew tired of the bustle of cities and the hustle of men.[33] She retired to a river, reveling in its cool depths as a mermaid. During her sojourn by the river, she occasionally came onto land, sitting on a rocker, weaving fish nets and baskets and cloth.

Oshun Ibu Yumu was powerful in her old age. She was the one who guided and supported women during pregnancy, from conception to delivery. She was the ruler over insects and animals that produced venom, from wasps to snakes.[34] Oshun Ibu Yumu was the wise woman who presided over the matters of life and death itself—she could bring new life into existence by making women pregnant and she could bring destruction through her venom.

This version of Oshun is another piece that helps us understand the long evolution of the conjure woman in America: from the Negro Mammies of slavery to the Voodoo Queens of the antebellum era; from the mojo-wielding conjure women during Reconstruction to African American midwives, called Granny Midwives, of the Jim Crow era. Like Oshun Ibu Yumu, the midwives of Black communities, from slavery to Jim Crow, were weavers. And it is through textiles that Black midwives have passed down our conjure for generations.

The aspects of conjure that we've seen so far in the American landscape were incorporated into the fabrics made by these women during slavery, from table linens to jeans worn by the enslaved. The dyes that colored their fabrics were made from the plants and herbs they also used for medicine. The patterns and symbols they wove into their fabrics drew upon iconography of their ancestors' gods, from mermaids like Oshun to the BaKongo cosmogram. And the fabrics themselves were considered to be spiritually potent. Fabrics like red flannel were a crucial part of the construction of mojos. Larger textiles like quilts served as amulets, offering spiritual protection. And in the hands of Granny Midwives, these quilts became a vital means of keeping our conjure tradition alive in the twentieth century as well as defying the racism and sexism in the nascent medical establishment of their time.

CHAPTER TWENTY

Enslaved Midwives as Weavers

I N HER 1938 INTERVIEW WITH THE FEDERAL WRITERS' PROJECT, AN African American midwife of Texas during the Jim Crow period, Lu Lee, tells us about a rich tradition of conjure she inherited from enslaved midwives who doubled as textile producers on the plantation.[1] Several interviews with the previously enslaved report that *de cotton, flax, and wool what our clothes was made of was growed, spun, wove, and sewed right dar on our plantation.*[2] And midwife-weavers primarily took the lead in textile production, hand-making fabric for all the plantation's textile needs: tablecloths and linens, undergarments and pants, blouses and dresses.

Different tasks of textile production were often divvied up along age and gender lines. Children and adults who could not handle the strenuous work in the fields (like the elderly or women who had just given birth) were tasked with "teasing" or *pickin' de burrs an' trash an' sich* out of raw wool or cotton, which replaced indigo as the primary cash crop of plantations and slaveholders at the turn of the nineteenth century.[3] They might also do the carding that came after teasing, which involved spreading a cloud of cotton onto a metal studded wooden board, called a card. The cotton-filled board would be placed directly against another card that was empty. Then they would rub the two cards together, alternatively pulling the cotton between them. This constant friction, pulling the puffy material between the cards, caused the fibers to lay flat.

Once carded, enslaved women would take the now flat fibers to a spinning wheel. If the plantation was small, they might do this work alone in their cabins. After a long day of work in the field, enslaved women practically *fell in at the door* because *[they] would be so tired*. Still, they placed one weary leg before the other as they marched to the spinning wheel. Because if they failed to churn out the amount of thread their slave masters required every night, they would face severe punishment. Many enslaved children fell asleep to the sound of the spinning wheel going late in the night, their mothers squinting in candlelight as they pumped and pumped and pumped.

Lee tells us that on the plantation where she grew up, *[t]here was a loom house made out of logs and there was looms and spinning wheels* where *the old granny women* tended to the *women [who recently] had babies*. At plantations that were large enough to have a separate location dedicated to textile production, many enslaved women transformed tufts of cotton into spindles of thread right alongside enslaved weavers. The loom room or house is primarily where enslaved midwives worked when they were in between deliveries.[4]

To pass the time and feed their souls, the spinners and midwife-weavers would sing spirituals like "Climbing Jacob's Ladder," filling the loom house with their voices.[5] *I'm climbing Jacob's ladder,* one woman would ring out as she began to feed the fibers into the spinning wheel. The midwife-weavers would join, *for my work is almost done*. As the spinners worked the wheel, calling forth thread like a spider issues silk from its gut, they sang, *every round goes higher and higher*. And the midwife-weavers would again join, *for my work is almost done*.

On long rainy days or cold winter evenings, the loom house was one place where midwife-weavers could share their West African heritage, through the shout in their Negro spirituals as well as their stories, awash with conjure. The children were kept busy, their tiny hands reaching out to keep the spinning wheel turning through its hitches, their feet pattering in haste to pass the finished bundles of thread to midwife-weavers. And the children were rewarded with the stories the old women told. Squealing with delight, the children would lean closer to midwife-weavers to hear stories of the harrowing escapes and tricks of Bre'r Rabbit (alternatively known as High John de Conquer), powerful snakes that could talk and were worshipped by witch doctors, powders and dolls that could make you lose your mind, and the mojos that could restore your sanity.[6]

It's likely that Lee first heard the story of her grandparents' kidnapping in the loom room. Lee tells us that *[b]oth [her] granny and grandpa came out of Africa*. Her grandparents were tricked onto the slave ship, lured by their love of red cloth. *They didn't know better than to love red*, Lee shares, so when *the mens come in a ship and showed the red handkies (handkerchiefs)*, her grandparents thought the ship was safe to board. But these white slavers had *fooled them onto the ship*, and before her grandparents knew it, *they was in the chains and don't see the land no more*.

We know from ex-slave interviews that this was a common story often passed down by enslaved midwife-weavers on plantations across the South.[7] The tale was deeply tragic, helping the children to see why they should remain wary of their white masters. But that's not all that we should take from the tale. The story also pointed to the rich spiritual context that midwife-weavers brought to their textile production, inherited from their West African ancestors. For in the enslaved midwife-weavers' tale, the fabrics they made were a way to commune with the spirit world, and weaving itself was a form of prayer.

Lu Lee's ancestors in fifteenth-century West Africa used textiles to communicate. The clothes you wore were considered "sacred skin" that spoke to those in the world of the living and the world of spirits.[8] In the world of the living, what you wore informed others of your spiritual status and political rank in your community.[9] In the world of spirits, the threads weavers pulled and twisted into cloth thrummed with power. The dyes that brightened the weavers' strings with vibrant colors, the decorative knots that adorned royal headdresses and spiritual amulets, and the animal and plant motifs they wove in their fabrics all conveyed messages to the spirit world. These features in their textiles often represented contracts and covenants, invocations and incantations, prayers and curses made within families and the larger community in the presence of ancestors and gods.

For many West Africans, the spiritual and physical worlds were in contact at various moments: during birth and death, where spirits transition from one realm to another, during religious festivals and ceremonies, and during sacred rituals. This belief in the junction of the spiritual and physical worlds was captured in images, such as the Yoruba and BaKongo cosmograms. The Yoruba cosmogram was made by drawing intersecting lines to represent the crossroads, the threshold where these two worlds touch.[10] Similarly, BaKongo cosmogram was drawn as a circle with a horizontal line that cuts a vertical line at the center.[11] The connection between the two worlds was denoted by the point of intersection in the BaKongo cosmogram. And in fifteenth-century West Africa, textiles were one way of channeling that site of intersection between the two worlds, drawing down divine power in hours of dire need.

One of the most prominent textiles of the Congolese that influenced the spirituality of the enslaved were magical bundles called *minkisi*, sacred medicines from the gods.[12] It was believed that a spirit inhabited these divine parcels, and if the practitioner gained power over that spirit, they could get it to do their bidding. *Nkisi* took many forms for the Congolese: small handwoven bags filled with potent plants, fingernail parings, and strands of hair, which were then stuffed into tiny wooden sculptures, clay bowls, or animal skins; pieces of metal, animal teeth, or herbs and roots tied to a string that hung around your neck or wrist or ankle; elaborately knotted strings that were fastened around your waist.[13] All of these amulets featured macrame-like knots or complex folds called *makolo* that were woven into the thin strips of cloth, raffia, rope, or chord used to bind and contain the spirit summoned into the *nkisi*.[14] The enslaved descendants of the Congolese in the Americas would feature these knot techniques centuries later in their own spiritual textile tradition, like the bundles called mojos.

The *makolo* of a *nkisi* drew the power of the dead down to a singular point on Earth, much like the intersection at the heart of the BaKongo cosmogram, harnessing spiritual power to heal or harm, to protect or curse.[15] For the Congolese, the weaving techniques used to make *makolo* were crucial, since they also served as incantations that invoked the spirit within the *nkisi* to action. The *makolo* of a *nkisi* told the inhabiting spirit how many days you intended to pray or the offerings you promised in return for your request or the parts of your body that needed healing.[16]

Much like their West African ancestors, the enslaved and their newly freed descendants would use textiles to communicate with the spirit world well into the twentieth century. The red handkerchief used to kidnap the grandparents of Lu Lee, a Black midwife during Jim Crow, would be used by their descendants to make mojos, sacred bundles derived from the Congolese *minkisi*. The red hue of the flannel primarily used to make mojos was perhaps favored because the color red symbolizes the liminal space between the spiritual and physical world.[17] These mojos would often feature nine folds or knots, and at each fold of the red flannel or knot of the mojo's strings, practitioners would repeat phrases that declared their intentions to the spirit within.[18]

Negro Mammies also used knotted red strings or strips of cloth for healing rituals.[19] Harriet Collins, a Negro Mammy in Texas, tells us in her 1937 Federal Writers' Project interview that she would *wear dat red flannel string all plaited up, [around] my wrist ter keep away de sprains*.[20] Collins also recalls that her mother would *tie er knot* and *put dat knot in de front [of] de head an' tie de string [around] her [head]*. And like the metal, bone, and herbal *minkisi* necklaces of the Congolese, Collins would tie a range of objects onto strings for various ailments and spiritual purposes. She would fasten rattlesnake tails, hog teeth, alligator teeth, chinaberries, or elderberries onto strings around the necks of teething children. To ease cramps in her legs, Collins would use *a dime on de string [around] [her] ankle*.

Sometimes these knotted strings leaned more medicinal, such as the asafetida bags worn around the neck, the most common healing string among the enslaved. The person wearing the necklace would inhale the fumes of asafetida, which has antibacterial and anti-inflammatory properties. Other times these knotted strings leaned more spiritual, addressing the psychological dimensions of illness. When used in this way, these healing strings did not supplant the medicinal components of healing that a Negro

Mammy offered—they were just one part of her healing rituals that might also include teas or the application of salves.[21] For instance, enslaved midwife-weavers often gave a red nine-knotted string to enslaved women who struggled with reproductive health issues such as miscarriages, irregular periods, or difficulties conceiving.[22] A woman suffering with infertility might be given this string in addition to sassafras tea to purify the blood and build up her immune system.

While healing strings primarily have a spiritual function—getting in touch with the divine—there are psychological effects that should not be overlooked. The knotted string ritual could induce a flow or trancelike state similar to meditation.[23] Feeling the knots when you were worried could ground you in the present and have beneficial psychic effects, like temporarily reducing the symptoms of anxiety and depression.

We know that chronic and acute stress, anxiety, and depression raise the risk of miscarriages.[24] Persistent psychological distress can also increase levels of cortisol, which reduces the amount of progesterone in women's bodies.[25] And if a woman doesn't have enough progesterone, periods will cease along with any chance of getting pregnant.[26] So in this scenario, the red nine-knotted string is not fixing some of the physical issues that cause miscarriages or issues in fertility, like diabetes or fibroids. Instead, the knotted string is establishing the conditions of mental health needed to sustain pregnancies and increase fertility.

KNOTTED STRINGS WERE ONE WAY that the Congolese and their enslaved descendants drew help down from the heavens. The designs and motifs woven onto the scalp or into cloth was another method to tap into the divine. Many of the hairstyles and fabrics made by Yoruba women were used for such purposes.

For example, *orishas* were associated with various hairstyles that men and women wore, and devotees would arrange their hair in these special styles to honor their gods.[27] Yoruba women had three main weaving styles used to structure elaborate coiffures (and they all continue to have an impact on African American women's hair): braids like cornrows, called *irun didi*; less intricate braids or large plaits upon the head, called *irun biba*; and hair that is parted into small bundles and wrapped with threads, called *irun kiko*.[28] The Yoruba hairstyle *agogo*, an arrangement of *irun didi* that resembled a rooster's crest, indicated that a woman was married or that she was a priestess of Oshun. Another style of Oshun devotees, along with ancient queens, was the *suku*, or "basket," which features cornrows on all sides of the head that rise to form a hump at the crown. The *suku* was often combined with the *koroba*, or calabash. This style had cornrows that start at the crown and go down every side. At the end of the cornrows, the braids were curled round and round till they resembled a calabash, the gourd considered to be the home of the *iyami aje* or secret witches when they turned into birds at night.[29]

Everyday cloth was also used to get the attention of *orishas*. The most common textile produced by Yoruba women was the *kijipa*, a rough slip of handwoven cloth that was often dyed. It was a multifunctional cloth and was used for bathing and cleaning, as a wrapper to work in the garden, head to the market, or attend ceremonies, and to fasten a newborn to the mother's back.[30] The cloth was also sacred. It was believed that women imparted spiritual power and medicinal potency to the *kijipa* they made—perhaps through the *aje* that Oshun grants to women, allowing them to bless or curse, to heal or harm, to protect or endanger others.[31]

Kijipa is what you took to the priest when you were suffering from illness or heartbreak or wanted to ensure success in a business deal. A priest would often perform rituals to invoke the *ashe* of the cloth through medicinal herbs and prayers.[32] *Kijipa* is what you turned to if you were having difficulties conceiving a child or had frequent miscarriages, one of the cloth's primary uses. A priestess might pray over the cloth and then instruct you to wear it on your belly as you continued to pray for a child, much like the knotted healing strings of the Congolese.[33] *Kijipa* is what you used to make costumes for the annual (or biennial) *egungun* festival, a masquerade event that honors the ancestors.[34] As devotees of the *egungun* sect danced, it was believed that the ancestors came down, for a moment, to inhabit the brightly colored strips of cloth in the dancers' costumes.[35] The *kijipa's* association with the prevention of miscarriages goes hand in hand with its use in honoring the ancestors, since birth and death were, to the Yoruba, transitions from one world to the other.

The handwoven cloths of Yoruba women also contained tales of women's empowerment. The *itagbe* cloth was said to have come from a woman named Poroyen who dared to bargain with the gods and secured a blessed future.[36] One day, Orunmila, the *orisha* of divination, prophecy, and wisdom, fell into a yawning pit. (One wonders how he didn't see that coming.) The hole was too deep for him to get out on his own. Day after day, for the span of a week, Orunmila walked listlessly about the underground cave. He was without food, without water, and without any assistance. On the eighth day, he began to sing a haunting tune about the foolishness of gods and men.

Poroyen was drawn to Orunmila's pit, enchanted by the delicate spell his song cast. She heard someone cry out from the deep cavern for help. But she knew the heart of man was fickle, how quickly men forgot the favors women extended to them. So she extracted a promise from the stranger in the pit—she would help him if he would marry her in return.

Orunmila agreed. As the god of wisdom, he surely appreciated her shrewdness.

Poroyen took off her wrapper, the *itagbe*, and lowered it down into the pit. Slowly, she pulled the stranger out of the cavern. And when she saw his face, she knew at once that she had looked upon a god. Orunmila kept his promise, and Poroyen soon had a baby boy. She took the same *itagbe* she used to rescue Orunmila to tie her baby on her back. The wrapper became a symbol of how she advocated for herself, securing a pact with the gods that cemented a good future for herself and her descendants.

Yoruba women who made the *itagbe* cloth wove motifs of mud fish (a fish that has lungs to breathe air) and frogs and crocodiles.[37] Animals that often live between land and sea, in swamps that are liminal spaces much like the crossroads. Animals that represented water spirits–Yoruba goddesses or *orisha* like Oshun and Yemaya and Olokun who gave women like Poroyen the *aje* to barter with a god.[38] Like the *makolo* of the Congolese, weaving these motifs was a way of invoking the crossroads so that these goddesses who live in the heavens may hear your plea. This is why the *itagbe* was considered to be a visual form of prayer and was often offered to the gods in shrines or placed on prayer altars.[39] Those who continue to make the cloth today weave written words of prayer into the cloth.[40]

Perhaps the most beloved fabric made by Yoruba women was *adire*, the sacred context for the indigo dye that gives your jeans its iconic blue. Indigo symbolized wealth, abundance, and fertility, which is why the Yoruba associated it with *orishas* like Oshun, Yemaya, and Olokun. *Adire* was made on *kijipa* cloth by dye-resist methods. Sometimes women would tie raffia along with rocks or seeds onto a *kijipa*, then dip the bundle repeatedly into vats of indigo dye. The raffia and small objects attached to the cloth would resist the dye, creating patterns. Other times, women would make a thick paste of a root vegetable called cassava and draw patterns on the *kijipa*. As they dipped this cloth into the vat, the cassava paste would also resist the dye, preserving the patterns drawn. It was said that Oshun is the *orisha* who "owns the dye pot" and taught the women how to make the stunning patterns in *adire*.[41]

These patterns included a wide array of motifs: geometric configurations that represented the crossroads, rebirth, or *orishas*; animals associated with witches (like birds, which symbolize the secret witches called *iyami aje*) or a desired outcome (such as an ostrich, which stands above other birds, if you want to gain power in your community); plant leaves, flowers, and symbols of spiritual and political power, like combs and crowns.[42] Like the *itagbe*, the motifs woven upon *adire* often represented prayers. A woman who was suffering from miscarriages might use a crocodile motif to reach out to water goddesses like Oshun.[43] A woman who was in a dire situation might use a fish motif, as fish were a common sacrifice offered to the gods to curry favor.[44] Once finished, the *adire* strip would be laid upon a prayer altar dedicated to the gods or used as a wrapper, the contact of the cloth immersing the woman in prayer whenever her troubles caused her to fret and worry.[45]

In the New World, the divine indigo strips of the Yoruba like *adire* were transformed into the jeans of the enslaved. Jeans are a vivid symbol of the trauma our enslaved ancestors endured. Under slavery, the indigo fabric of West Africans became associated with a lifetime of bondage, supplanting the rich spiritual traditions from which they came. The harsh labor that slave masters foisted upon our ancestors turned what was once a sacred ritual into painful drudgery. The holy indigo that came from the *aje* of Yoruba women became the "blue gold" that Europeans had kidnapped Lee's grandparents along with millions of other West Africans for, earning it the nickname "the devil's dye."[46]

ALTHOUGH BLUE JEANS MARKED ENSLAVEMENT, they also became associated with rebellion and the struggle for freedom. Advertisements crafted by slave owners to recapture the enslaved often included jeans in the descriptions of what the enslaved wore when they ran.[47] For those who stayed, like midwife-weavers, jeans were also a symbol of the struggle for survival and dignity in the face of cruel treatment. The toils of slavery may have effaced the sacred context of the indigo in our jeans, but midwife-weavers managed to give these denim pants a new spiritual meaning that drew upon the textile traditions of their foremothers.

When these jeans were worn out, riddled with holes, and no longer salvageable by patchwork, they were given a new life in our textile tradition as material for quilts. Many of the enslaved joyfully recall gatherings called quilting bees, where the old women would gather to make the quilts that would keep the enslaved warm come winter. These quilts supplemented the meager bedding provided by slave masters, which was barely enough to cover the enslaved, let alone protect them from harsh winter elements. While snow was not too common in the Deep South, there were still biting winds that brought the danger of frostbite in the heart of winter.

Sometimes quiltings would be grand occasions, occurring alongside corn-shucking competitions. The enslaved from nearby plantations from miles away would join. Other times the gatherings were held in the secrecy of cabins, during the *dancing and singing on Saturday nights* that Lu Lee remembers fondly.

It took only one enslaved woman to get a quilting bee started on a given Saturday night. She would whisper to another woman, *I's gon'a step over to one or another's cabin*.[48] Then that woman would whisper her plans *to step over* to another enslaved woman. Soon enough word would spread to the cook of the plantation. Throughout the day, the cook would slip a little something here and there into her pockets, sewn extra large for this purpose, so that she and the other enslaved would have food for the quilting bee. Another woman might cajole her husband or brother to bring his banjo so that they would have some music to sing to while they quilted and to dance to when they were finished. On those evenings, the cabin would be filled with women who worked together to produce quilts for the entire slave quarter. It was understood that this huge task would be easier to accomplish if done together in a group, where *everybody took a part of the quilt to finish*.[49]

When Lee assisted the women at the quilting bees, she learned a tradition whose roots stretch back to West Africa. The top layer of quilts usually consisted of long strips of rectangular cloth that were pieced (sewn together to make a larger piece of cloth) or appliquéd (sewn on top of another piece of cloth), in keeping with the vertical strip structure her West African ancestors used.[50] The enslaved would often tear old jeans or overalls, skirts, leftover material, and even rags into strips to be pieced or appliquéd.

Unlike European quilt traditions—which emphasized symmetry and uniformity, prioritized staying within grids, and valued how closely the quilt maker could replicate the same image over and over again—African American quilts often intentionally deviated from these norms.[51] Like jazz, these enslaved quilters improvised, repeating images with stylized differences.[52] In some West and Central African textile traditions, it was believed that improvising upon or rupturing patterns was an instance of the ancestor "breaking through" or possessing the artist.[53]

For many enslaved women, the quilting process was just as sacred as the spinning and weaving that made the original materials. They prayed and sang and perhaps even shouted as they quilted. While they were likely to say that during the shout the Holy Spirit had fallen upon them, moving them to create striking designs, their West African forebears would have said this was an instance of their ancestors taking hold of them to break the pattern in their stitching.

These quilts were steeped with conjure. They carried our herbal knowledge, as it was known that enslaved women often *got the pattern [for quilts] by goin' out into the woods and getting a leaf to cut it by*.[54] And the quilts sometimes were designed to provide spiritual comfort, functioning like amulets. For instance, enslaved quilters believed that evil spirits couldn't follow straight lines, so sometimes they intentionally introduced asymmetry and busy patterns to sidetrack the spirits that could bring bad luck upon them.[55] Quilts also featured large, bulky knots that resembled the *makolo* of the Congolese.[56] And quilts were used in spiritual rituals meant to bring good luck to the household and to facilitate peaceful transitions during death.[57]

Many quilts the enslaved made also featured symbols that carry spiritual significance in Yoruba, Vodun, and Congolese religions.[58] Among the enslaved, the BaKongo and Yoruba cosmograms merged with Christianity and were represented by the frequent diamonds, crosses, and pinwheels featured on their quilts.[59] Weaving these cosmograms into their textiles made these fabrics an instance of the crossroads, a locus where power from the gods could be channeled on Earth. Like the sacred cloths of the Yoruba, these strips, woven into quilts by the midwife-weavers, were prayers that summoned spiritual power into their warp and weft. This was how, for generations, enslaved Black women were taught the power that lay in the things their white slaveholders so easily discarded, the things they could not see right under their noses.

CHAPTER TWENY-ONE

Black Midwives and the Nineteenth-Century Brawl over Abortion

ENSLAVED MIDWIFE-WEAVERS SAW ENOUGH IN THEIR LINE OF WORK to need to pray constantly. They witnessed how slavery developed for the worse at the turn of the nineteenth century.[1] They saw slave doctors delve deeper and deeper into Black women's wombs, experimenting on them with grotesque and risky surgeries, at the behest of slave owners looking to maintain and increase their workforce.[2] They saw fetuses flee the wombs of young, enslaved girls who had been violated by their masters and were far, far too young to ever be pregnant.[3] They witnessed morbid innovations in torture, like enslaved pregnant women being forced to lie down on the ground with their bellies in a pit while they were whipped within an inch of their life.[4]

These practices were most prevalent during the cotton boom at the turn of the nineteenth century. From the 1740s to the 1790s, indigo was the most profitable crop on slave plantations, over and above rice, sugar, and cotton.[5] But the onset of the American Revolution in 1775 made England, one of the United States' biggest buyers of indigo, search elsewhere for that blue hue, like India.[6] And new inventions like the cotton gin (1794) made cotton production both easier and faster. With the increase in production, cotton became more affordable for the everyday American, which, in turn, drove up demand for the crop, outstripping the demand for indigo.

At the height of summers, the enslaved would break, beat, soak, and transform deep green stalks of indigo into blue dye. Come fall, the enslaved were forced to wade through a sea of white, prying cotton bolls from their thorny husks. Once they harvested the cotton, their slave masters shipped bales of it to northern mills to be processed. Slave owners became instantly wealthy—along with the northerners who owned the mills.

In the Deep South, the maze of rivers that made their way to the Gulf of Mexico made the land especially fertile. This was delta land. This was the land that made cotton king and those who knew how to husband it supreme. Those who worked this soil knew that you could lay anything into this river silt, and it would grow (good *God*, would it grow). In this land, it wasn't just cotton that was laid, but the American dream itself.

But the American dream has always had a dark underbelly. An increase in the demand for cotton during the boom resulted in an increase in the demand for slaves. With the ban on the transatlantic slave trade in 1808, slave owners could no longer legally buy enslaved peoples from Africa. So they turned to the enslaved women on their plantation and decided to "breed" them instead. They interfered with enslaved women's wombs to increase the number of slaves to continue the backbreaking work of harvesting the cotton that filled their dreams. Slave owners would resort to tactics of reward and punishment to force the enslaved to have children.[7] They might offer couples a separate house with extra bedding or offer perks to enslaved women, like time off or extra food. If the couple refused to have sex, the slave master often brutally whipped them until they relented.

Slave masters began to settle their financial accounts based upon the number of children enslaved women had. They even went so far as to will the unborn children of enslaved women to their descendants.[8] But slave masters could never truly be sure that the enslaved mother and child would survive childbirth. During the nineteenth century, a host of problems could arise during and immediately after pregnancy. Many women suffered painful, prolonged deliveries that caused vesicovaginal fistulas, small tears that effaced the separation of the vagina from the urethra, leading to incontinence and, if left untreated, infertility.[9] And most women feared puerperal fever, an extremely common bacterial infection of the reproductive system that could develop quickly after giving birth and often resulted in death.

Slave owners turned to doctors to ensure some measure of control over the hazards that haunted childbirth. When slaveholders were deciding whether to buy an enslaved woman, they sought doctors to validate whether she was healthy and likely to bear children. And if the woman slave masters bought failed to produce children, they sought doctors to treat her apparent infertility. It was in this context that James Marion Sims, the father of gynecology, experimented on three enslaved women, Betsey, Lucy, and Anarcha, in Alabama in the 1840s.

During Sims's attempts to develop treatment for vesicovaginal fistulas and thereby curtail infertility, he operated on these women without anesthesia, even when his colleagues who performed the same surgery on pigs gave their animals that courtesy.[10] For nearly two centuries, Sims was lauded in the medical community for his innovations in surgery and contributions to the field of gynecology. In New York City, a statue dedicated to his legacy was set up across from the New York Academy of Medicine in Central Park. That statue stood for nearly a century, finally taken down in 2018, after protestors demanded the removal of such a blatant racist on a pedestal in a public square.[11]

Slave doctors like Sims earned a steady paycheck when they were hired by slave owners, often the only people wealthy enough to pay for their services. Their investment in the system of slavery often made these doctors fail in their attempts to remedy the very cases of infertility that they were trying to cure. For example, these doctors routinely refused to acknowledge how rape of girls who were far too young to have children could lead to deformities in the pelvis.[12] These girls also suffered severe malnutrition that caused rickets, a disease in which the bones become soft and deformed because of a vitamin D deficiency. Both these factors led to deliveries that were painful and long, making conditions ripe for developing vesicovaginal fistulas.[13] Slave masters, who overworked enslaved women, uually did not give them enough time to recover in between pregnancies, which led to frequent miscarriages.[14]

The presence of a doctor during this period did not ensure a safe delivery for any woman in America. Often doctors relied on heroic methods and tools such as bloodletting to hasten delivery and cure fevers or performing incredibly risky C-sections. They were also known to use roughly handled forceps with unwashed hands that could cause lacerations in the vagina along with infections.[15] These methods greatly endangered women in the throes of labor.

So, when slave doctors could not deliver the results that the slave owner expected, they cast about for someone to blame. They did not consider how their heroic methods might have contributed to the problem, nor did they care how the trauma of slavery could place catastrophic stress on our bodies and quite literally shrivel our wombs. Instead, slave doctors used enslaved midwives as their scapegoat for the high death rate. Doctors claimed midwives were needlessly interfering when labor began. And they complained that midwives called them too late to do much good when complications arose. As much as they could, doctors tried to paint enslaved midwives as a danger to pregnant women, unaware of and unwilling to grasp the midwife-weaver's essential role in labor and delivery.

But it was enslaved midwife-weavers who truly cared for the well-being of mother and child on the plantation. They were Negro Mammies who specialized in women's reproductive issues. And like other Negro Mammies, they primarily relied on noninvasive methods to address problems that arose during pregnancy, delivery, and postparturition.[16] Their practices were largely shaped by their West African ancestors and are still practiced by traditional birth attendants on the continent today.[17]

Negro Mammies were especially skilled in combining their herbal remedies with massage techniques for alleviating sprains and assuaging congestion. And Negro Mammies often coupled these massages with herbal baths to provide further relief to achy joints. Midwife-weavers drew upon this knowledge when they prepared enslaved mothers for delivery by giving them steaming baths and performing massages on the womb to get the baby in position for delivery or even to turn a breech. To prevent painful lacerations, midwife-weavers applied herbal salves and gave women perineum massages to relax the vagina during labor.[18] Midwife-weavers would also give women teas to adjust the speed of delivery. For instance, black pepper tea was given to make women sneeze and hasten contractions.[19]

Enslaved communities also looked to midwife-weavers to provide spiritual comfort. Like their West African ancestors, the enslaved believed that during moments of life and death, when the threshold between the spiritual and physical was open, many things could go wrong. The spirit of the child that was coming could be harmed by the curses and ill wishes a neighbor might have against the pregnant woman.[20] And malevolent spirits, like the Yoruba *abiku*, could come through the spiritual threshold and cause mothers incredible grief. *Abiku*, those "born to die," were children who died shortly after or during birth. The Yoruba believed that if the appropriate spiritual remedies were not offered, the *abiku* would return again and again to the mother in future pregnancies, causing all of her children to die.[21]

But the midwife-weaver was born with the power to stand in the crossroads, and the enslaved knew to look for signs that indicated this spiritual gift. One common sign was the midwife-weaver's own birth. If the midwife-weaver was born with a caul over her face, it was believed that she would have second sight or be able to see spirits and ghosts.[22] That second sight was valuable if you were assisting a birth; it meant that you could access the crossroads and direct the child that was coming safely to its new life.

The midwife-weaver also performed rituals to fortify the spiritual threshold during a vulnerable time for the mother and child. Early in labor, midwife-weavers would start a "birthing fire" and throw in herbs to keep away malevolent spirits.[23] And shortly after birth, midwife-weavers would bury the placenta to keep the child tied to Earth.[24] This was in keeping with many West African societies that believed newborns dwelled in the liminal space between the living and the dead for several days after birth. Practices like burying the placenta in the family's land and sacred naming rituals secured the child to their new life.[25] These rituals made midwife-weavers the spiritual leaders of their communities when it came to reproductive matters, making them the perfect ally for enslaved women who wanted to wrestle control over their wombs away from slaveholders.

Midwife-weavers often taught enslaved women tactics that gave them some reproductive autonomy. They taught these women to prolong breastfeeding, which hindered pregnancy, so that they could give their bodies time to recover. They helped these women keep their deliveries a secret to prevent the interference of slave doctors while giving birth. And they even provided emmenagogues to cause abortions, what they would call "restoring" the menses or "bringing the woman right."[26]

THE MIDWIFE-WEAVER DID NOT JUST bring new life into existence; she also knew the herbs that could cause miscarriages and abortions. To induce an abortion, women would be given the roots of plants like black haw to chew or teas of dogwood, rue, or pine straw (for turpentine).[27] When midwife-weavers made indigo dye for our blue jeans, they would also parcel out some of the plant to give to enslaved women who wanted abortions. Lu Lee, a Granny Midwife during Jim Crow, recalls several women who *got pregnant and didn't want the baby* during slavery. Lee tells us *they used to take indigo to unfix [miscarry] themselves.*[28] Midwife-weavers understood that slavery provided several reasons why a woman might want to abort a child—pregnancy by rape of a slave master or forced coupling with another enslaved person or an outright refusal to bring a child into a state of perpetual bondage.

Out of all the herbs and roots that enslaved women used to ensure their reproductive freedom, cotton was by far the most popular. Cotton roots can make the uterus contract and cause the cervix to soften and open to expel the fetus.[29] So, midwife-weavers often gave enslaved women cotton roots to bring on contractions during labor. By this same principle, cotton roots could be taken to perform an abortion. Taken early in a pregnancy, cotton roots would coax the cervix to open prematurely and push out the fetus, causing a miscarriage.

In a way, using cotton to cause abortions was a form of poetic justice. The cotton that enticed the slave masters to put pressure on their reproductive labor also gave these women a way to assert a sliver of bodily autonomy. That's the way that previously enslaved Mary Gaffney tells it to her Federal Writers' Project interviewer.[30]

When Gaffney was brought to Texas in 1860, her slave master tried to force a man upon her so that she would increase his number of slaves. *I just hated the man I married but it was what Maser said do.* Like so many white men who flocked to the West, her slave master had come to Texas seeking a vast fortune. *When [the master] came to Texas he took up big lots of land and he was going to get rich.* Gaffney resented that her womb was her master's get-rich-quick scheme, and at first, she tried to resist his plan. *I would not let that negro touch me and he told Maser and Maser gave me a real good whipping.* The whipping demoralized her so greatly that later that night she *let that negro have his way.*

Under these conditions, it is no surprise that many of the enslaved ran away. Gaffney reports that *they was one or two slaves that tried to run off and go to the north.* The men ran, wearing the same jeans they wore as they worked in the fields. The same jeans they wore when they buried their loved ones whose bodies had been worn ragged by years of backbreaking labor. The same jeans that they wore when they were forced to "marry" at the master's orders.[31] But for those who did not run, like Gaffney, there were other ways to enact revenge.

I cheated Maser, Gaffney proudly tells her interviewer. *I never did have any slaves to grow and Maser he wondered what was the matter. I tell you son, I kept cotton roots and chewed them all the time.*

Slave masters soon became aware that enslaved women were using cotton root to prevent or end pregnancies, so they began to keep careful watch. Enslaved women were severely punished if caught. Slave masters even enlisted white doctors to prescribe medicines to counteract the effect of cotton.[32] So Gaffney was *careful not let Maser know or catch [her], so [she] never did have any children* while *[she] was a slave.* Many enslaved women would get around the slave master's watchful eye by simply gathering cotton roots at night from the fields or the little cotton patch they raised in their yards, so they could chew the root secretly in their quarters.[33]

Gaffney likely got this idea from the midwife-weaver on the plantation, an old Black woman who would *gather all the medicine out of the woods.* This old woman was also responsible for making clothes for the enslaved out of the cotton that Gaffney, along with others, picked from the fields to the point of exhaustion, from sunrise to nine or ten o'clock in the evening. And as the principal textile producer on the plantation, this enslaved midwife-weaver frequently handled raw plants and herbs that could be transformed into beautiful tapestries—or used for subversion.

So the midwife-weaver who made Gaffney's clothes would have been intimately familiar with cotton in all its uses, as a textile fiber and as a curative element. She knew how to dissect the plant in its raw form. She knew what it took to transform cotton from a fluffy cloud to long threads to an intricate tapestry. And her skill as a weaver required the same precision she used in making her medicines for the enslaved on the plantation. To cause a miscarriage, she only needed *just enough [of] that root to get one flower.*[34] Cotton root could be deadly if too much was taken; it was her conjure that gave her expert knowledge of just how much to use, which she passed on to desperate women like Gaffney.

During the antebellum period, the use of cotton as an abortifacient was so widespread in Texas that many of the enslaved joked that the women would inadvertently end slavery in this way—because there would be no new generation to enslave. Anna Lee (previously enslaved in Texas) tells her Federal Writers' Project interviewer that *our negro women they like to have depopulated this country on the negro race* due to their chewing cotton roots.[35] Because of this, Anna Lee surmises that *[i]f slavery had lasted much longer they would not have been slaves except the old ones they had here left, cause when [it] was ended they was not being any new slaves born, we had done quit breeding.* The "depopulation" of the enslaved was likely an exaggeration on Anna Lee's part, but we know from medical journals that doctors witnessed the use of cotton as an abortifacient by enslaved women.[36] And these doctors thought the method was so effective it merited scholarly investigation.

Anna Lee informs her interviewer that these abortions were such a threat to slavery that *they finally made a law against that but it did not help much.* She was likely referring to the abortion ban in Texas, a statute instituted in their 1857 penal code. At this time, abortion was a widespread practice in the United States, and it was generally acceptable among white women up to the point of the quickening, the moment in the pregnancy when a woman could feel the fetus moving, usually at fifteen to twenty weeks.[37] Even some doctors prescribed cotton roots to their white women patients after learning about enslaved women's use of the crop from medical journals.

For the most part, however, Black midwives were the ones who offered cotton roots.

Under the Texas abortion ban, anyone who helped women have an abortion would be jailed for two to five years.[38] The bill defined abortion as any actions where *the life of the fetus or embryo shall be destroyed in the woman's womb or that a premature birth thereof be caused*. The only exception provided was when the life of the mother was in danger: *nothing in this chapter applies to an abortion procured or attempted by medical advice for the purpose of saving the life of the mother*. According to this exception, the only legal abortions were ones determined and provided by "medical advice" or doctors—not midwives—meaning that after this statute, it was white male doctors who determined when an abortion should or should not be attempted.

The 1857 abortion ban in Texas redrew the nation's ethical lines of what were acceptable abortions and what were illegal ones. Before this statute, the ethics and feasibility of abortions were determined by women—both the pregnant woman who alone knew when the fetus had quickened and midwives who, in several communities across the nation, possessed expert knowledge on how to restore the menses. It is not an accident that the new statute appeared precisely at a time when white male doctors were striving to professionalize medicine. In fact, one doctor in particular, Horace Storer, was largely responsible for the increased restrictions of abortion found in Texas's 1857 penal code. As president of the American Medical Association, founded only a decade earlier, Storer launched a nationwide campaign against abortion.[39]

Doctors who wanted to study midwifery had a particularly steep hill to climb, since for centuries it was understood among the general public that midwifery was a distinctly female practice. Not to mention, in many rural communities, both Black and white, enslaved midwife-weavers were revered, their special skill considered a divine gift. In these rural communities, midwife-weavers were valued for their ability to both assist birth as well as terminate pregnancies. It was Storer who devised a devious plan to get the midwives out: criminalize abortion and, thus, rob them of their moral (or divine) high ground among the public.

In 1857, Horace Storer wrote an anonymous letter from the American Medical Association to the governors of every state, stating strong opposition to abortion.[40] This letter moved governors to create laws that imposed greater restrictions on abortions like the 1857 statute in Texas. But his move did not eradicate Black midwives as he had hoped. During Anna Lee's lifetime, Black midwives would remain the preferred reproductive health care provider in rural southern communities, relying upon the herbal, spiritual, and noninvasive methods of their enslaved foremothers to bring new life into the world. Everything changed, however, after the Civil War.

MARY GAFFNEY RECALLS HOW, UPON learning that she was "free," her elation quickly turned to worry and fear. *When Maser came home he told me that I was free, I just hollered because then I could go where I wanted to or I could get on a log and jump off if I wanted to, but my merriment did not last long.* She began to think about what it would mean to leave the plantation with no money to purchase food or clothes or pay for a doctor if she or her husband became deathly ill. So she, along with the other newly freed, *began to ask Maser and cry as we didn't know what we was goin' to do.* The master washed his hands of them, saying *the government had done freed us and he didn't have any more to do with us.*

This was a major failure of the Reconstruction period. The government never built the infrastructure needed to support the newly freed as they transitioned to citizens who could secure a paycheck, travel without restriction, and, in the case of Black men, vote. Without this infrastructure in place, the former slaveholders simply introduced slavery in a new form: sharecropping.

This new system is why Gaffney claims that they *was freed one way to go in worse slavery than ever.* Under slavery, it was in the master's interests to keep those they held in bondage alive, to feed them and clothe them and secure a doctor if they were gravely ill. Under slavery, if they died, the slave master considered it a loss of "property" and therefore their money. But when the enslaved were freed, their new bosses had no incentive to treat them with any decency. Under sharecropping, previously enslaved men and women leased land, tools, and crops from their former slave owners. Since the newly freed were now considered "employees," their previous slave masters felt they no longer needed to supply health care, clothes, or food as they had done (in the most miserly manner) during slavery.

Under this new system, the bosses barely paid the newly freed and ballooned their debt, year after year, until it was impossible for the enslaved to ever repay it. *[A]fter the [Civil] war we did not have anything to eat half the time,* Gaffney tells us. There was *no money to buy clothes with muchless money to have a doctor with when we got sick and no one cared what became of us, we could have died for all our white man cared.* So the newly freed often felt that they had been shortchanged on the freedom and rights that had been promised to them by the thirteenth amendment.

Many of the newly freed refused to work as sharecroppers, having seen that it was like being enslaved all over again. But cotton was still booming, and the bosses needed workers. So former slave owners began to look overseas for a new workforce. During the 1860s and 1870s, hundreds of male Chinese laborers immigrated to the delta South. They were largely Cantonese, from South China.[41]

Prior slave owners threatened the newly freed population, saying they could replace African Americans with this new labor force. Because of this threat, many of the newly freed simply took what they could get by way of jobs, even if it was not very much. *If we got work which we had to do,* Gaffney tells her interviewer, *half the time we never got payed for that so we had to take just what they would give us.* Former slave owners resented the newfound freedom of African Americans, so they were not willing to cede the demands of the Black population for better pay and working conditions and the respect they deserved as laborers.

Doctors also lost their massive paycheck upon slavery's demise. The government wouldn't pay for the health care of the newly freed and neither would the sharecropper bosses. And the previously enslaved population simply didn't have the money. It was largely Granny Midwives who shouldered the burden of health care for the newly freed in this gap. These midwives also tended to white communities in rural areas that did not have ready access to hospitals. Doctors resented the presence of these women healers in the rural South, who they saw as "stealing" their jobs.

So, after the Civil War, doctors like Horatio Storer redoubled their efforts to attack midwives. We can see how in his book *Why Not? A Book for Every Woman*. Storer sought to convince the public that life begins at conception, an uncommon belief at the time. If life begins at conception, then committing an abortion, even before the quickening, meant taking a life and so was clearly immoral. Midwives, who were by far the most likely to offer this service, became further tied to immorality.

This idea especially attacked Black midwives, who had been suspected of abortion practices during slavery. In fact, in medical journals doctors suggested that enslaved women's tendency to miscarry was not due to the harsh conditions of slavery but to midwives who encouraged enslaved Black women to abort.[42] When enslaved women miscarried, the plantation doctors assumed that they did so on purpose and were degenerate mothers with a tendency to kill their offspring.[43]

These claims downplay how enslavement informed Gaffney's decision to have abortions. During slavery, she chewed cotton roots and never once gave birth. She tells the interviewer that *after freedom we had five children*. She valued children, as did many enslaved women.[44] But slavery was so horrible that she resolved not to have children in those conditions. For her efforts, she ended up with a large family.

Doctors like Storer ignored the role slavery played in Black women's reproductive choices and, instead, tapped into the popular ideas and fears of white Americans to press his point. After the Civil War, white Americans began to fear that the newly freed and immigrant populations would soon outnumber them. And the newly emerging pseudoscientific theory of eugenics that appeared in newspapers, magazines, and government-funded research institutes across the nation gave white Americans arguments that bolstered their fears. Eugenics convinced them that their race was superior because of their genetic composition and that they had a duty to ensure that the most "fit" (i.e., them) survived.

And yet, at this time, white birth rates were falling in various parts of the nation.[45] Storer blamed these lower birth rates on white women receiving abortions from midwives. He claimed these white women who sought abortions were not only insane, but that they were also shirking their moral duties as wives and propagators of the white race.

In *Why Not?*, Storer bemoaned *[a]ll the fruitlessness of [his] present generation*. He looked around at the *great territories of the far West, just opening to civilization, and the fertile savannahs of the South*. He thought about these parts of the country, full of the newly freed and immigrants, and how they *offer homes for countless millions yet unborn*. Storer was likely talking about men like my great-great-great grandfather, Thomas "Papa Sing" James, a Chinese man who migrated to the delta South in the 1870s. Because of men like these, Storer beseeched the white women of America to have more babies. *Shall [these homes] be filled by our own children or by those of aliens?* Storer asks, for *[t]hat is the question that our women must answer; upon their loins depends the future destiny of the nation.*

It is no accident that today we face an increase in antiabortion rhetoric and legislation in tandem with a steep surge in anti-immigration speech and law. As evidenced in Storer's remarks, these two stances have always been linked in our country and continue to be perpetuated by the profound fear of whites.[46]

This fear was so permeable among white Americans after the Civil War that it shaped laws for the next hundred years of the country, laws that severely disadvantaged women of all races, as well as immigrants, African American men, and the disabled. White supremacists did not want Black people mixing with whites, which gave rise to Jim Crow laws in the South that promoted social segregation. They did not want white women to stop having babies, so they restricted access to contraception and abortion via the Comstock Act of 1873. And in the late nineteenth and early twentieth centuries, they also forcibly sterilized those in the population who they deemed "undesirable" through state laws—those deemed criminals, the "feeble-minded," and "promiscuous" women. They also severely restricted Chinese immigration with legislation like the Page Act of 1875, which barred Chinese women from entry to the United States, and the Chinese Exclusion Act of 1882, which barred Chinese laborers from entry.[47]

In the end, Storer's crusade against abortion failed to get rid of midwives. To his dismay, in the 1920s, the government launched a program that sought to integrate midwives into the medical profession via the Promotion of the Welfare and Hygiene of Maternity and Infancy Act, also known as the Sheppard-Towner Act. Under this new law, Black midwives were forced to work with the doctors who despised them. If they could not end midwifery, doctors resolved to absorb it into the country's burgeoning for-profit medical system. Doctors began a campaign to change the public perception of Black midwives and used their rich conjure traditions as a way to demean and denigrate the legitimacy of their practice. This struggle over which group had the moral and legal authority to perform midwifery—white male doctors or Black rural, southern Granny Midwives—would come to a head at the height of the Jim Crow period.

This fight between doctors and Granny Midwives during Jim Crow is a pivotal point in our four-hundred-year voyage through Black women's magic. Upon emancipation, different kinds of conjure women stepped into the roles the Negro Mammy previously served in enslaved communities. There were women like Aunt Caroline Dye, who primarily offered spiritual comfort through mojos and nursing minor ailments. Granny Midwives were another. With two generations' worth of reproductive care, the work of Granny Midwives spanned the entire Jim Crow period, and some Granny Midwives delivered babies well into the 1970s. The first generation of Granny Midwives were the daughters of enslaved midwife-weavers. They were women like Lu Lee, a Granny Midwife who was a child when slavery ended. The second generation were the granddaughters of enslaved midwife-weavers, like Onnie Lee Logan (1910–1995). These second-generation Granny Midwives were a crucial link to our enslaved past during desegregation, a great transition that reconfigured American society.

The conjure of their enslaved grandmothers—the roots and herbs, the prayers and spiritual rituals, the salves and massage techniques, the medicinal teas and baths, the rich textiles—informed this distinctive tradition of midwifery in the rural South. During a time when the integration America promised to Black people was premised upon assimilation to whiteness, Granny Midwives were largely responsible for keeping our conjure tradition alive in the twentieth century.[48]

CHAPTER TWENTY-TWO

The Quilt of Motherwit

ONNIE LEE LOGAN (1910–1995), A BLACK MIDWIFE DURING JIM CROW, tells us about the origin of the title, Granny Midwife. *That's yo granny. That's yo grannymother. She delivered you. She was the first one to put her hands on you. She's the one that made you cry, got the breath in you.*[1] Granny Midwives were responsible for nearly 80 percent of Black and white births in rural, southern Black towns.[2] If you were born in the South in the first half of the twentieth century, Black or white, it's likely you would have been ushered into the world by a Black woman.

Logan was responsible for the delivery of hundreds of babies during her over fifty-year career as a midwife.[3] By the time Logan became a midwife in the 1930s, the tradition of midwifery she'd inherited from her mother (who was already one generation from enslavement) had undergone major changes. Unlike her grandmother, an enslaved midwife-weaver, Logan not only made her own salves and teas, but she also regularly bought ready-made mixes like Vicks VapoRub at stores.[4] And Logan no longer made her clothes and household items from raw materials or handmade cloth like her grandmother's generation did. Instead, Logan bought prepared fabric like denim and gingham from stores, and then sewed her clothes at home.

But perhaps the most profound change to the African American tradition of midwifery was the midwives' helter-skelter integration into the emerging medical establishment in the rural South, such as hospitals and maternity clinics installed in major cities like Atlanta and Montgomery. With the change brought on by the Sheppard-Towner Act, Logan found herself between two worlds—a mediator between a predominantly white medical establishment and the Black community she served. And in this movement back and forth between two communities, Granny Midwives like Logan were forced to reevaluate the midwifery tradition of their grandmothers, deciding what they should keep and what they should let go so that they could pass on a tradition that was still relevant and feasible for the generations to come.

As Logan moved between these two groups, she often displayed what Toni Morrison describes as a blended cosmology, "an acceptance of the supernatural and a profound rootedness of the real world at the same time with neither taking precedence over the other."[5] Morrison explains that Black people are primarily practical in how we approach life, but "within that practicality we also accepted what [she] suppose[s] could be called superstition and magic, which is another way of knowing things." Logan called this blend of practical wisdom and otherworldly insight "motherwit."

With motherwit, Granny Midwives adapted the conjure of their enslaved grandmothers to the changes in medicine, society, and technology during the twentieth century, like the discovery of antibiotics, namely penicillin, in the 1920s. Unlike their grandmothers, Granny Midwives did not hold onto conjure because of its ties to Africa. It's likely that Granny Midwives were several generations removed from ancestors who had living memory of Africa. And Granny Midwives, by and large, replaced the African gods of the Yoruba and Congolese with the demons, angels, saints, and the Holy Spirit of Christianity.[6] The bits of conjure that Granny Midwives decided to hold onto in their birthing practices were a matter of survival in an anti-Black health care system and a means of defiance of a medical institution, the Board of Health, that belittled the traditions of their ancestors.

The Board of Health became heavily involved in obstetrics and gynecology by way of the Sheppard-Towner Act of 1921. The act was proposed by the Children's Bureau, tasked with reviewing the state of maternal and infant health care across the nation to figure out what was causing the high rate of maternal and infant death. In the act, legislators displayed a large degree of ambivalence toward midwives. They blamed midwives for the infant and maternal deaths across the country, but they also understood that midwives filled an important gap in medical care for poor, rural communities that did not have access to hospitals or doctors.[7] In their minds, midwives were a "necessary evil," a temporary fix, while they worked to set up medical institutions in these rural regions.[8] So these legislators decided to temporarily support the work of midwives by supplying funds to create prenatal care clinics and hospitals, where they brought the Board of Health in to supervise and medically train midwives on matters of hygiene and maternal-infant care.[9]

Logan agreed with some of the Sheppard-Towner Act's arguments. She concurs that in her mother's day, *there was no hospital that they could go to have a baby. They didn't have clinics. They didn't have doctors. And if a doctor could be found, [w]hen you call one, even if you call one today, he* might *come tomorrow.* Logan, too, saw midwives like herself as standing in this gap of sorely needed care.

Logan understood that her foremothers did the best they could with the few resources that were available to them, even if the medical establishment deemed their conjure practices crude as well as barbaric. Like many Black midwives of her generation, Logan agreed that several procedures from the Board of Health would decrease the infant mortality rate. So she incorporated practices the Board of Health dictated, like scrubbing your hands, removing the infant from the parent's bed for sleep, and adhering to a strict prenatal care regiment that focused on supplementing the mother with nutrients like calcium and vitamins.[10]

But Logan did not think that all of the methods of her foremothers needed to be abandoned. Logan was proud of the massage techniques that she had inherited from her mother. These techniques allowed her to turn a breeched baby in the womb, eliminating the need for a traumatic C-section. Her perineum massages and salves helped prevent the mothers from getting lacerations that could lead to vesicovaginal fistulas. And during deliveries, Logan recognized the comfort that spiritual rituals brought to Black women in the throes of labor. So she did things like swing an axe into the floor to "cut the pain" of labor, much like the contemporary practice of placing combs in the hands of birthing mothers, who squeeze the combs to take their mind off the pain.[11]

Logan tells us that *[w]hen [she] was a lil girl the midwives used all those kinda things because they had nothin' else.* Her foremothers took what was available and *through God it worked.* So Logan understood her Black women clients, who still preferred herbal salves of animal fat rather than ready-made products like Vicks VapoRub and Vaseline. The *old grandparents [of her clients] brought 'em up on [home remedies].* She recognized that *[i]t hadn't been too long since [we] got away from* them, which is why Logan didn't blame her patients for wanting to *do like what mother said and grandmother said*. Unlike white male doctors who would ridicule their Black women patients for their conjure rituals, Logan accommodated these patients, sticking to many home remedies for much of her midwifery career. She had seen for herself that some of these home remedies—teas, salves, and offering spiritual comfort—still worked during deliveries.

The enduring success of these home remedies motivated Logan to object when the Sheppard-Towner Act placed the blame for infant and maternal deaths at the feet of Black midwives like her mother and grandmother. *That was not the midwife. That was the lack of prenatal care. No vitamins, no calciums. No prenatal care whatsoever. It was not havin' proper food. Not havin' enough calcium for her and baby.* Much like doctors during slavery, the Sheppard-Towner Act blamed midwives for maternal and infant deaths while they ignored harsh conditions that racism placed upon Black women's wombs. Logan must have grasped the irony of this study. When they were enslaved, Black midwives were considered valuable. But now that Black midwives were free, placing them in competition with white doctors for a wage, they were painted as the bane of reproductive care.

Although the Sheppard-Towner Act brought much-needed resources to these rural areas in the South, it also complicated the already precarious relationship between Granny Midwives and white male doctors. Although some rural doctors were able to maintain a somewhat positive relationship with local midwives across the South, the Jim Crow system ultimately undermined their collegiality. Granny Midwives were privy to the segregated waiting rooms and stark difference in treatment that followed.[12] Granny Midwives, who went with mothers to the doctors for prenatal and emergency visits, witnessed how doctors prioritized treating white patients over Black ones. Often, these overlooked patients had been waiting long before the arrival of their white counterparts, who were seen immediately.

When Logan worked under the supervision of doctors, she witnessed how sternly Black patients were treated. *[T]hey was treated so bad and so cold by the doctors. The doctors thought the black person was mostly too filthy for him to put his hands on. They talk to 'em just like they was a dog that didn't have human sense.* But under the new laws, Logan could only work with birthing women who had received prior authorization from these doctors to seek her services, on the basis that the doctors were a licensed authority.

The licenses of midwives were more like that of nurses today: They were allowed to attend some aspects of pregnancy and childbirth, but major decisions on treatment, complex diagnoses, or the ability to perform surgery belonged to doctors. In order to get a license, midwives were expected to attend meetings arranged by the Board of Health; to follow all instructions, even those that forbade their conjure rituals like teas and salves; and to meet the education requirements.[13] And licensing became a major tool used to phase out midwives during Logan's career.

Granny Midwives were in a perilous position. The same government that was enforcing Jim Crow laws also relied upon midwives to be their eyes and ears within rural communities that had, until now, been beyond their reach due to lack of access. At this time, the government, still enthralled by the eugenics movement, strove to ensure that "good stock" (read: rich, Christian, and white) stayed high in the nation's population. With a newly freed Black population and rising immigration, many whites thought that the way to maintain their political power was to increase their own numbers in America. And one way that the government worked toward this goal was monitoring births through the Board of

Health. Midwives were already expected to report every birth they assisted to the board. Even before birth, hospitals had information on who was pregnant, since midwives had to get prior authorization from doctors to begin their work early during women's pregnancies. This means that the government now had the data necessary to make policies to control birth rates across the rural South.[14]

The Board of Health was especially interested in births that were deemed "undesirable"—births out of wedlock, births of people with disabilities, and births from mixed-race couples (still illegal in many states at the time). As the daughter of a midwife, Logan understood that love often crossed racial boundaries that were erected by the government. She regularly accompanied her mother to deliver the babies who were the result of these interracial unions.

There was one heartbreaking case where Logan's mother delivered one of these babies to a married white woman who had had an affair with a Black man. Because miscegenation was a crime, Logan's mother helped the white woman hide the evidence of her affair (the baby) by placing the child in the care of Logan's aunt. The Black man who was suspected of the affair skipped town to avoid a lynch mob. But, out of spite, the white woman's husband reported the baby to the Board of Health, and *[t]hen the government got a hold to it and come and taken that lil girl away from my aunt. It liked to have killed her.* Often, when the Board of Health received reports of these kinds of births, the birthing women were declared insane and forcibly sterilized to prevent more "undesirable" offspring.[15]

The government also sought to monitor abortions through the midwifery program. If a midwife was suspected of providing abortions, her license was revoked. Like Horace Storer did on the eve of the Civil War, doctors during Jim Crow publicly linked midwives to miscarriages. So people came to believe that miscarriages were evidence of a midwife's supposed incompetence or ignorance. Others believed that midwives caused abortions on purpose, rendering them "evil."

Logan tells us that the Board of Health and her supervisors thought *some midwives was doin' something to bring on the miscarriages.* The Board of Health claimed that *there was quite a few miscarriages looked like uncalled for.* Mere suspicion was enough to put a bull's-eye on the midwife's back. Some midwives decided to resign under increased scrutiny; others were driven out by the revocation of their licenses. *They've taken licenses from much older women durin' that time. They taken licenses from a couple that they suspected. And I don't know whether any of 'em was doin' it or not.*

White male doctors also threatened to revoke the licenses of Granny Midwives to belittle them during hospital visits. Many women still opted to deliver their babies at home rather than a hospital, so midwives authorized to work with them only interacted with the medical establishment during their patient's mandated prenatal clinic visits or when something went wrong during labor. Under the midwifery program established by the Sheppard-Towner Act, Granny Midwives were expected to report to doctors when any complications arose.[16]

Doctors demanded this, but they also secretly resented this. Doctors wanted all the credit when the cases went well, but they also feared the blame that was to follow when the difficult cases went horribly wrong. So when the midwives called doctors during emergencies, the interactions were often volatile.

Logan often experienced this abuse. Once, she had a patient who was hemorrhaging so badly that she thought it best to bring her to a doctor. Dr. Jones, the doctor assigned to care for the woman Logan brought in, was livid. *He came in and mostly told the wall how mad he was.* He was yelling at the wall, but Logan knew his complaints *referred to [her].* Sure enough, the doctor turned around and advanced on her. *He came on in and drug his chair up and he had a seat. Drunk. Got him a chair. Drug it up right in front of me. And he said what he wanted to say.*

He immediately blamed Logan for bringing in the hemorrhaging woman.

I'll have you arrested—brought that dead woman in here.

Logan replies out of surprise, *What dead woman? Who is this?*

The woman she brought in was not yet dead, but the doctor had revealed his hand: He was not worried about helping this woman. He was worried that her imminent death would be a stain upon his medical career.

Well, Dr. Jones, Logan continues, *I didn't bring you a dead woman in here and if she done died I want to know that.* He continued to yell at Logan, all the while threatening to take her license and to call the police. Logan knew she did the right thing with bringing the woman in, so she did not budge, saying *I'll be sittin' right here when [the police] come.*

That riled the doctor even more. So he got right in her face and yelled at her: *You uncompetent nigra woman. You don't know what you're doin'. If you want to deliver any mo babies go back to Africa where you come from. Go back to Africa where you come from.* He attacks the source of her conjure, a tradition that stretches back to Africa, to undermine her ability and authority to deliver babies. In his America, Granny Midwives like Onnie Lee Logan had no place in the medical profession.

LOGAN MIGHT HAVE TAKEN DR. Jones's disparagement to heart if she had not watched her mother and learned what it meant to be called by God to do the awe-inspiring work of *catching babies*. Logan was impressed with how important her mother was to the community who valued her knowledge—even when doctors called that knowledge "superstition." When Logan was young, this same community uplifted her with stories of her grandmother, who was *such a good midwife and did so much work, nurse work and he'p people in the country from one place to the other when they gotten sick*.

Logan was inspired when her mother was called to deliver a baby. *I could just see right now my mother workin' and goin' on delivery. I could see it right now. I can just see when they came for her.* While her mother was bent over her gardens, tilling the soil or harvesting greens for their meals, there would be *a man comin' for her to ride in that wagon for miles*. No matter the weather or situation, her mother would always respond to the call and get up and go. At a time when women were largely restricted in how they traveled, what they wore, and how they expressed themselves, the divine calling to be a midwife gave some Black women a great degree of independence.

So when doctors like Jones told Logan she had no place in the medical profession, two generations of midwives in her blood prepared her to reply back to the medical establishment: *[you're] not gonna stop me from doin' the gift God give me to do*. As long as she was in good health, she wouldn't let *no man stop [her] hands from doin' what says the Lord*. This view—that midwives needed to be called by God—highlights the irrevocable tension between how the medical establishment and Granny Midwives viewed the profession of midwifery.

The medical establishment saw pregnancy as a sickness that must be managed.[17] They stressed efficiency and replicability—they wanted to control as much as they could during the birthing process to prevent any complications. So doctors wanted the pregnant woman herself to have very little to do with the event. Women were rendered immobile—laid out flat on a table and sedated with drugs—while the doctors did the work of retrieving the fetus from the womb. Doctors denigrated the spiritual rituals (like use of the axe to "cut pain") that would have provided comfort and put the mother at ease during the distressing event of childbirth. In the eyes of a doctor like Jones, rituals such as these marked Granny Midwives as "incompetent."

Granny Midwives, however, saw pregnancy as a normal process that women are already equipped to do—they simply need to be supported while doing it. So they helped women remain active participants in their labor and retained a preference for the noninvasive methods of their foremothers. Their central metaphor, "catching babies," demonstrates this sensibility.[18] They did not need to go into the womb; they only needed to create the conditions for the emergence of the baby that they then "caught."

Those conditions were spiritual as well as physical for Granny Midwives. They needed to sanitize the birthing room according to the Board of Health's standards, yes, but they also needed to be in touch with the divine, to guide the child from the world of the spirits into the world of the living. Which is why, during Logan's lifetime, Black communities believed that divine calling is what gave midwives their ultimate authority.

Logan heard the call from God through the spiritual textile traditions of her foremothers. She tells us: *I've always from a lil girl wanted to be a nurse. Bein' a nurse started young when I was a child, nursin' my lil sick baby doll.* These dolls were made by Logan's own hand. The hair of the dolls was made from a weed that has long roots beneath the soil. She would *lay it out in the sun and let it dry and that was the hair and we would tie this lil string around the green part of it.* Her mother would supply buttons that had fallen off old clothing for the eyes and the mouth. The body of the doll was made of old rags that they would tear into strips and sew together.

When Logan played with her doll, she *was always a nurse for [her] baby cause [her] baby was always sick.* As she nursed her baby, she caught glimpses of her purpose in life through visions. *The Lord deal to me in visions to be a person to he'p somebody. When I was young I had that vision over and over and over again. I'd get those visions that my doll was sick and I was the nurse with the doll.*

Her mother's tradition of midwifery was passed down in the very rags and scraps that Logan used to construct her doll. She remembered her mother's wizened hands, which caught babies, thumbing through the same fibers that Logan would pick and sew together to find a rag to treat a cold. When there was a cough going around the house, her mother would take down a jar of herbal salve. To make these salves, her mother would take the *tallow fat from animals,* boil it down to a thick paste, and *put a lil turpentine in it* along with some herbs. Logan remembered how her mother would *cook it up and put it in a jar and put it up on the shelf among the other vegetables and things so she'd know where it was when it come time to use it.* Logan's mother would take that salve and grease a rag that she then rubbed upon the chest of the sick.

Sometimes her mother would tie the rag onto a string, placing it *around the neck so it would always be right [here] on the chest,* similar to the asafetida bags the enslaved wore around their necks as both medicine and to ward off bad luck. The string amulet Logan's mother devised was believed to *absorb some of the cold.* Logan explains that the fumes from the salve on the rag would also *[o]pen up the chest from the smell of the turpentine*, much like Lunsford Richardson's original Vicks VapoRub. Logan underscores the connection between Vicks VapoRub and the healing salves countless enslaved and newly freed Black women made: *you could go buy Vicks salve for fever and for colds but I have always said it's made out of the same stuff that lil [jimson] weed is.*

Logan also recalled how her mother would set aside scraps of cloth that she called *shoestrings*. These bits of cloth were taken from *material they would have set aside. You know when you buy material—the end of it. Well she would tear that all the way down and she would cut it into pieces.* Her mother would then sterilize the strips by boiling them in water to use during the deliveries she assisted. The shoestrings could be used in several ways during the birthing process: to bundle the herbs she brought with her to make teas that would hasten contractions or ease labor pains; to grease the vagina to prevent lacerations; or to clamp the birth cord to prevent hemorrhaging of the mother.

Granny Midwives like Logan's mother also used these shoestrings for spiritual purposes during their work with birthing mothers, which began long before conception and continued long after a child had arrived. If a woman had several miscarriages, Granny Midwives would take a red rag and tie nine knots.[19] They would instruct the woman to wear the string around her belly during pregnancy, much like their Yoruba ancestors used the *kijipa* cloth and their Congolese forebears used knotted healing strings. If a woman wanted an abortion, a Granny Midwife might take a knotted string and dip it in turpentine to be worn around the woman's waist.[20] And if a woman had a man who was threatening to run off on her upon discovery of her pregnancy, a Granny Midwife might make a nature (or nation) sack, a powerful mojo believed to control a man's erections. This mojo was considered a specialty of Granny Midwives, and it caused widespread fear in Black men.[21] Even a man who professed not to believe in it would react violently if he caught his woman trying to do this, perhaps because it told him just how far his lover would go to keep a hold on him.

The nature sack reached its height in popularity in the 1930s with Robert Johnson's blues song about it, "Come On in My Kitchen."[22] But this potent charm was widespread across the South well before then. In New Orleans, it was a common trick performed by the famous Voodoo Queen Marie Laveau, who was also said to perform midwifery work.[23]

The central part of the nature sack was a knotted string that was initially the length of a man's erect penis. Gathering the measurement had to be stealthy and was tantamount to betrayal (that perhaps the men already deserved)—for it had to be measured during sex. A woman would secure a string and bring it to a Granny Midwife. Zora Neale Hurston tells us that after a woman secured the string, the Granny Midwife would curse the "other woman" threatening her patient's relationship or command the man to stay true to her client. At each curse and command, the Granny Midwife would wind the string in on itself again and again. She would continue until she tied nine knots into the string, much like the *makolo* of the Congolese, awakening the spirit within the mojo to restrict the man's erections to only that of her client.

This type of mojo is one example of how Granny Midwives mediated intro-communal conflict, much like Negro Mammies did for enslaved communities. And with mojos like these, Granny Midwives placed a potent weapon of revenge in the hands of women. Logan does not mention any use of the nature sack in her autobiography, but she encountered several situations that would have driven women to request it of her. Logan was well acquainted with the heartache that made women turn to these desperate means. She knew several women who *had babies and their husband lef' after they were pregnant*. And as a midwife, she stayed around after babies were born to help the family adjust to a newborn in the house. During her time with these families, Logan always discovered the skeletons in their closet, like men who would *stay out after [they received their] paycheck and get rid of all that. Here he'd come in with a brand-new baby and other small chil'rens with nothin' to eat*.

LOGAN TREASURED THESE METHODS OF midwifery that her mother passed down to her. She trusted motherwit, the *[w]isdom [that] come from on high. You got it and you [cain't] explain how you got it yo'self*. She couldn't explain *exactly how [she] got it*, nor could she tell you *exactly how Mother did it*. Logan might not be able to tell you with words, but she can show you through the rich textile tradition she inherited from her mother. Those rags her mother used were scraps of motherwit, a living record of our conjuring tradition that you could hold in your hand and use to heal or usher new life into existence. This is why it's important to understand that our conjure, and African American culture as a whole, is not only oral; it's also visual.

Like their enslaved foremothers, Black women in the community sewed these strips of motherwit into their quilts. When Logan tagged along with her mother for deliveries, she would help her mother boil and sterilize their old quilts. *[I]n the country you know they had these quilts that they pieced up*. The women used *[t]he old clothes that we wore and wore out, the skirt part a the dress wasn't hardly tore up. We would take that and cut it into blocks and sew it together to make quilts*. As Logan washed these quilts with her mother, she noticed the bits of work clothes that had been repurposed, especially the bits of jeans and overalls the sharecroppers wore in their daily work.

The beliefs and values of Granny Midwives were laid into these quilts, when they, like their enslaved foremothers, wove in diamonds, pinwheels, and crosses that recall the BaKongo and Yoruba cosmograms. The West African ancestors of Granny Midwives would have recognized these symbols as that in-between space where they believed new life came, the crossroads where God could be called upon for help. And like their West African ancestors, the quilts Granny Midwives made were often visual prayers.

Sometimes you had to peek at the corners of Granny Midwives' quilts to clock their prayers. In hoodoo, the four corners of an object or space are considered sacred, as they represent the four angles made by the crossroads symbol.[24] It seems to be a holdover from the Yoruba, who also revere the four corners of the world as the domain of the *orisha* Eshu, the god of the crossroads. Hoodoo practitioners revere that spirit of the crossroads by making offerings at the four corners of a room for blessings or to remove curses. These beliefs blended with the Congolese's sacred knots, *makolo*, in a striking ritual of the enslaved. In their Federal Writers' Project interviews, many of the enslaved took the screeching of night birds, like owls, as a sign of bad luck. To turn that bad luck away from them, they would tie knots in the corners of their bedsheets, invoking the spirit of the crossroads to protect them.[25]

This practice sheds light on another frequent quilting custom. Many of the enslaved and the newly freed would sew pennies into the corners of their quilts.[26] Among hoodoo practitioners, copper is a sacred metal that is used in mojos to draw luck and success, offered to spirits at the crossroads as payment, and thrown into the four corners of the home to ward off evil spells.[27] This ritual was still common during Logan's mother's lifetime. It's likely she taught Logan, too, to put pennies in the corners of her quilts, perhaps as a request for help from God.

Granny Midwives prayed with their hands. And they believed God answered them by blessing those same hands with the power to catch babies, which is why Logan often said that she's *just usin' God's hands He gave [her]*. She believed when she midwifed, God's spirit was flowing through her, much like the rituals of spirit possession her West Africans ancestors revered. Logan declared that *if the Lord wasn't guiding [her] hands and this mind of [hers] that He lent [her] for a short while, [she] wouldn't've had that much success*. And every time she wrapped a quilt around a birthing mother, every time she made a quilt for a new birth in the community, Logan was reminded of where her ability to catch babies came from.

The medical establishment denigrated the much-revered quilts of Granny Midwives. Medical journals reported these quilts as dirty and a source of infection—even though they were often meticulously sterilized, as Logan reports of her own deliveries.[28] With their vibrant colors and bold patterns, the medical establishment saw these quilts as an exotic eyesore. They seemed to understand that the quilts were part of conjure, so they painted them as relics of "African barbarism" in the pamphlets given and instructional skits performed during midwifery meetings.

The quilts especially reminded the medical establishment of the willfulness of Granny Midwives exerted when they deviated from protocol. The quilts were used in ways that starkly contrasted with the Board of Health's official instructions for assisting births, where the birthing mother was to lie flat on her back during labor. Quilts were often laid on the floor to support the mother's knees as she squatted forward or leaned on an overturned chair or to cushion her feet while she sat on a collapsible birthing stool. Logan witnessed how many women *want[ed] to have babies in that sittin' position. It's not unusual. It feels good. Mother gets mo' relief.* Even white women preferred Logan's home visits rather than go to the hospital, where *doctors just don't do that. In a hospital, you cain't move.* The quilt midwives laid under the mother reminded these white male doctors that women, still, knew better than them. These quilts were a symbol of the spiritual authority of Granny Midwives to deliver babies and, ultimately, a threat to the medical establishment.

Logan watched how nurses from the Board of Health performed procedures, all the while *see[ing] it a lil different that you could do or you could add to it.* At midwife's meetings, when she received instructions, *in [her] mind [she] was addin' a lil bit mo to it.* This was how Logan honed her skills as a midwife, taking what she learned from the medical establishment and adapting it to the tradition of conjure her mother passed down to her. *That's how come I say God give it to me. The Bo'd a Health didn't give it to me. Readin' books didn't give it to me.* Like an expert seamstress, she took scraps of motherwit and medical insight and pieced it together to make a quilt of knowledge in her mind. And it was knowledge that she believed could usurp the doctor's authority. Because it was ultimately given by God.

CHAPTER TWENTY-THREE

The Midwife's Bag, a Tool of Rebellion

MARGARET CHARLES SMITH (1906–2004), AN AFRICAN AMERICAN woman in Alabama, loved to say that she was the last licensed midwife in the state. She got her license in 1949, when Granny Midwives were being aggressively erased across the country, their craft supplanted by doctors and hospital births. At the beginning of the 1940s, virtually all births were still at-home deliveries attended by midwives."[1] By the end of the following decade, almost 90 percent of births occurred at hospitals.[2]

Over the years, the medical establishment steadily upped the education requirements of Granny Midwives, who were often *poor people who missed an opportunity to pursue an education*.[3] The lack of equal access to higher education during Jim Crow all but ensured that Granny Midwives would not be able to reach the rising requirements put forward by the medical establishment. And when Granny Midwives failed to meet these ascending stipulations, their licenses were not renewed.

This put Granny Midwives in a difficult position. Black women in the South still largely preferred to work with Granny Midwives over doctors, but if Granny Midwives continued to practice when they lost their license, they could be fined or, worse, jailed. Smith's position gives us great insight into how Granny Midwives negotiated a hostile medical system to deliver the care that Black women sorely needed, even while they were on their way to being phased out.

The midwifery tradition that Smith inherited was steeped in conjure practices that instilled a sense of dignity to the cycle and passage of Black life when Jim Crow rendered us "filthy animals" that could be put to death with impunity. Sometimes, Granny Midwives would wait nine days after a birth to walk counterclockwise around the birthing mother's house. During this walk, they would hold the newborn, "calling the baby's spirit" to tether it to the Earth. The counterclockwise walk in this ritual traced the BaKongo cosmogram on the ground, enabling Granny Midwives to draw down the spiritual power needed to guide the newborn in its transition from the world of the dead to the world of the living—a transition that their West African ancestors believed took the newborn at least a week to complete after the infant's birth.[4]

When a Granny Midwife was called for a delivery, it was common to see her *[s]itting up all night long, [with] the door cracked, [as she] spread a quilt down*. And on these quilts, it was common to find diamonds and pinwheels and crosses in the patterns.[5] These symbols represented the four points of the sun in BaKongo cosmology: our dawn or birth, our noon or the middle part of our lives, our sunset or settling into old age, and our midnight or transition from death to rebirth, starting the cycle once again.[6] For many women's lives, the BaKongo cosmogram's cycle takes a particular shape. Those four moments become our birth, the onset of our menstruation, menopause, and death. And quilts were often present at each stage.

Smith tells us that her grandmother made her a pad for her first period from a quilt. Smith's grandmother, a previously enslaved midwife who had been kidnapped directly from Africa, both raised Smith and delivered her first child. Smith confides that *[t]hey used to give you an old piece of quilt to make your pad and tie a string around your waist.* When Smith first saw her blood, she thought she was dying (as did I!). But as her grandmother tore down a quilt into strips for her baby girl's pads, she told Smith, *now you seen your flowers, that's what they call your period, you're old enough to get a baby.* Her grandmother's explanation of the female cycle relied upon the language she knew best—the plant life she relied upon for midwifery. When Smith began to experience the onset of menopause, the end of her menses, she also picked up a quilt. When there was breakthrough bleeding, Smith tells us *you have to have a quilt. You have to have a nice piece of quilt to soak up that blood.*

During her own pregnancies, Smith participated in a ritual similar to "calling the baby's spirit" called "taking up the mother." When the baby was two weeks old, Smith's grandmother *brought [her] the thimble of water, and [she] had to carry it all the way around the house.* This counterclockwise walk also marked the BaKongo cosmogram, allowing the new mother to channel the strength of her ancestors to fortify her spirit (and perhaps stave off the postpartum depression that we now know so many new mothers experience).[7] Smith held the thimble in her hands as she walked, and at the end of the walk, she had to drink water from the tiny cup. In this sacred practice, even the tools used had significance. The thimble—a small metal cap put on the finger that pushes the needle through the fabric to protect it while sewing—invokes our textile tradition, especially quilting.

Midwives were also a comforting presence at death. Smith not only healed minor ailments and delivered babies, but she also cared for the elderly and offered spiritual support as they died. The midwife's hands were a steady witness to the cycle of life. In those days, one midwife's hands caught you as you came into this world, swaddling you in a quilt as she helped you take your first breath, while another midwife's hands tucked a quilt around you for solace as you took your last.

WHEN MARGARET SMITH DECIDED TO become a midwife, she attended mandatory midwife training meetings every Saturday, from 8 a.m. to 11 a.m., for three months. At these meetings, Smith sat among a mixed group that included Granny Midwives, white women nurses trained by medical doctors, and prominent white women of the community, such as the wives of sharecropper bosses. Together, they sang songs that carried simple messages about hygiene and reminded midwives to wash their hands. They watched live skits that ridiculed many of the Granny Midwives in the audience, calling their teas and reliance on quilts not only superstitious but deadly.[8] And they awaited the dreaded inspection of the government-issued midwife's bag, which came at the conclusion of the meeting and was, in a way, the meeting's underlying point.[9]

In the midwifing community, this government-issued bag was a symbol of your license to practice.[10] The state-issued bags were black and a little over a foot in length, with inner pockets for state-approved instruments and tools. Smith lists the things that the state would allow midwives to pack in it: *your scissors and a tray, your scales, your orange sticks, and your soap, your cap, and your mask.* There was a space at the bottom of the bag to put bigger items, like your white medical gown.

The government-issued state bag was an attempt to replace the tradition of the midwife's bag from slavery. Across ex-slave interviews, the first thing a Negro Mammy or midwife-weaver would do when tasked to care for the sick was to *get her sack and hoe and go to the woods and get herbs to make our medicine out of.*[11] These bags were not merely functional. They were part of our textile tradition, like quilts. Onnie Lee Logan, a Granny Midwife, tells us that midwives in her mother's generation crafted their bags themselves. *The midwives would always make them a sack.* And these bags were starkly different from the state-issued bags. *They didn't have bags naturally like that I have. But they would make them a sack and they would put their stuff in there and put a drawstring on it and draw it.*[12] Like quilts, these bags were made of rags, scraps, and leftover work clothes like jeans. The textiles of the bag, woven together in the quilting tradition of their foremothers, reminded Granny Midwives that they had a higher authority—God—that gave them permission to deviate from the state's methods when necessary.

The state's obsession over the midwife's bag begat stringent inspections when Granny Midwives were absorbed into the medical establishment. When the doctors searched the state-issued bag, they flipped out its linings as well as its pockets to verify that only what the state authorized was packed. Those who were caught carrying teas were severely punished—from public ridicule to hefty fines to losing their license. And "turning in your bag" became a euphemism for getting fired, losing your license, or simply quitting the midwifery profession.[13] Smith recalls how one woman was *ripped about them teas* in front of everyone else at a last-minute midwife's meeting. *They told her the best thing you do when you go home, get your bag and come back to town. Bring your bag in because you're going to kill somebody.*

The medical establishment especially feared that abortions could be induced by the teas. Smith tells us that she *remember[s] [midwives] giving them teas to make their period come, and when they have cramps.*

She mentions that they used a root, but she's careful, even in her memoir, not to disclose what that was. She tells us that she learned about this root from her grandmother, who she heard *talking to older women, her friends* about it.

Smith certainly understood why some women would be moved to have abortions. During her first pregnancy, she was brought to the brink of despair. She absolutely did not want the baby. Not only was she, at sixteen years old, too young to have a baby, but she also despised the man who had gotten her pregnant. So she decided to try to kill the baby. *I jumped off logs. I climbed trees. Thought I'd lose it.* But all her attempts came to nothing. *[T]he more I climbed, the bigger [the baby] got.*

The worst part is that she suffered a lot of this alone. She was too ashamed to tell her grandmother what had happened. When she began to show, a girlfriend of hers *stole [her] a sack, wrapped it like a girdle, pinned it up on [her] in the woods, so you couldn't tell there was a baby in [her] belly.* In the end, it was another midwife, a friend of her grandmother's, who outed her secret so that Smith no longer had to face this problem by herself. During a Sunday dinner, Smith *was drawing water, toting water, and the midwife asked [her] did [she] have a baby in [her] belly.* Smith denied it, of course, but *one night [she] woke up and Mama had pulled all the covers off [her] and found the sack.*

Smith must have felt a sense of déjà vu when, as a midwife decades later, she came upon a frightened young girl who had done the very same thing. At this time, if you were in school, they would put you out if you were pregnant. So the girl tried to keep her pregnancy a secret, wrapping her belly in a sack like Smith had done years ago. *She got a plain sack, like yellow domestic, folded that thing, and she got somebody to fix her up with safety pins, real nice and neat.* But the sack put so much pressure on the fetus that it came out premature and alarmingly underweight. Smith tells us that she *had to cut the sack off of her before she had the baby to give the baby a chance.*

Stories like these are one reason why Smith, along with other Granny Midwives, refused to give up administering her teas. These midwives saw that these teas helped women who were suffering all sorts of problems, from unwanted pregnancies to painful deliveries. At one of the midwives' meetings, Smith saw a midwife inform the nurses that she was quitting rather than carry on without her teas. This midwife said to her supervisors, *I think I'll bring my bag in and give it to you all because you all are not there when this labor is going on.* She insisted that *[r]ubbing helps and teas help. If I can't give them some hot teas which I know will help, I just well ought to give it up.* But some Granny Midwives, like Smith, found ways to work around the system.

These midwives often kept two bags—one that was state issued and the homemade bags of their enslaved foremothers. During meetings, they would present the state-issued bag and pass the test with flying colors. But during the home call deliveries, where there usually was not a state official or medical personnel present, they brought the state's bag, but they also packed the second, secret bag with them. In these bags were secret tools of conjure: roots and herbs for teas to bring on contractions, castor oil or Vaseline for perineum massages, knotted strings or red rags for women who had a history of miscarriages, even *coins tied into the corners of a handkerchief*, which called upon the spirit of the crossroads to help them guide a new life into existence.[14]

The two-bag trick is likely how Smith continued to furtively supply teas to her patients. But her patients started telling other pregnant women about how good Smith's teas were. And eventually, through word of mouth, Smith's covert use of teas got around back to her. People couldn't keep a secret and *[her] name was getting where [she] could hear it*, which meant it wouldn't be long before the medical establishment got wind of it.

So I quit. I quit trying to do anything but what they gave me to work with. I had been working a good while when I threw that root out my bag. It must have broken her heart to stop offering something she knew would help her patients. Still, Smith worked as long as she could within the system, believing that she ought to uphold her oath to perform midwifery. *I figured I done took the oath, and I'm going to work on anyhow til the end.*

She kept on until 1978, when the state declined to renew her license, along with all other Granny Midwives across Alabama in one final sweep. When a Granny Midwife could not meet the bar, the medical establishment would not renew her permit. But even Granny Midwives like Margaret Smith who could indeed keep up with the new requirements faced challenges. In the 1970s, several doctors conveniently "forgot" to sign new licenses for Granny Midwives.[15] And sometimes, hospital boards aggressively "retired" midwives, claiming that women like Margaret Smith were "too old" to continue this line of work.[16]

Without the license, they were forced into formal retirement. But many Granny Midwives, like Smith, continued to work underground. *The underground is you working, you deliver the baby, but you aren't supposed to be there,* Smith explains, because *[y]ou don't have a license to be there.* Many Granny Midwives operated underground because they believed that God ultimately gave them the right to deliver babies, not the government, not the Board of Health, not the medical establishment.

DURING THE 1950S AND 1960S, *Brown v. Board* and federal benefits programs like Medicaid granted Black Americans more access to hospitals and medical care. When Black women began to transition to hospital and clinical care, Granny Midwives like Margaret Smith were a constant presence during their doctors' visits, offering them support. *I'd be standing right 'side the head of the examining table, and the doctor at the other end.* The loss of this advocate put us in the direct line for harm from doctors who still resented us and disavowed the federal government's social programs.

Smith remembers when the Civil Rights movement came to a small town near Demopolis, Alabama. An old hunting lodge had been turned into a makeshift clinic, and it's here where she worked as a midwife. As Smith dressed one of her patients, she paused, hearing singing. *The school buses come in. I believe it was about six or seven buses, and commenced to parking all the way around, and they started singing that we'll overcome.* The community had organized to demand their right to adequate medical care, which had not yet been ratified into the American framework. This makeshift clinic had failed to address the inequalities in medical access that was prevalent in this area—the clinic was only open a few days a week, not nearly enough to service the large, Black rural population that depended on it.

The white male doctor at the clinic was outraged at the protest. *The doctor got so mad couldn't say nothing.* Perhaps he was especially put off that the hunting lodge had been converted to a clinic in the first place. The lodge had been an exclusively white club that doctors like him once enjoyed. Now his recreational space was replaced by a government run clinic that serviced poor and rural Black folk free of charge, where he himself had to service patients he felt were beneath him.

Out of spite, the doctor shut down the clinic completely. *Made the doctor mad, and he left. Made the nurse mad, and she left.* Smith tells us that the medical personnel even abandoned the patients they were currently serving. *They closed [the clinic] up from that day on. Left the patients lying on the table with their legs up in the air.* By closing the clinic, the medical professionals exacerbated the rural Black community's problems. Without Granny Midwives or grudge-holding doctors, Black women now had nowhere to go to service their reproductive needs unless they could afford to pay for travel and services at the major hospital in Demopolis, twenty-five miles away.

These activists were not only protesting the lack of care provided by the makeshift clinic. They were also protesting the kind of care they did receive when the clinic was open. The doctor's response to their protest—his blinding anger, his withholding of treatment, his abandonment of his patients—was part of the anti-Blackness that was widespread in the medical establishment. The doctors who sat on the local Boards of Health crafting state policy, the doctors who advised hospital boards, and even the doctors who managed these makeshift clinics had a lot of power. And many of these white male doctors openly contested the government's attempt to remedy deep racial inequalities, from medical care to housing, in the nation's Civil Rights Act.

These doctors especially resented the rise in taxes due to institutions like Medicaid. Due to their belief in eugenics, many of these doctors did not believe that these social benefit programs could help the poor.[17] If you were at the bottom of the social hierarchy, according to these doctors, it was because of your social degeneracy, passed down through your racial makeup.[18] So these doctors often took out their anger stealthily upon the Black population.[19] Under the guise of government services, these doctors sterilized us without consent to prevent, in their mind, their "hard-earned" tax dollars going to waste.[20]

Fannie Lou Hamer (1917–1977), a civil rights activist, famously called these clandestine procedures commonly performed on Black women in the 1960s "Mississippi appendectomies." When she was forty-four, she went to the doctor to be treated for fibroids, a condition that many Black women still suffer from today.[21] She went in to get a fibroid removed, and she left the hospital without a uterus. These procedures were even performed on children. In 1973, Minnie Lee Relf (age fourteen) and Mary Alice Relf (age twelve) were sterilized without consent. Their parents filed charges against the government for its gross violation of their daughters' reproductive rights. Their lawsuit brought the wrongs done to Black women in shady hospitals to public light. We know now that over one hundred thousand Black women had been sterilized without their consent during this period.[22]

One of these women was my grandmother, Mary Ann Wooden Perkins. In 1970, she went to the doctor to be treated for a bladder infection. The doctor tried administering some medicine, but the infection returned. So she went back to her doctor, who asked her, "How many kids do you have?" She replied, "Two." He told her, "Two is enough," and pressured her to have a hysterectomy. She was only twenty-three years old. She still thinks on that doctor's visit to this day. If a Granny Midwife had been present at the visit, I can only imagine how wildly different the results would have been. Thankfully, other Black women soon stepped into the spiritual void created by the removal of Granny Midwives from our communities. One woman was someone my grandmother loved to visit: the hairdresser.

CHAPTER TWENTY-FOUR

Black Women's Hair, the Everlasting Textile

Although Black women are turning more and more to home births and requests for doula services, the era of Granny Midwives and their birthing quilts are long gone. Groups like Crescent City Quilters in New Orleans and textile artists like Bisa Butler have worked to uphold the quilting tradition of our foremothers and spark communal interest. Even celebrities like Tatyana Ali have joined in these efforts by founding Baby Yams, a company that makes upcycled quilts from African prints. But the majority of us no longer enter the world on the quilts of Granny Midwives, coverlets that called down spiritual power to guide our transition to Earth. Once-prized heirlooms, these quilts are no longer passed from one generation to the next. Instead, we get our bed coverings from department stores like Macy's, supercenters like Walmart, or online at Amazon.

Enslaved midwife-weavers used our clothes, once "sacred skin" to our ancestors, to channel the spirit world for our protection, help, and guidance as we moved through a hostile, anti-Black world. But our clothes are now largely a product of fast fashion—cheap, mass-market products chasing the latest trends. Our clothes are a revolving door of consumption. And once we are done consuming in the United States, the squalor of our fast fashion is washed up on the shores of Ghana and Nigeria and Uganda, in the hundreds of tons of waste dumped by "developed" nations. When I see pictures of these massive landfills on the coasts of West Africa, it's always the blue jeans, peaking through the mounds of trash, that haunt me—a sorry return for what enslaved African women contributed to America by way of those iconic pants.

So it may seem like African American women have been cut off from the conjure that lay in the fabrics woven by our foremothers. But there is one place where the conjure of our textiles lives on. And you don't have to go any further than a Black woman's scalp. The hairstyles of our West African ancestors have had staying power in the Americas—along with the spiritual role of the hairdresser.

Oshun's occupation of dressing hair elevated the hairdresser to the status of priests in Yoruba society.[1] It was thought that hairdressers had the capacity to affect your luck since they spend their days handling the threads of your *ori*, or destiny. Through braiding styles, arrangements of cornrows, and materials woven into the hair (like cowries or beads or brightly colored strings), the hairdresser put you in touch with the gods, making your requests and desires visible upon your scalp, much like the visual prayers of the *itagbe* and *adire* cloths. And like the *iyami aje*, the hairdresser drew upon herbal knowledge to create shampoos to cleanse your scalp along with elixirs to strengthen, smooth, and grow your hair. Because your hair was your *ori*, when the hairdresser was performing these grooming rituals, she was also cleansing and feeding your spiritual head.[2]

So it was serious business when someone put their hands in your hair—it was as if they were touching the most sacred and vulnerable part of you. Which is why the Yoruba said for centuries, *one does not plait or cut a person's hair without the consent of the owner of the head.*³ Those who were skilled at manipulating hair, the fragments of your soul, held an esteemed position among the Yoruba. The hairdresser held your fortune in her hands, so you did not haggle with her over the price—you paid her whatever she wanted.⁴ These beliefs about the spiritual power of our hair informed our conjure traditions in the United States, from the hairstyles and mojos of the enslaved to the role of the hairdresser in African American communities.

MUCH INK HAS BEEN SPILT over the politics of Black women's hair in the United States. For decades debates have waged over what Black women were saying with their hairstyles. From the days of slavery, mainstream America has privileged straight hair (notably blond along with blue eyes) as the standard of feminine beauty. So, were Black women straightening their hair during slavery and Jim Crow because they had internalized these Western beauty standards? Were Black women saying they were down with the cause when they finally ditched their hair straighteners and sported Afros in the 1960s and beyond? Were the billowing weaves and hair extensions of the 1990s merely a symptom of the fact that, over a hundred years removed from slavery, Black women have still internalized the belief that long hair is what makes women desirable?

Today, even with the overwhelming trend toward natural hair among millennials and Gen Z, the questions about the politics of Black women's hair remain. The 2023 television show *The Other*

Black Girl, based on the novel by Zakiya Dalila Harris, rehabilitates the old theory that Black women straighten their hair due to internalized racism and the desire to assimilate to whiteness. Throughout the series, a toxic hair grease made Black women compliant with the norms of mainstream white society. After the hair grease was applied, these Black women were more reticent to speak out against the racism and sexism they faced in the workplace; instead, they became demure, meeting every insult with a servile smile. At the beginning of the series, the main character, Nella Rogers, tries to resist the grease. At the end of the series, we are left to wonder whether Rogers's apparent change in personality—from shy and politically progressive to a confident sellout, marked by her now straightened hair—is the result of the grease or a ruse to gain influence in her profession.

Lurking beneath this series, I hear the incessant question about the politics behind Black women's hairstyles. If Black women went back to their perms after going natural, does that mean they've internalized anti-Blackness? And when Black women such as myself wear dreadlocks, are we signaling that we are pro-Black?

As an educator, I often see these debates unfold in my classroom. One time, I heard a Black male student rail against a Black woman about hair straightening. He told her that Black women should not straighten their hair because it showed they have rejected their natural texture to "become" white. The Black woman rallied back, pointing out how long it takes to care for and style natural hair. She also mentioned that we might perm our hair because our careers don't afford us much time for the hours it takes to perfect twist-outs and wash-and-gos. I understood where the young man was coming from—we are still bombarded with television shows, movies, commercials, social media, and novels that tell us that straight hair makes women beautiful. But it did not sit well with me that this Black male student felt like he had the right to dictate what Black women should do with their bodies.

I struggled to mediate the debate between those students that day. But if I could do it all over again, I would point out to these students that a central aspect of our hair traditions—our ever-present conjure—is missing from these endless questions about the politics (or rather, policing) of Black women's hair. It seems to me that if you really want to examine the relationship Black women have to their hair, you have to go to our spirituality. Whether or not the various methods we use to adorn our hair—straightening by hot comb, flat iron, or perm, blowouts and twist-outs, the bevy of products and hair extensions used in weaves and complex hairstyles—can be said to emulate whiteness, I maintain that our relationship to our hair is still greatly informed by the conjure in our textile traditions and, hence, our ties to our West African ancestors.

THE STORY WE OFTEN TELL about Black women's hair assumes that enslaved women were forced to accept white beauty standards and that each advent of hair care has been a response to a shifting goalpost meant to lock us out. But, in fact, hair grooming was one space where slave masters tended to leave Black people to their own devices.[5] Slave masters tended to have problems with Black hair when it looked too much like white people's hair—not when the enslaved used hairstyles that our textured hair favored. There are many stories of jealous white mistresses who cut the hair of enslaved Black women who had hair textures a little too similar to theirs. Perhaps the straight, wavy hair of the enslaved confirmed the mistresses' suspicions that their husbands were forcing Black women into their beds.

So on Sundays, the only day slave masters allotted to the enslaved for grooming rituals like tending to their hair, styles from their homelands were common. If the weather was pleasant, the women would sit outside and *comb and roll each other's hair [while] the men cut each others hair.*[6] First, enslaved women would take pains to comb their hair thoroughly. They had lost the combs of their ancestors that had teeth sharp enough to part their curls with precision and wide enough to move through their curls smoothly, without intense pain and snagging.[7] Instead, enslaved women combed their hair with "Jim crow cards"—the same cards they used when they stretched tuffs of cotton to make the fibers lie flat before feeding them to the spinning wheel.[8]

It's unclear whether their slave masters gave them the cards in place of actual combs, or whether enslaved women took up the cards as combs on their own. If the former, slave masters undoubtedly gave enslaved women cards to mark their "inferiority." This would have been in keeping with how slave masters denigrated enslaved women's hair texture by calling it wool—as if the enslaved were animals, not human just like them. If the latter, the use of the cards as combs underscore that enslaved women saw their hair as yet another textile to be threaded, sewed, knotted, braided, plaited, and woven like the cloth they made daily.

Once their hair was untangled, enslaved women would arrange the hair in styles that protected their strands from strong winds or harsh heat.[9] Sometimes enslaved women and young girls wore their hair *plaited in tiny braids* or *neatly parted into squares [with] dozens of little plaits, wrapped with yards of twine*, much like the Yoruba's *irun didi*.[10] Or they might take portions of the hair and *roll it up on cloth and in little light cobs*. Once rolled in this way, *if they wet the [cobs], [the hair on them] would stay curled*.[11] And it was very common for the women to parcel out their hair and wrap the gathered strands tightly with thread or strings of cloth, similar to the Yoruba's *irun kiko*.

Enslaved women and girls would wear their hair like this for a week, tucked under head rags to protect the exposed parts of their scalp from the scalding sun in the field. After a week, they would unwrap or unbraid their hair *and comb the hair out fine*.[12] Gus Feaster, once enslaved in South Carolina, remembers that enslaved women styled their hair this way for special religious occasions, like weddings, church revivals, and camp meetings.[13]

Enslaved women did not always see methods of styling that straightened the hair—such as "wrapping"—as trying to imitate whites. Rather, in Federal Writers' Project interviews, enslaved women often wrapped their hair to make it *naturally curly*. Stretching their hair in this way also allowed them to be even more creative and experimental with further styling, like gravity-defying updos.[14] Interviews with Negro Mammies and midwife-weavers like Lina Hunter also suggest that enslaved women often saw their hair texture as holy, *'cause de Blessed Lord sont [them] here wid kinky hair, and [they are] gwine 'way from here wid dat same old kinky hair*.[15]

On Sundays, when enslaved women did one another's hair, they created an environment much like quilting bees. They gossiped and shared secrets. And they passed down their conjure rituals. It was likely that young Black girls learned the awesome spiritual power of hair while they sat between the knees of their mothers and grandmothers and aunts who were busy styling their hair. As enslaved women tugged and twisted their hair, young Black girls learned that people can make *powerful medicine* with their hair.[16] They learned that when someone meant them harm, *dey [would] sneak round and git de hair combin' or de finger or toenail, or anything natural 'bout your body, and works de hoodoo on it.*[17]

So young Black girls were taught on Sundays to *burn their hair combins* after their hair had been styled for the coming week.[18] Older enslaved women stressed to their descendants how important it was not to leave hair lying around. Even if no one was trying to conjure you with your hair, enslaved women believed that if you didn't dispose of your hair properly *and the birds get them to put in their nests, you'll have a "wanderin' mind"* that will drive you crazy.

This is something that African Americans still feel strongly about. A few years ago, I watched an older second cousin, Andrea Perkins, do my great-grandmother's hair. When Andrea was finished, she carefully removed my great-grandmother's hair from a comb and shaped it into a ball. Andrea then handed the ball to a young girl to dispose of the hair. Andrea leaned into the young girl's face and said gravely, "Take this here, and don't let none of it drop." Considering that hair contains your DNA material, perhaps there's even more reason to be careful about where you leave your hair.[19]

The close tie between conjure and hair drew its apex in the figure of the hairdresser, who became a conjure woman in her own right during slavery. It is no accident that one of the most famous conjure women in America was a hairdresser. In New Orleans, the Voodoo Queen, Marie Laveau, ran a beauty parlor in the French Quarter.[20] As she dressed hair, Laveau would listen to her clients' problems—heartache or law trouble or illness—and sell them *gris-gris* that would give them power. The Yoruba ancestors of Black folks in New Orleans would have said that part of Laveau's power to make *gris-gris* came from her daily handling of the souls of white and Black folks through hairdressing.

After slavery, Black women hairdressers continued to rely on this connection between conjure and hairdressing. Consider Annie Turnbo Malone (1869–1957), a Black hairdresser who revolutionized the beauty care industry at the turn of the twentieth century. Malone drew upon the herbal knowledge she gained from a Negro Mammy when she was young.[21] She incorporated herbs like sage into her products designed to treat hair issues such as loss, breakage, and eczema.[22] Her hair care line was widely successful, drawing the attention of Sarah Breedlove (1867–1919), known as Madam C. J. Walker, who became one of the first self-made female millionaires in America.

After some time in Annie Malone's employ, Walker created her own hair care line. These products were a hair care system, from shampoos to salves for the scalp, designed to be used with the hot comb, originally invented by a Parisian hairdresser. Walker maintained that the purpose of her care line was not simply to straighten the hair in an imitation of whiteness. And she strove to keep the term "straightening" out of the ads that promoted her products.[23] Instead, Walker argued that the aim of her products was to make the hair healthy for whatever way a client may want to style their hair—straight *or* curled.[24]

Walker also claimed that her formulas were given to her by divine revelation.[25] She asserted that she had a dream where *a big black man appeared to [her] and told [her] what to mix for [her] hair.*[26] Our conjure tradition is implicit in Walker's story about how she got her recipe. She reported that *some of the remedy [comes] from Africa*—herbs and roots that she *sent for* and mixed into her products. And the reference to the "big black man" who gave her a special plant from Africa bears striking similarity to the black man blues musicians met at the crossroads—the devil they sold their soul to for success in their career, for musical talent that would rival the gods. Walker's ancestors would have called this "big black man" Eshu, a Yoruba *orisha*, or Papa Legba, his Voodoo counterpart.

The association between hairdressers and conjure was so common that white men sometimes tried to co-opt it in advertising schemes, much like Aunt Jemima and the Negro Mammy's hoecakes. In 1925, William H. Brown saw that cosmetics for Black hair was a lucrative market. So he made up a hairdresser, Madame Hightower, who had been given a mojo by a conjure woman, Aunt Nancy. This mojo, the story goes, secured Hightower's success in doing hair and enabled her to create the incredible Golden Brown hair care line. Brown's scheme came tumbling down when the true identity of Madame Hightower was revealed. In 1926, an internal letter of the company, which had disparaging comments about African Americans, was leaked to Black newspapers. It turns out that Madam Hightower was really the wife of an employee of Golden Brown Chemical Company—a janitor by the name of Zachary Hightower.[27]

THE HAIRDRESSER WAS ONE OF many women who took up the spiritual responsibilities of conjure women when Granny Midwives were removed from our communities. For Black women, the beauty shop was not just a place where you could get the latest hair style. The beauty shop was a spiritual place, where your soul could be uplifted—with prayers as the hairdresser massaged your scalp or with hoodoo paraphernalia she might sell you out the back of the shop.[28] The beauty parlor was a place where you could get much-needed advice on how to handle the conflicts in your closest relationships—friends, lovers, children. And it was a place where you could get health advice, for the hairdresser was often the first person who noticed and pointed out chronic problems whose early symptoms show up in the hair, like diabetes, lupus, and polycystic ovarian syndrome.

These experiences led feminist and cultural critic bell hooks to argue that getting her hair straightened or "pressed," as was the trend of her day, was not "a sign of our longing to be white."[29] At the beauty shop, bell hooks learned that our hair was magic. When she was a child, she saw customers at her aunt's salon "bring in little brown paper sacks to put their hair in after it was cut."[30] Some of these clients told hooks that "it will make the hair grow to burn it." Others told her about the dangers of letting stray hair lie around. These clients were careful to gather their cut hair "so no enemy will get it and use it to work an evil charm." So, for bell hooks, getting her hair done was a sacred ritual, "an exclusive moment when black women (even those that did not know one another well) might meet at home or in the beauty parlor where they would be comforted by the parting hands that comb and braid, comforted by the intimacy and bliss."[31] Like the quilting bees of our enslaved foremothers, the beauty shop was "a space where black women could share life stories—hardship, trials, gossip; a place where one could be comforted and one's spirit renewed."[32]

Many of us have busy careers that keep us from slowing down enough to linger with other women for the hours a visit to the beauty shop often requires.[33] Our options now are more isolating than communal: solo stylists who get us quickly in and out of chairs with minimum chatter; "African auntie" braiding shops with Nollywood flicks filling the space where conversation would have been; and following YouTube tutorials, alone in our bathrooms, working late into the night. But many of us remember going to the hairdresser with our mothers.

So you might also remember another conjure woman who frequented the beauty shops, selling her wares all throughout Black neighborhoods. This woman was responsible for the plates of fried fish that bell hooks remembers being served at the beauty parlor. In my lifetime, she was known as the Candy Lady. And she was not just a keeper of African American food traditions. She used the conjure of her foremothers to bring sustenance and freedom to Black communities in every meal she served.

PART FIVE

The Candy Lady's Soul Food

CHAPTER TWENTY-FIVE

Oshun's Legacy in the New World

WHEN I WAS AN UNDERGRADUATE IN COLLEGE, I LIVED FAR AWAY from home. I had moved from Baton Rouge, Louisiana, to Grand Rapids, Michigan, an entirely different region of the country. So of course I got homesick. And the best way to cure it was comfort food from home. But I was without many of the ingredients for the dishes I craved, the vegetables and spices that were easily found on any grocery shelf in the Deep South. But what I *could* find in the stores up North was Zatarain's rice mixes.

With the help of Zatarain's rice mixes, any American family across the nation can savor dishes that, two hundred years ago, could only be found in the South. The company was founded in 1889 by Emile A. Zatarain, a New Orleans businessman of French descent.[1] Zatarain expanded his neighborhood grocery business by trademarking and mass-producing Creole staples like root beer (which came from the Choctaw people in Louisiana), Creole mustard, and pickled vegetables. The company continued to augment its product lines for well over a century to include its famous rice mixes and frozen meals. In 2003, Zatarain's was bought by McCormick and Company for $180 million.[2]

If you go down the aisle of "international foods" in any major grocery store in the nation, you'll find Zatarain's rice mixes in the white and red box with the black silhouette of a jazz man promising to bring the "soul of New Orleans" into your kitchen: jambalaya, red beans and rice, dirty rice, gumbo, black-eyed peas and rice. Many Americans add a little bit of sausage or shrimp to their rice mixes and dine on these one-pot meals without any inkling of what these foods have spiritually meant to African Americans for generations.

You may recognize these dishes as common staples of soul food: the meals that enslaved West Africans cooked on plantations for both Blacks and whites. Many of the foods served on plantations became fixtures in the southern diet during the Jim Crow period. This fare traveled with African Americans during the Great Migration, transforming the food landscape in the North as the cuisine melded with the culinary influences of African, Caribbean, and European immigrants. And in the 1960s and 1970s, these foods took on an explicit political valence during the Black Power movement, when "soul" was coined as a euphemism for "Black."[3]

Soul food's culinary ties to West Africa have long been observed (most recently in shows like Netflix's *High on the Hog*).[4] But much less has been said about the spiritual traditions that have influenced soul food.[5] Quiet as it's kept, there was one Black woman in your childhood whose kitchen was filled with conjure. Do you remember the Candy Lady?

THE CANDY LADY WAS A staple in many of our childhoods, known for expertly transforming her kitchen into a makeshift diner, church bakery, or candy store. Her prevalence is salient for 1980s babies like me, but she's been sweetening up Black communities for over four hundred years. The Candy Lady was the centuries-removed descendant of women who sold their wares of pottery and dyed clothes and street foods in village markets along the coast of West Africa. At the dawn of the transatlantic slave trade, West African market women had total command over these open-air markets.[6] Their successful trades helped shape the local economy of their community. And so, African market women were not only vital to the wealth of their household, but they were also the lifeblood of their villages. And their economic participation gave them a powerful position in their communities, where they wielded great social and political influence.[7]

To see the market woman in the pantheon of African American conjure women, we have to dive back into the myths of Oshun. In this four-hundred-year-long foray into Black women's magic, we have seen Oshun's legacy show up in many ways: in the skilled herbalists and lay nurses of slavery, the Negro Mammies upon whom the stereotype Aunt Jemima is based. In the vengeful mermaid, Mami Wata, who was worshipped among Voodoo Queens in antebellum New Orleans. In the mojo-wielding women of Reconstruction, like Aunt Caroline Dye and Bessie Smith. And we have seen Oshun in the Granny Midwives of Jim Crow, the weavers who sewed symbols of conjure into patchwork quilts of jeans.

But in Yoruba mythology, Oshun was also an extraordinary market woman due to her many skills of weaving, herbalism, and dying cloth. She traded in the kola nut, and her calabash overflowed with cowrie shells, two of the most desired commodities on the eve of the transaltantic slave trade.[8] The kola nut and cowrie shell served multiple functions for the Yoruba people. As units of currency, they were a status of wealth. As tools of divination, the kola nut and the cowrie shell were the very power of gods.[9]

Divination is a rich knowledge of self and world that gives you, as Toni Morrison describes, "this canny ability to shape an untenable reality, mold it, sing it, reduce it to its manageable, transforming essence."[10] This wellspring of knowledge is ultimately what helps conjure women manage their luck, staying afloat on the waves of good and bad fortune that crash over all our lives. One of my favorite myths of Oshun tells us how she learned the art of divination by making an incredible trade that only the most proficient market woman could pull off.[11]

Long ago, Obatala, the *orisha* of the white cloth of peace, noticed that humans were beginning to fall into all sorts of problems—illness, neighborly disputes, family brawls, brutal wars. So Obatala asked Orunmila, the *orisha* of divination, to share a bit of his *ashe* with him. With some of Orunmila's foresight, perhaps the humans Obatala created could learn how to solve, if not outright avoid, these troubling situations. And for a while, that worked.

Obatala had an imagination as vast as the sky, so he was always on the move. It was his habit to roam all over the Earth, like the clouds that inevitably drift to the edge of the horizon. So often, when the people came to find Obatala for guidance, he was not there to give it.

Oshun was moved by the people's despair. She saw how they perished without a firm vision of the future. So she decided to follow Obatala on his grand journeys one day to see if she could convince him to teach her the art of divination. That way, the people would no longer have to rely on Obatala's whims to address their problems. If she could pass the art of divination into the hands of the people, they would be able to draw upon the wisdom they needed to tackle the tough issues that arose in life whether or not Obatala was around.

So she stepped over gnarled tree roots and ducked swinging vines, keeping a steady pace behind Obatala as he trekked through the woods. On and on he went, leaving her to wonder when this maddening journey would end.

Finally, Obatala reached the edge of a river. He slipped off his blinding white robes and dived in. Oshun crept closer to the shore, peeking around the trunk of an Ube tree. She saw Obatala gliding through the water. His nakedness was that of a child when they enter the world and an elder when they depart from it. His nakedness was the breathtaking vulnerability of all humans, who he shaped in his likeness. The vulnerability that Obatala saw in himself when humans drew breath. The same vulnerability that he tried to hide with palm wine and then the purest robes of white.

A giggle, high in the branches, disrupted Oshun from her thoughts. It was Eshu (also known as Elegua, who is not gendered).[12] She immediately recognized the laughter of the *orisha* of crossroads and chaos and luck. She moved to shush Eshu before they gave her hiding spot away, but then it dawned on her that Eshu, as the sacred messenger of the gods, might actually be able to help her in her quest.

Oshun crooked her finger at Eshu, beckoning them to her. Eshu raised their eyebrows and climbed down the tree.

Will you help me convince Obatala to teach me the art of divination? Oshun asked as she winked at them. Eshu's greatest delight was to be involved in trickery, and they hated that Obatala would never indulge their desire for mischief. Eshu got down into a squat to think and rested their face on their fist. *What to do? What to do?* Eshu muttered.

Eshu looked up and saw Obatala drawing closer to the shore. His swim was quickly coming to an end. Eshu looked to a low branch of the Ube tree that held Obatala's white robes.

Suddenly, Eshu's eyes glistened with pleasure. *Oshun, they said, why don't you go back to your house? I'll make sure that Obatala meets you there.* As Eshu winked at Oshun, she caught on to their devious plan.

At her home, Oshun took a bath. When she stepped out of the tub, she found Obatala's robes laid out neatly on a chair. And then she knew exactly what to do.

She reached for her honey pots on a shelf. When Obatala finally stumbled through her door looking for his robes, he beheld the honey dripping from her breasts. Honey dripped, dripped, dripped down her thighs. He heard the honey droplets as they hit the floor. She pointed to his robes just behind her on the chair. But by then his whole being was consumed with longing for a taste of honey. So when Oshun offered Obatala his clothes in exchange for his lessons in divination, he could not help but oblige.

When Oshun bartered with Obatala, she learned how to use what you've got on hand—her honey—to shape the future, which is the task of any diviner. And the success of her bargain furthered her empowerment and that of others. When Oshun learned the art of divination, she did not keep the mysterious knowledge to herself. Instead, she shared it with the other *orishas* and the humans who suffered without it. And she taught women how to use their *aje* to mold their destiny with their own hands, to transform the bitterest of sorrows into a nourishing sweetness. This lesson was passed on among West African market women for generations. When forcefully brought to the Americas, their descendants did not forget the power of their mother's cooking pots. In the United States, conjure women turned the food they served into a source of strength for their communities, continuing their foremothers' tradition of gastronomical alchemy.

THE CONJURING OF AMERICA

LIKE WEST AFRICAN MARKET WOMEN of the seventeenth century, Oshun was *a marvelous cook*.[13] In Yoruba mythology, Oshun used food in every arena of life, from the bedroom to the village market, to amass great wealth and power in the process—for herself and the communities she took under her wing. And like all the *orishas*, Oshun had special foods that captured aspects of her essence in Yoruba folklore. Consider the story of a village woman who saved her community by making an offering of some of Oshun's favorite foods.[14]

Long ago, the people of Oshogbo were struggling with infertility. As much as they tried, they could not bear children. And without children, they struggled to envision their future. So of course they cried out to Oshun, the goddess of fertility.

She heard their cries, and she was moved. So she blessed them with children and wealth. But like humans are wont to do, after a few years, they began to forget how Oshun had helped them. They neglected Oshun's altar in their homes, even though she had filled their houses with the tinkling laughter of children. They did not call Oshun's name during their harvest festivals, even though it was she who guaranteed their bounty.

And there's nothing Oshun despises more than a lack of devotion.

So, soon, their children began to fall ill, their bodies ravaged by fevers. A gloomy silence fell over the town. The celebrations that marked coming-of-age rituals, the lively banter among neighbors in the street, and the jaunty cries of market women all ceased.

The people began to flock to their village priests, asking what they should do. But the priests only scratched their heads, for they, too, had forgotten Oshun, along with the joy she brought in her wake. Even those with the gift of divination did not know how to turn back this tide of bad fortune.

So Oshun took it upon herself to show the people what to do to please her. She transformed into *an ordinary woman* in their village. This woman called the people to her house. Then she made a sacrifice to Oshun, reminding them that they had turned their backs on the *orisha* who had given them so much. This mysterious woman told the people to bring Oshun offerings of the foods she loved most: wild lettuce, black-eyed-pea fritters called *akara*, cornstarch porridge, and kola nuts. Shortly after the offerings, the people returned to their homes and found that *their children were cool*, their fevers gone. In thanks to Oshun for healing their children, they began to make weekly offerings. Every fifth day, *[t]hey were taking five portions of cornstarch porridge; they were taking fritters; they were taking wild lettuce; they were taking kola nuts; they were going to give them to Oshun*, placing these gifts upon her altar in their homes.

Oshun was appeased by their show of devotion. With her blessing, the people *had money, and their children were uncountable*. These children chattered in excitement at the cornstarch porridge their mothers prepared for breakfast. Market women returned to the streets, their baskets full of *akara* to be sold as midday snacks. Cheered by the return of good fortune, the elders of the town gathered under the stars at night around large pots of greens stewed with fish heads. They dipped *fufu*, pounded yams, into the pots as they ate.

During their celebrations, the elders passed around gourds of kola nut tea to mark their joy. For Oshun herself was the essence of the kola nut. This small brown nut is both sweet and bitter, much like Oshun, who can be just as kind as she is vengeful. Peel back its green skin, and ruby red or white flesh is reveled. That's the part you chew. It has an acrid taste at first, but it makes everything you consume afterward toothsome.[15] The kola nut was the promise of abundance nestled into the palm of your hand. If you were hungry or thirsty, the kola nut gave you the sensation of fullness.[16] That's because consuming the kola nut, as a tea or eating it raw, made you feel satiated due to its ability to refresh the body through and through.

These foods—wild lettuce, cornstarch porridge, fritters, and kola nuts—show up repeatedly in Oshun's lore. In some myths, Oshun taught Obba, another river *orisha* and fellow wife of Shango (the *orisha* of lightning), how to secure a man's love by putting a little something "extra" in Shango's favorite dish *amala*, a porridge of cornmeal, okra, and palm oil. In this case, the secret ingredient was Obba's own ear.[17]

In another myth, Oshun transformed into a market woman who sold poisoned leafy greens called *efo yanrin* to political enemies trying to invade and conquer her town.[18] And at times, Oshun was simply the everyday village woman who made delectable fried bean cakes of black-eyed peas.[19] She rose early to feed these fritters to her family for breakfast or peddled them in the market as a popular snack.[20]

Greens, black-eyed peas, corn for porridge, and kola nuts could be easily purchased from market women, as they were common staples of West African (especially Yoruba) diets.[21] And enslaved West Africans brought these food preferences with them across the

Atlantic. On slave ships, the enslaved would often refuse to eat food that they were not used to, even risking severe punishment.²² Slavers knew that if the enslaved looked sick and famished when they arrived in the Americas, no one would want to buy them on the auction blocks. So the captains of slave ships enlisted Black women to cook the foods the enslaved desired. On the ships, enslaved Black women cleaned the rice and ground the corn for their meals.²³ They stewed beans like black-eyed peas in *dab-a-dab*, a dish of rice, beans, peppers, or yams.²⁴ They molded the ground corn into patties for frying.²⁵ They peeled the kola nuts given to the enslaved to curb their hunger and thirst on the long, long journey.²⁶

IN THE NEW WORLD, MUCH of the American diet was the result of the agricultural and artistic innovation of those who survived the Middle Passage. Colonists like the British had dietary preferences that differed starkly from West Africans. In the seventeenth century, the basic diet of West Africans was a soup or stew of leafy greens or beans, seasoned with a bit of smoked fish, peppers, onions, and garlic, and served over a starch, such as *fufu*, a bed of rice, or cornstarch porridge.²⁷ But the ideal diet for British people was lots and lots of red meat, some potatoes or oats to supplement, and very little fruits and vegetables.²⁸ They considered stews and soups of vegetables like greens to be poor people's food. But on plantations, these colonists were continually exposed to mainstays of West African cuisine.

In fields along the East and Gulf Coasts, enslaved West Africans used knowledge from their homelands to cultivate staples like rice that soon found a permanent place at their slave masters' tables.²⁹ And in the Big House kitchens, Negro Mammies slowly Africanized the American palate. They took *French and Spanish dishes* and applied their *typical Negro skill at making a fine dish out of a little added*.³⁰ That little something extra added was drawn from West African cooking techniques, the *certain knowledge or instincts* that we *brought from the wilds of Africa*, such as *rare flavoring herbs*.³¹ These "instincts" included spicing things up with cayenne pepper or hot sauce, deep frying in vegetable oils, seasoning soups and stews with bits of smoked pork or fish, thickening those soups and stews with leafy greens or okra or sesame seeds, and adding immense complexity and depth of flavor by simmering it all in one pot.³²

It was Negro Mammies who *went into the woods and brought forth the leaves and roots that, wisely prepared, added new half-tastes and quarter tastes that, like the [nuanced shades] of a painter, add a subtle attractiveness* to the overall dish.³³ And with their tantalizing fare, Negro Mammies also introduced West African fruits and vegetables like okra, eggplants, and black-eyed peas into the diets of generations of white Americans.³⁴ It's striking that, in the kitchen, the enslaved held influence over their master's meals. Slave masters did not cook, so they had to eat whatever Negro Mammies prepared.

Throughout the history of the United States, Oshun's foods show up again and again. Some of Oshun's foods were absorbed by white corporations and then stripped of their spiritual contexts in Black communities. The cornmeal porridge Oshun loved became the hoecakes of the enslaved; during Reconstruction, Pearl Milling Company co-opted those hoecakes with the figure of Aunt Jemima.

And although the enslaved in the United States did not grow kola nuts like their counterparts in the Caribbean, they still remembered the joy of kola nut tea.³⁵ At parties and frolics, the enslaved prepared a bevy of red drinks reminiscent of their beloved kola nut, like strawberry lemonade and red molasses mixed with water.³⁶ I find it deeply ironic that the kola nut our enslaved ancestors revered was formally introduced to American culture by way of a former slave owner, the pharmacist John S. Pemberton. In 1886, Pemberton created Coca-Cola, with the kola nut as one of its principal ingredients.[37] And once again, something that was deeply African was absorbed by American capitalism, with Coke products now earning billions of dollars in revenue.

Today, it's more likely that you'll sample other foods of Oshun, like greens and black-eyed peas, with a lonely box of Zatarain's, rather than dine on them at soul food restaurants, which served these dishes to Black communities during Jim Crow. By the 1990s, many soul food restaurants that once flourished in Black neighborhoods were no longer in business. Desegregation largely eroded these Black eateries.[38] One of the gains of the Civil Rights movement was the freedom to eat wherever we like, which expanded our range of dining options. And our patronage of soul food restaurants in the latter half of the twentieth century waned as a result. So in my childhood, I didn't have access to all the soul food restaurants my grandparents enjoyed in their youth. But at least people in my generation had the Candy Lady.

Our Candy Ladies largely retained the cultural meaning of Oshun's foods in Black communities. Candy Ladies have been cultural bearers, upholding Oshun's legacy in the New World. Through *aje*, the magic that Oshun grants to women, generations of Black Candy Ladies in America transformed their cooking pots into vessels of freedom, empowering Black communities just like Oshun did in her food myths.

CHAPTER TWENTY-SIX

The Candy Lady

I F YOU GREW UP IN A BLACK NEIGHBORHOOD, THERE WAS ONE HOUSE you probably loved to visit: the Candy Lady's. She was a central elder in Black communities, stepping into the roles that Granny Midwives once filled by offering spiritual support to families, along with childcare and a bit of tough love if you needed it. Although the Candy Lady was a soul food cook extraordinaire, she got her name from the sweets she sold to the children of our neighborhoods for chump change.[1] Candy Ladies were women like my great-grandmother, after whom I am named: Margaret "Booie" Lindsey Perkins (1921–2014). She was a Candy Lady in Darrow, Louisiana, well known for her *popcorn, candy, and pies*.[2]

Every winter, my family and I would stop by my great-grandmother's house for some of her confectionary specialties. There were pralines, candy made of sugar, butter, and pecans, and date roll candy, a sweetmeat of dates and pecans that was as dense and smooth as fudge. There were apples and popcorn drizzled in a homemade caramel that made the tongue rejoice. And my great-grandmother always had a homemade batch of strawberry lemonade in her fridge to welcome us too. These treats were things that she, like other Candy Ladies, would sell throughout Black communities: in beauty and barber shops, in the local drugstore or corner grocery, outside of church after regular worship service and revivals, or even from their house on weekday afternoons to children getting out from school.

When the Candy Lady sold kids treats, she was giving them much more than mile-high sugar rushes and the cavities that were likely to follow. The Candy Lady cared for children during those critical hours when they had arrived home from school and their parents were still at work. And, at times, she was the only defense against hunger in that long stretch between paydays for families or when breakfast and school lunches were missed for lack of funds. When you were at the Candy Lady's house, there was almost always something warm and filling like beans or greens going in a pot on the back burner of the stove, the kind of food often found at soul food restaurants.

When we were children, the Candy Lady was also our lay nurse and our therapist. She nursed us with the home remedies passed down through her conjure forebears, adapting to what was at hand. There was potlikker (a broth left from hours of cooking down greens) for colds and salt water for sore throats. To settle an upset stomach, there was ginger ale, now more readily available than the ginger teas of her foremothers. And when we were congested, there was Vicks VapoRub, like the herbal salves of Negro Mammies, which she smeared under our noses and over our chests. The Candy Lady could make us sit our behind down with only a stare while she treated us for sickness or scrapes from play. And, truth be told, we were grateful to sit down on her couch, pristinely preserved under a thick layer of plastic, because she always listened patiently when we chose to share the things on our heart.

She taught us about money and entrepreneurship and the power of saving up our dollars. You never knew just how much money she had tucked away from this side hustle over the years until you saw her reach into her cookie tin for a few crumpled dollars to lend to families in need. She was often the first businesswoman we ever saw who looked like us, a tangible model of economic independence that we could aspire to.[3] My great-uncle and *griot* of our family, Daniel Perkins Jr., tells me that my great-grandmother was one of the first caterers of the area.

Her world was shaped by the Granny Midwives of her childhood. So when her children had colds, she wrapped a string of asafetida around their necks. When her children had fevers, she rubbed their chests with a homemade salve that my mother remembers was "stronger than Vicks Salve" and smelled like menthol. Then my great-grandmother sat her children down in front of the radiator to sweat the fever out. During the winter, when her neighbors were in need, she and her sisters sewed quilts and prepared hot dinners.[4]

Like other Candy Ladies, my great-grandmother was a phenomenal cook. She honed her culinary skills through years of serving as a cook at a restaurant in Houmas House Estate and Gardens, a former plantation, now tourist destination. It is likely that this plantation is where many of my ancestors were enslaved. Working for whites who likely owned members of her family during slavery must have been humiliating and tough. But she turned what was meant to denigrate her into a source of income and a step toward self-determination. She scrounged up enough money from those years at Houmas Plantation to set up her own country store. My mother tells me that for ten years, my great-grandmother ran Watts Delicatessen, which sold tea cakes, pralines (or what we in the rural areas called pecan candy), pickles, pig lips, pies, and popcorn.

Great-Uncle Dan told me that "there was nothing [my great-grandmother] put her hand to that she couldn't do." This was the legacy she passed down to me. And like other Candy Ladies across the country, she was one of the very first people in our community to teach us that in order to lay hold of our future potential, we have to understand where we come from.

✿

CANDY LADIES LIKE MY GREAT-GRANDMOTHER have a long history in Louisiana. They go all the way back to black market women called *marchandes* or *pralinières*, who sold a bevy of sweet and savory delicacies in the French Quarter during the eighteenth and nineteenth centuries. In New Orleans, *marchandes* appeared early on, becoming a vital part of the culinary and economic development of the city during slavery. Sometimes *marchandes* were free women of color. More often, they were enslaved women *too old to be of other use*, or Negro Mammies. They were routinely *put out into the city streets to peddle the surplus produce of the plantations.*[5]

In the French Quarter, *marchandes* didn't just sell sweets. They hawked a range of items: vegetables, herbs, flowers, handmade trinkets like dolls or toy skeletons, candies and pastries, prepared meals, and even their laundering services by *waving their washboards above their heads as signs of their trade.*[6] The steady gaits of *marchandes* walking throughout the French Market were as constant as the sun's trek across the horizon. Just before dawn, the market opened with their cries of *Café au lait! Café noir!*, as they doled out coffee with steamed milk or simply silky black.[7] At dusk, the market closed with their cries of *Belle chandelles!* to any tourist or neighbor who needed a candle for reading or sewing late into the night.[8]

Much of the wares that *marchandes* sold in the French Quarter came from leftovers and excess goods from plantations that they then put their spin on. The treat that is most synonymous with New

Orleans, pralines, were born from such innovation. Negro Mammies took the humble pecan, abundant on plantations, and turned them into a delicacy that rivaled the best of European confections.

Negro Mammies who worked as *marchandes* at the end of the eighteenth century were sometimes able to turn street vending to their advantage. Some slave owners allowed the enslaved to keep a portion of what they earned from their sales in town.[9] Under Spanish law, the enslaved were also allowed to negotiate a price for their freedom through the courts.[10] These factors created a path to freedom that several *marchandes* took, especially when years of cooking and nursing gave them an advantage over white and immigrant street vendors in pressing their homemade wares on the market.[11]

Consider the life of *marchande* Rose Nicaud, the first person to sell coffee outside of the home in New Orleans and who made enough money to purchase her freedom at the end of the eighteenth century.[12] Coffee that was usually roasted, ground, and brewed at home could now be purchased from Nicaud's cart, parked outside of St. Louis Cathedral, just in time for congregants who needed to perk up after a long Mass service.[13] Years of making medicinal teas helped Nicaud make her own special blend of coffee, spices, and chicory that made her the envy of the French Quarter.

And as a Negro Mammy, Nicaud's cooking duties gave her direct access to the *luscious "open kettle" sugar, that dear, fragrant brown sugar* that made Creole coffee irresistible.[14] This sugar was made through the open kettle process, where the enslaved poured boiling crushed sugarcane from larger to smaller cauldrons in succession.[15] For the last pour, the enslaved drained molasses from brown sugar crystals. Both products were highly sought after by confectioners of New Orleans.[16]

Nicaud also sold *calas*, sweet fritters made from leftover rice. In nineteenth-century New Orleans, *marchandes* also sold a savory version of *calas* made of cowpeas, much like Oshun's *akara*.[17] *Calas* are precursors to the beignets that many of us still enjoy today in Louisiana. These *calas* are seldom served commercially in New Orleans. But to this day, pralines are still one of the most beloved candies of New Orleans. Pralines also enjoy national prominence, as their flavor has informed a range of other desserts Americans love. There are praline cakes, praline ice creams, and even praline liqueurs.

To draw the eye and direct smell to the nose, *marchandes* would wave palmetto fans to and fro over these delicious candies, made of coconuts and pecans.[18] A *marchande* during Nicaud's time, Tasie was known for her extraordinary pralines, and her story hints at how this French delicacy came to be sold primarily by Negro Mammies.[19] When people asked Tasie how she learned to make her candies, she frequently pointed to her years as a Negro Mammy. In this role, she nursed the children of her master, and *it was for their delectation [that she] learned of vieille maîtresse [an old mistress] to make the toothsome sweets she sells*.[20]

French women slaveholders learned how to make pralines from Ursuline nuns, who originally brought the candy over to the Americas.[21] Negro Mammies learned how to make the candy from their French mistresses, and with years of cooking and nursing under their belt, they soon made the candy their own.

It's said that pralines were originally developed by a French chef.[22] He candied almonds for a French duke to treat his constant stomach pains. Negro Mammies, too, were familiar with making candies to persuade reluctant children to take their medicine.[23] And Negro Mammies were particularly well suited to innovate on the once medicinal praline. They switched the then-scarce almonds for the copious pecans they picked on plantations and in neighboring forests. And they substituted the candy's white sugar for the open kettle sugar that they had access to in their masters' kitchens.

By the 1890s, the most famous type of *marchandes* were praline ladies, dressed in the familiar garb of Negro Mammies, *starched white aprons and tignons*, even though they were no longer enslaved.[24] Whites who approached these Candy Ladies in the streets viewed them as innocuous and docile with their wide smiles and soft Creole patois, but there was more to these women than what met the eye. For praline ladies were also an integral part of the ecosystem of Voodoo in the nineteenth century.

IN HIS FEDERAL WRITERS' PROJECT interview, Joseph Alfred remarks that the famous Voodoo Queen of New Orleans, Marie Laveau, *had a black woman living with her who sold peanuts, pralines, potato pones, and I believe she sold powders and herbs.*[25] Shortly after emancipation, most conjurers no longer needed to go into the woods or swamps to gather their own roots and herbs. Instead, they bought their supplies from the praline lady or from *regular supply houses*.[26] Praline ladies also supplied clients for Voodoo Queens. Alfred tells us that the praline lady who lived with Laveau *directed people to Marie Laveau's house* while she made her sales *all through the French Quarter*.

The association between Voodoo Queens of New Orleans and *marchandes* like the praline lady started long before Laveau rose to prominence. Sanité Dédé, the Voodoo Queen of New Orleans before Laveau usurped her, bought her own freedom by selling *calas*.[27] It's rumored that after her fall from queendom, Sanité Dédé became Zozo LaBrique, another type of candy lady who roamed the French Quarter.[28]

In the 1850s, Zozo LaBrique frequently walked through the French Quarter with three buckets of powdered redbrick dust, one in each hand and one atop her head in perfect balance. Children were drawn to LaBrique, much like they are often captivated by witches in fairy tales. They would sneak up behind her and yell "Zozo," which means bird, and LaBrique seemed to accept the title they bequeathed to her. Instead of chastising the children, she would reward them with a peppermint stick. The children did not know the truth they spoke, considering that the *iyami aje*, Yoruba witches, were also thought to transform into birds at night.[29]

Perhaps she was, indeed, a witch—as a *marchandes*, LaBrique supplied a crucial ingredient used in conjure. Redbrick dust was used to cast spells of protection and attract luck.[30] And as Toni Morrison observed, the worst kind of bad luck Black women wanted to avoid was white people—having the law or the landlord or their bosses show up at their door and wreak havoc on their families.

One *marchande* who was apprenticed to Marie Laveau, Mary Washington, can help us understand how women peddlers like Zozo LaBrique, praline ladies like Rose Nicaud, and Candy Ladies like my great-grandmother navigated the perpetual racism and sexism they faced as they sold their wares. White people took LaBrique's eccentricity to be the madness they thought lurked behind every Black woman who defied their "place," who dared to stand out and refused to be demure. White people expected Nicaud to fulfill their fantasy of *awaken[ing] every morning* to a Negro Mammy *standing beside [their bed], her round black face broken with a white smile and a tray in her hands on which was piping-hot drip coffee*.[31] And white people who toured Houmas plantation wanted my great-grandmother to play the part of the "faithful slave" so they could be transported back to the "good old days." When my mother accompanied my great-grandmother to Houmas plantation, the restaurant owners would put her to work waiting tables while my great-grandmother was ensconced in the kitchen—and they gave my mother "slave clothes" to wear as she greeted their white patrons.

Candy Ladies were stuck between a rock and a hard place. Money was crucial for their dreams of freedom. LaBrique and Nicaud needed money for their manumission. My great-grandmother needed money to secure some amount of economic independence to support her family during Jim Crow. But this way of getting money was demeaning and belittling. So how did they do it without letting these encounters with white people destroy their souls?

Mary Washington gives us some insight into how these Candy Ladies might have pulled this off. Marie Laveau once told Washington how she became *the most powerful woman in the world*. How did Laveau rise to the upper echelons of New Orleans society, bending policemen and judges and politicians to her will? Laveau told Washington: *[w]hen [you] can fool 'em, be sure to fool 'em.*

Washington explains that *[Marie Laveau's] associating with the white people made her learn how to fool them. She had a way with white people.* Laveau was well aware of the delusions of the white people she encountered on a daily basis. *She would learn the ways of the men from the women and the ways of the women from the men.* And then she would use that information to trick them in any manner she saw fit. In this network of praline ladies and Voodoo Queens, Laveau's shrewdness was passed around in gossip and folktales until it become a lucrative business model women like my great-grandmother drew upon well into the twentieth century.

Marie Laveau's approach to white people reminds me a lot of Black anthropologist Zora Neale Hurston. In *Mules and Men*, Hurston tells us that Black people in the South often had to deal with nosy, racist white people. But during Jim Crow, openly defying whites could lead to imprisonment or lynching. So Black people came up with a different tactic. They would not reveal their innermost thoughts to white people; they would not let white people take up space in their minds and hearts. Instead, when a white person comes, poking their nose in Black folks' business, Black people would *offer a feather-bed resistance*.[32]

Rather than tell white people directly to leave us alone, *we smile and tell him or her something that satisfies the white person because, knowing so little about us, he doesn't know what he's missing.* So Zozo and Rose Nicaud and my great-grandmother could give the white folks the fake smiles and honeyed speech that racked up sales. They could play this role, *sett[ing] something outside the door of [their] minds for [white people] to play with and handle.* They understood that white people could not *read [their] mind*. And as long as these Candy Ladies did not let white people into their minds, they remained free to *say [their] say and sing [their] song*.

This is how these Candy Ladies "fooled the white folks," all the while filling their purses with coins that secured freedom not only for themselves but also for their communities. But that's not all that Candy Ladies did. I think the greatest trick of these Candy Ladies was fooling white folks into consuming the conjure in many of the dishes found on the average American's dinner table. If they had eyes to see, a terrifying realization would befall white folks: this conjure woman, the Candy Lady, is forever a *brown specter [who] pulls up a chair beside [them] when [they] sit down to eat*.[33]

CHAPTER TWENTY-SEVEN

From Black-Eyed Peas to Red Beans and Rice

THE PLACE WHERE CONJURE HAS SHOWN UP MOST IN MY LIFE IS THE kitchen. And if you've ever eaten a meal of black-eyed peas, leafy greens, and corn bread to usher in a lucky New Year, then conjure has showed up in your kitchen too. My family often had some variant of this meal on New Year's Day. And over the meal, family elders always offered an important life tip: Don't let the New Year catch you with your house out of order. This ritual has roots in African American conjure traditions, which are all about how to manage your luck—how to ensure good fortune and how to keep all the stuff that you don't want far away from you. So every New Year, my family took stock of our relationships to make sure we were entering the coming year on a good foot, swept and mopped until our floors shone, and ate the dishes that our enslaved ancestors believed to be luck enhancers.

In Louisiana, we have our own take on this luck-enhancing ritual. I also grew up eating red beans and rice on Mondays, a common tradition in South Louisiana that is strictly adhered to in households, school cafeterias, and restaurants featuring local cuisine. If you ask anyone there why we eat red beans and rice on Mondays, they'll tell you that a long time ago, it was tradition that, on Mondays, women would put on a pot of red beans while they did the laundry. The story goes something like this.

In the eighteenth and nineteenth centuries, laundry used to be done outside in large cauldrons that were also used for cooking. The arduous task would take all day: filling up a huge cauldron with water from rivers or bayous or wells, stoking the fire under the cauldrons to make the water boil, steadily stirring submerged batches of clothes, scrubbing the clothes with handmade soap over washboards, and then hanging them out to dry. So the women would often set up two pots of water, side by side.

In one cauldron, the women placed bits of ham left over from Sunday dinner along with red beans and the seasoning base we call the "holy trinity"—bell pepper, onion, and celery. In the other pot, they placed the filthy clothes. Cooking red beans is a slow process that, thankfully, doesn't require too much attention once you've set up the pot. So the women could tend to the laundry, giving it their full attention, while a hefty pot of red beans puttered slowly beside them, ready just in time for family supper.

In tourist pamphlets and books on New Orleans culture, you'll likely get some version of this story. Even Zatarain's Red Beans and Rice mix spreads this tale, describing the meal as *[a] quintessentially New Orleans dish, traditionally prepared on Mondays when a long stovetop simmer gave home cooks time to do the laundry.* But this lore often leaves out the role that Candy Ladies and their conjure have played in shaping this tradition that spread throughout South Louisiana.[1] What the story doesn't tell you is that eating red beans and rice on Mondays was a conjure practice among Black people in New Orleans—doing so was lucky, just like eating black-eyed peas on New Year's Day. Conjure is the reason why red beans, as opposed to other types of beans, were cooked on Mondays; why Mondays were an auspicious day to wash; and why these beans were believed to be lucky in the first place. And conjure, remember, is all about managing your luck in an already bad situation, like the staggering oppression Black people faced in America for centuries.

To understand how red beans and rice came to be lucky, we have to recover the hidden origins of this dish. During slavery, Hoppin' John, a spicy dish of black-eyed peas and rice, was one of the preeminent dishes of African Americans. Some believe this dish to have evolved from what the enslaved ate during their horrific journey across the Atlantic.[2] By the nineteenth century, Hoppin' John had become the chief fare of our conjure traditions.

Negro Mammies like Harriet Collins reported that her grandmother always told her that *[d]ose black eyed peas is lucky / when et on New Year's Day, / You'll allus have sweet 'taters / and 'possum come you way.*[3] Although black-eyed peas were eaten regularly by the enslaved and slaveholders alike on plantations, the enslaved were often not given enough to eat by their slave owners, so to have sweet potatoes and possum in your possession all year long was good fortune indeed.

Across the West, traditions around winter holidays like Christmas and New Year's Day have long been treasured for their ability to forecast the rest of your year.[4] Slave owners brought this tradition to the Americas. And then Negro Mammies altered the traditions of their slave masters according to their own spiritual beliefs, making Hoppin' John one of the central dishes to bring in the New Year across the nation.

In Louisiana, we put our own twist on Hoppin' John and called it *jambalaya au congri*.[5] Central to both dishes are black-eyed peas, also known in the South as cowpeas, crowder peas, or field peas. The black-eyed pea is a much beloved bean across the African diaspora. Beans have long been associated with fertility and abundance, both in parts of the West and parts of Africa.[6] So it is no surprise that the West African forebears of the enslaved, especially the Yoruba, wove black-eyed peas into their spiritual traditions. The black-eyed pea was considered a favorite food offering for certain *orishas* like Oshun, Yemaya, and Oya.[7] All of these *orishas* were thought to bring wealth, fertility, and good fortune to those who worship them.

In West African lore, it was believed that the black pit of these beans, the "eyes" so to speak, brought protection.[8] Their eyes could shield you from the evil eye of neighbors and malicious spirits that could bring misfortune upon your life. And the black-eyed pea was revered among the enslaved, too, for its usefulness in keeping all that *shit* off you.

The beans' nutritional value could definitely help stave off bouts of physical illness and medical issues that enslaved people faced. They suffered wounds from whippings that oozed blood; there was endless pressure on enslaved women to bear children; and when they grew old, their bodies broken from years of hard labor, their slave masters preferred to sell them off rather than provide the medical care they needed. But these tiny beans are a powerhouse of vitamins, minerals, and metals that support blood clotting (vitamin K), pregnancy (folate), and bone strength (calcium).[9] They are filled with fiber, which helps regulate blood sugar and lower cholesterol, reducing the risk of diabetes and cardiovascular issues. And they provide a robust amount of protein, helping the people who eat them feel full.

It's no wonder that black-eyed peas became a staple of the diet of the enslaved. There was many a night that the enslaved would gather outside around a large pot of black-eyed peas cooked with a slab of salt pork. Like their West African ancestors, they would eat with their hands, scooping out mounds of beans with corn bread. And if there were any leftover peas, they might *mash 'em up right soft [and] make little cakes [that they] rolled in corn meal and fry 'em up for breakfast*, much like the *akara* of their West African forebears.[10]

Dining on the nourishing black-eyed peas, the enslaved might have swapped stories about their role in overturning enslavement, perhaps the most terrible form of misfortune you could experience in this life. They might have told tales of men who used black-eyed peas to make *gris-gris*, magical amulets, that would draw money to them so they could purchase the freedom of their loved ones.[11] They might have told stories of how women used Hoppin' John to "poison" their masters—either spiritually through mojos or physically through herbs.[12]

Or they might have bantered over how the dish Hoppin' John got its name.[13] Some people say the dish came from an old, enslaved man named John. He had such a bad limp it looked like he was hopping as he walked. Old John's slave master gave him a little patch to raise his own crops. So Old John raised black-eyed peas. Day after day, he'd dote on those peas until, months later, they were finally ready. His patience and careful tending gave him so many peas he was able to sell some off to his slave master. Then Old John cooked up the rest and took his delectable dish of black-eyed peas into the streets of town to sell them.

When he returned to the plantation, after selling his peas and rice, Old John tucked away the bit of money he earned. Year after year, Old John continued to sell his pot of black-eyed peas in hopes that one day the bit of money he had saved up would be enough to buy his freedom. This kind of story would have resonated with the enslaved in New Orleans, where street vending created a (narrow) pathway to manumission.

At the turn of the nineteenth century, Haitian and Cuban immigrants arrived in New Orleans, bringing a fare with them that was quite similar to Hoppin' John. It was called *congri*, a dish made of red or black beans and rice.[14] New Orleanians quickly fell in love with the new red bean. And soon, Negro Mammies in Louisiana began to incorporate the new red beans into their culinary repertoire. They swapped the black-eyed peas traditionally served in *jambalaya au congri* for red beans. And over time, the red bean slowly began to absorb the association with luck that the black-eyed pea held.

Published in 1899, *Mrs. Owens' New Cook Book and Summary of Helpful Information* demonstrates that by the end of the nineteenth century, the red bean switch was well established. In the cookbook, Chicagoan Frances Emugene Owens gives us a recipe of *jambalaya au congri* that uses red beans rather than black-eyed peas.[15] By the time Owens wrote her book, *jambalaya au congri* was going by another name in New Orleans: *haricots rouges au riz* or "red beans and rice."[16] We can see from Owens's cookbook that the tradition of cooking beans while laundering was also well established. Owens suggests that housewives should *boil a large ham, if possible, and bake a big pot of beans* while they're doing the washing and ironing for their household.[17]

Cookbooks like Owens's were designed to inform housewives across the country about "proper" (read: Protestant and middle-class) domestic customs. Owens's instructions for cleaning suggests that, at the end of the nineteenth century, the weekly coupling of laundry with the luck-drawing power of beans was becoming a national trend—one that Black women in New Orleans were well ahead of. I often chuckle to myself, wondering what these prim white housewives would have done if they had realized that this custom was born from the very same Vodou that Haitians had taught them to fear.

Mrs. Owens's cookbook marks a tremendous change that occurred over the nineteenth century that was brought about, primarily, by Black market women. Consider New Orleans fare. It's easily available today, so it might be hard to imagine a time when it wasn't widely enjoyed. But during the eighteenth and early nineteenth centuries, many white people across the country considered dishes like gumbo to be "exotic" and strange because of their African base. While slaveholding families regularly dined on these foods, most white people in the United States did not live on plantations or have access to the Big House kitchen cooks, Negro Mammies.

But after the Civil War, Black Candy Ladies called *marchandes* began to expose the American public to a culinary tradition that was once *the hereditary lore of our negro mammies*.[18] In the French Quarter, these former Negro Mammies moved what whites termed the *occult science* of African American cuisine from secluded plantations to the public market, preparing the way for the fare that we still enjoy in New Orleans today: gumbo, red beans and rice, beignets, pralines, and exceptional coffee.[19] And when they brought these foods into the public square, these Candy Ladies also planted the conjure that informed these dishes into the soil of American culture.

For instance, in New Orleans Voodoo, Mondays are favored by the *loa* Papa Legba. He was syncretized with the *orisha* Eshu-Elegua, the god of crossroads and chaos and luck, along with St. Peter of

Catholicism.²⁰ So, like Eshu-Elegua, Papa Legba has the ability to shift bad luck to good fortune. This made Monday a good day to clean out bad luck and bring in good luck. Papa Legba was also known to enjoy rice and beans as an offering.²¹ The combination of the two, washing the laundry and cooking red beans, can be seen as a conjure practice in plain sight during the nineteenth century: both preparing the space for good luck to enter and offering thanks to Papa Legba for his hand in the blessings to come. And this is how many Black women spent their Mondays in South Louisiana, from the days of slavery to emancipation.

Early Candy Ladies or *marchandes* in New Orleans were largely responsible for spreading this ritual far beyond Black communities after slavery. Due to segregation, white communities continued to have very little access to what Black people did in their own homes. So most white people had no idea how Black people arranged their private lives. But *marchandes* carried red beans and rice, along with their association of Monday luck, beyond the color line and into the kitchens of the average (white and immigrant) New Orleanian. Sometimes, *marchandes* sold red beans and rice as cooked food. Other times, *marchandes* supplied the ingredients directly to people's houses.

The Kleinfeldts, a Jewish family in New Orleans, tell us that this is how they began to eat red beans and rice on Mondays.²² They hired a Black woman by the name of Pearl Jones to be the cook, nanny, and general housekeeper of their home. These domestic workers were almost always Black women. Jones taught Mrs. Kleinfeldt how to cook many of the vegetable staples of African and African American cuisine: *butter beans, squash, eggplant, black-eyed peas*. Jones also made adjustments for the Kleinfeldts' religious observances, such as *substitut[ing] corned beef or brisket for ham hocks*. Pearl took pains to prepare red beans and rice on Mondays, which might have seemed odd to Mrs. Kleinfeldt. However, Mrs. Kleinfeldt took this quirky habit of her cook in stride. *There was nothing in our religion that said you couldn't eat red beans and rice on Monday,* she confides, *and that's what we did.*

Jones likely got her ingredients from *marchandes*, as was the custom of the time. In the bustling French Quarter, housewives and domestic workers got their groceries from *regular peddlers or basket'totin' Negresses who [came] daily to the kitchen door.*[23] All day long, it was common to see Black women *carrying baskets upon their heads and calling at the doors of houses.*[24] These *marchandes* were preferred, in part, because they supplied households with what they needed to make meals on the cheap.[25]

In Louisiana, *lagniappe* was the tradition of giving customers a little something extra for free with their main purchase. And a common *lagniappe* when ordering vegetables for a dish was the seasoning herbs, like *a bit of parsley or a small bunch of shallots.*[26] From *marchandes*, you could buy *soup vegetables, a bit of cabbage, a leek, a sprig of parsley, a tiny carrot, a still tinier turnip, all tied in a slender package* for ten cents, about four dollars today.[27] For the same price, you could buy *a quartee [nickel's worth of] rice, a quartee beans, and a little lagniappe to make it nice.*[28] These bundles were a precursor to the rice mixes Zatarain's would begin to sell in the 1980s.

By selling the cooked dish or its ready-made bundle of ingredients with *lagniappe* on Mondays, *marchandes* made the dish of red beans and rice accessible to those outside their community as well as created the market demand for red beans and rice that stands to this day.

While *marchandes* were bringing red beans and rice into the public market, Marie Laveau was busy shoring up the dish's place in New Orleans Voodoo. Many of Laveau's ceremonies include invoking Papa Legba or St. Peter to *open the door*.[29] This was crucial because Papa Legba was the messenger of the gods. Only he could *open the door* of communication that would put Laveau in touch with the mermaid goddess or *loas* she worshipped. His role was so central to communication with other *loas* that it was customary to begin and end ceremonies with his invocation along with an offering.[30]

Marie Laveau made these kinds of offerings regularly. You could often spot Laveau *late at night on an unfrequented road outside the city, carrying a plate of food* like *congri*.[31] She would take this dish and place it under a tree to *pay off* or thank the spirits who gave her power. In Cecile Hunt's 1940 Federal Writers' Project interview, he remembers that Laveau also *made a sort of jambalaya out of cowpeas and sweet oil, no salt, and scattered it around the street.*[32] Another conjure woman in New Orleans who was interviewed in the 1940s by Harry Middleton Hyatt helps provide some context for this ritual.[33] She tells us that black-eyed peas can be used to *get in connection wit' de fo'k of de road* and the spirit who resides there.

If you're brave enough to stay at that spot after throwing those beans, you'll meet the devil, or Papa Legba.[34] *You'll see a man appear to yo' in black, in a black gown. Dat's dat man dat controls dat fo'k of de road an' den he appeahs tuh yo' if yo' wants a gift—anything yo' want yo' ask him at de time.* The power of the crossroads, the help of Papa Legba when you need it most, was precisely why *when yo' git in touch wit de fo'k of de road, yo' gettin' in touch wit a whole lot.* If you could reach Papa Legba, the whole world was yours.

To thank Papa Legba for *open[ing] the door*, Marie Laveau often prepared dishes of *congri* that used black-eyed peas and red beans interchangeably.[35] Laveau's flexibility in her usage of the beans in her Voodoo practices reinforced the spiritual context of red beans and rice, where it plays the role of the black-eyed pea to call upon Papa Legba to help us manage our luck. The Candy Ladies in Laveau's orbit moved these beliefs about the luck of red beans into the public square, until this conjure tradition seeped into the overall culture of New Orleans. And sure enough, in South Louisiana, we still have our red beans and rice on Mondays, without fail, as fastidiously as a religion.

CHAPTER TWENTY-EIGHT

Wild Lettuce, the Greens in My Gumbo Pot

BY THE MIDDLE OF THE TWENTIETH CENTURY, THE ORIGINAL Candy Ladies of New Orleans had all but disappeared from the city's streets.[1] Many whites had been trying to get rid of *marchandes* for over a century. During slavery, the enslaved could obtain a license to sell their wares through their slave masters, who *were required to purchase licenses for their slaves, but often added thousands of dollars per year to their incomes by doing so.*[2] But urban whites in New Orleans grew fearful that the enslaved who peddled goods in the city would cause "unrest" by rebelling against their oppression.[3] So white politicians introduced a law in 1817 that banned giving street vending licenses to the enslaved. Without a peddler's license, selling your goods in the street was illegal. But many enslaved people continued on without a license, risking fines for the chance to earn their freedom.

When praline women rose to prominence at the end of the nineteenth century, there was another push to get rid of them. White women who were looking to cash in on the lucrative candy business wanted to oust the Black women who had first introduced pralines to the market.[4] And white men who had their eye on commercializing candy for their grocery stores and drugstores saw Black businesswomen like Rose Nicaud as competition. So new laws that cracked down on food vending were introduced, making it nearly impossible for *marchandes* to continue selling their wares in open-air markets.[5] But another type of African American market woman soon stepped into their place. In the 1940s and 1950s, Black women began to dominate the kitchens of humble eateries and mom-and-pop shops.

During Jim Crow, Black people were severely restricted in where they could dine out. When they went to white-owned restaurants, the owners took every opportunity they could to humiliate them. Whites made Black people order through the back door. And if Black people decided to dine in the restaurant, white people rushed their orders and frequently hurled racial slurs at both the Black diners and the Black waitstaff who served them.[6] The chicken shacks and lean-to diners that African Americans set up along the side of the road, in bars and juke joints, and even in their houses, became both sanctuary and solace.[7]

A common menu item of these Black eateries was stewed greens, which has been a source of physical sustenance, lay medicine, and spiritual nourishment for African Americans for centuries. The enslaved often grew greens in their provision gardens, small patches of land given to them by their masters.[8] They used these bits of land to supplement the meager rations of cornmeal, molasses, and pork meat that their masters allocated. Sometimes, the enslaved even had a surplus in their provision gardens, which they sold to their masters or in town markets.[9]

Potlikker, broth made from cooked-down greens, was used by Negro Mammies as a much-needed immune system booster, both when you were ill or to fortify you against the flu and colds.[10] We know now that most of the nutrients from the leaves is distilled in the potlikker left behind, so it really is the best part.[11] Formerly enslaved Gus Feaster remembers *ole lady Abbie*, a Negro Mammy who raised him, using poke leaves to support and regulate digestion.[12] And it was common to use large leaves, like cabbage and collard greens, to treat fevers by wrapping them about the head or wounds as well.[13]

It was greens that sustained us through the devastating poverty of the Great Depression and Jim Crow. In the South, Granny Midwives like Onnie Lee Logan and Margaret Charles Smith recall how they were fed leafy greens from their families' own gardens. Smith remembers her diet during the Depression: *[Y]ou got that cornbread with those peas and greens, every day, every day. Lord, turnips every day.*[14] Logan recalls that, during the Depression, her family had *three big gardens* where they raised *string beans, butter beans, turnip greens, English peas, sweet potatoes, Irish potatoes, okra*, in a word, *ever'thing*.[15]

Logan's family were not sharecroppers, so they were in a better position than many of their neighbors. Logan tells us that her mother, also a Granny Midwife, took it upon herself to share with those who didn't have enough food. *Mother didn't give [her neighbors] time to come. She would take 'em vegetables, she would take 'em [corn] meal, flour, piece of meat, whatever.*[16] Midwives like Smith and Logan continued cooking greens in their communities, especially for the birthing women they attended during and after their pregnancies.[17]

Granny Midwives were also active in the kitchens of their churches, which connected them to other market women in their communities. Midwives were among the many women who fried chicken and prepared greens during worship services so that church congregants could share a meal together when the preacher finally turned them loose.[18] These women could no longer openly peddle their goods in the streets like their foremothers in the nineteenth century, but they could sell their goods on the sly from their churches, beauty and barber shops, and even their own kitchens.

Underground market women were vital to moving money and resources into our communities where we needed it. They could be relied upon to produce mouthwatering cakes and candies for bake sales to raise funds for schools or political campaigns or to fix up the local church. They were who you called to cook pigs' feet and collard greens, Hoppin' John and gumbo, fried fish or stewed chicken for rent parties, where heaping plates of food were sold for a few dollars to help you make up the rent money you lacked that month.[19] They were the ones who sweat out their perms in the small kitchens of Black eateries when they had scraped up enough money from their side hustles to set up their own establishment. These restaurants, where dining booths were as spirit filled as church pews, sold soul food long before the term appeared in the 1960s.[20]

LEAH CHASE (1923–2019) WAS ONE of the most famous underground market women turned soul food restauranteurs. Her remarkable life served as the inspiration of Tiana in Disney's *The Princess and the Frog*. During Jim Crow and the Civil Rights movement, Chase ran the kitchen at Dooky Chase, a soul food restaurant in New Orleans. During her long career as a chef, Chase became known as the "Queen of Creole Cuisine." To Chase, Creole heritage meant taking part in culinary and textile arts, two crafts that had been shaped by previous generations of conjure women, from Negro Mammies to Granny Midwives.

These conjure women were models of strength, ingenuity, and power for Chase.[21] She admired Negro Mammies, the women called

Aunt So-and-So, Aunt Jane, whatever. Chase understood that *all the whites would call [Negro Mammies] Aunt Jane*, in efforts to deride and belittle them, but she also knew that Negro Mammies weren't powerless. *Honey, Aunt Jane could do anything she wanted.* She looked up to the market women of the generation before her, like the *Creole ladies [who] used to sell Calas.*[22] And she adored her grandmother, who was *a midwife and a registered nurse in New Orleans,* along with her mother, who was *a genius with a needle and thread* as a seamstress.[23]

The conjure traditions of these women—the herbs and mojos of Negro Mammies, the textiles of Granny Midwives, the spiritual alchemy of Candy Ladies turning pralines into the sweetest of freedoms—all got distilled into Chase's approach to food. Many of the beliefs of these women were passed down from generation to generation, informing Chase's relationship to key ingredients found in her kitchen. Chase calls these beliefs *superstitions*, and she provides plenty of examples of them across her cookbooks and in her biography.[24]

In *The Dooky Chase Cookbook,* Chase reminisces about animal fat, how it was both a crucial part of the flavor base of her dishes as well as a common cure for colds. For whooping cough, her mother *rubbed [them] with goose grease or elderberry syrup.*[25] Similarly, it's likely that Chase became a *tea fanatic* because of the Creole tradition of *tisanes,* medicinal teas of herbs and roots used to treat fevers, common colds, and digestive issues.[26] Sassafras, a mainstay of cooking that Creoles adopted from the Choctaw people in their area, was also used to treat burns.[27]

While these ingredients shone in the African American culinary landscape for their multiple uses, the highlight of Creole cooking was gumbo. A dish passed down among the women in her family, Chase observes that *[e]very Creole woman took pride in her gumbo making.* On Sundays, they looked forward to a bowl of gumbo after attending Mass. When they came home after church, they had *a hot cup of coffee and a hot Cala.*[28] After that bit of refreshment, *every female who was old enough helped prepare the Sunday dinner.*[29]

Chase watched older women pull crabs from the icebox, examining them closely before they were dropped into boiling pots. She did not yet have the responsibility of tending the pots. Instead, Chase tells us, her *job was cutting onions and the other seasonings*, like bell pepper and celery. Beside her, women prepared the meat, *cleaning and chopping up chicken necks and gizzards,* slicing sausages and hams. Over the skillet's steady sizzle and the rhythmic rise and fall of knives, Chase likely overheard stories about the medicinal value of sassafras, how to make *tisanes* for whatever ails you, how black-eyed peas could bring you good luck in the New Year, and how to dispose of your hair so that others can't use it to curse you.

As she watched her mother make the roux, Chase learned what it meant to be intimate with your cooking vessel. Walking away from your pot as you tended to other things in the kitchen was the easiest way to burn a roux. You had to coax a roux from your pot with the kind of steadfast attention you would give a lover. So Chase's mother always *took extreme care to get [the roux] just right.* With all these years of making gumbo at the elbow of her female elders, it's no wonder that this was Chase's most famous and acclaimed dish.

Her gumbo was but another variant of the leafy greens that we have been eating for centuries. This assertion might make you scratch your head but consider the function of leafy greens in the one-pot dishes of our West African ancestors. The leafy greens were crucial to the texture and taste of the meal. The greens gave the dish a bitter taste that was much loved in West Africa. They thickened the soups and stews. And they gave the dish a velvet mouthfeel due to their mucilaginous texture.[30]

In the New World, we adapted to new ingredients, but we continued to cook leafy greens in a manner similar to our ancestors. In the Caribbean, we made *callaloo*, a soup or stewed greens dish that substituted the bitter leaf (*V. amygdalina*) used in West Africa for its cousin, spinach.[31] In the United States, those of us in the Black Belt region did not always have access to the fish our West African ancestors typically seasoned their greens with, so we stewed collards, mustard, and turnip greens with smoked pork instead.[32] (Then we swapped our ancestors' *fufu* for corn bread, as yams were not as readily available either.[33]) And in New Orleans's gumbo, the central ingredient of okra provided a bitter taste, thickened our soups, and gave us the same velvet mouthfeel as greens. This is why African American food scholars Judith A. Carney and Richard Nicholas Rosomoff consider gumbo, "in which okra substitutes for greens as the principal vegetable," to be a variant of the Caribbean *callaloo*, cousin to our southern greens.[34]

New Orleanian green gumbo or *gumbo z'herbes* was a sacred dish that bridges *callaloo* and more traditional gumbo. This dish combines leafy greens with okra. And when okra wasn't available, powdered sassafras—which has a similar taste, texture, and thickening property—was substituted.[35] Chase explains that green gumbo was prepared just like traditional gumbo: *gumbo z'herbes, we just do the greens, grind 'em up, put all the meat in 'em, and turn 'em to a gumbo.*[36] During Chase's lifetime, you could only get green gumbo once a year. On Holy Thursday, the day before Good Friday, green gumbo was served to strengthen devotees for their fast that follows from Good Friday until Easter.[37]

Green gumbo was also influenced by New Orleans Voodoo. *Gumbo z'herbes* must be prepared by an uneven number of green varieties. Chase explains, *I guess it is part of a superstition we have at home.... You can't have two, four, or six. You've got to have five, seven, nine, eleven, because it is bad luck if you don't have the numbers.*[38] To shore up their luck, most people would use nine varieties of greens.[39] Nine was a holy number in conjure. In many conjure rituals, a thing had to be done nine times or there had to be nine objects included—nine knots tied on a sacred healing string or nine needles stuck into mojos or nine days devoted to fasting or prayer or ingesting specially prepared tea blends.

Even the more traditional gumbos had a supernatural aura in the minds of many Americans. It's likely that Chase did not bat an eye when, in 1942, a group of Tuskegee Airmen refused to eat her gumbo. They were scared that her gumbo was a Voodoo charm. She heard one man tell the others at the table, "Don't eat the gumbo! If you eat the gumbo, you'll never leave New Orleans."[40] The men thought the Voodoo power lived in the sassafras, which was frequently a part of mojos in New Orleans.[41] I doubt that Chase was trying to conjure them that day. But they weren't wrong to observe that her gumbo pot held spiritual power.

IN MANY WEST AFRICAN RELIGIOUS traditions, the cooking pot was a vessel they used to communicate with spirits. Among the Dogon, pots were seen as the containers of spirits.[42] The pot may be a spirit's home, such as the shrine of an ancestor. Or the cooking pot may simply be a site where a spirit could be summoned to perform a certain request, much like a charm. In Bantu and Congolese mythology, the great god Ne Kongo first mixed his sacred medicines or *minkisi* in a cooking vessel.[43] His magical clay pot stood on three stones as legs while a fire blazed underneath, much like the stereotypical witches' cauldron.[44] And among the Yoruba, Eshu-Elegua, the god of crossroads and chaos and luck, was represented by and invoked with an upside-down cooking pot with a hole in it.[45]

These range of beliefs shed light on a peculiar practice of the enslaved.[46] During their secret worship sessions where they shouted and prayed for freedom, the enslaved often turned over a large iron pot used for cooking or washing and placed it in front of the door or in the middle of the room. When praying and worshipping alone, some of the enslaved would turn a pot upside down and crawl under it.[47] This was one way that enslaved children witnessed the psychological toll that slavery wrought upon their elders, the inner turmoil produced when freedom is so desired yet callously denied. Formerly enslaved Rachel Fairley remembered her mother would take *a large pot which she used to cook with* and *put her head under the pot and pray for freedom*.[48] It was common to see *de women stick dere heads in de wash pot and talk out loud, prayin' for de Lawd to take dem out of bondage*.[49]

If the children asked the adults what this ritual was about, the adults would say that these pots *held de sound in* or *kept the noise from going out* or *took up all the sound* or *caught the voice*.[50] The enslaved were careful to prop the pot up on sticks to make sure the sound was directed into the pot. The idea was to *leave a little hole under [the pot] so de sound o[f] their talkin' would go [u]nder de pot*.[51] They knew that *[i]f they'd put [the pot] flat on the ground, the ground would carry the sound*.[52]

It's common lore that the enslaved did this to prevent their masters from hearing their worship. But it's doubtful that the pots reduced their sound enough to thwart detection (in fact, the hollow pot probably amplified the sound).[53] And in many cases, slave masters already knew that the enslaved were doing this.[54] However, in light of these West African beliefs about the spirit of the cooking pot, this ritual might not have been about the master at all. Perhaps the enslaved wanted the pot to *hold de sound in* because they were trying to communicate with the spirit in the pot who could carry their petitions to God—much like you would want the person ferrying an important message for you to capture every word you're saying.[55]

The shout of the enslaved during secret worship sessions was taken as evidence that their message had been received by the spirit of the pot, the Holy Spirit (or Eshu, according to their West African ancestors).[56] This is because they considered the shout to be the possession of their bodies by the spirit of the pot—what we call "catching the Holy Spirit" or "falling out in the Holy Ghost" today. The shout of the enslaved was confirmation that the god(s) had descended upon them in answer to their prayers. This would explain why the formerly enslaved believed that the pot ritual *showed dat Gawd wuz wid dem.*[57]

I suspect that, over time, as we became more Christianized, the idea of communication with the spirit in the pot was lost.[58] In the absence of this spirit, the theory that the enslaved used the pots to ensure secrecy has become a mainstay in the story we tell about the lives of our ancestors. But the idea that cooking pots have spiritual power was *not* lost through the centuries.

During Marie Laveau's time, the cooking pot was a weapon that women could wield to enact revenge and justice upon their partners. To give her women clients this power, Laveau often performed a ritual that used food. In her 1930s Federal Writers' Project interview, Marie Dédé remarks that lovesick women would *take [their blood] to Marie Laveau for some kind of blessing.*[59] After the blood was blessed, *women would put [their] blood in [their lover's] food.* In this ritual, the cooking pot itself becomes a mojo or container for the spirit sent to bend the will of the woman's romantic partner.

The cooking pot was also one way that Creoles during the nineteenth and early twentieth centuries managed their luck. New pots needed to be prepared for use in a manner that would enhance their luck-drawing capabilities. This involved a spiritual ritual similar to redbrick dust floor washes. *First the pot was washed thoroughly, then red brick-dust was rubbed in.*[60] Wash the pot again. Then apply a layer of animal fat like pork and *place the pot on the fire to "season" it.* The seasoning, or the thick layer of grease baked into the pot, makes the surface nonstick and shiny and prevents rusting. Once that pot was seasoned, it was *ready for the cooking of the red beans and the black-eyed peas* that would usher luck into the house. This process was done for generations, the seasoned pot *often handed down from mother to daughter.*

By the time we get to Leah Chase and her pots in the 1960s, the original sources of these conjure beliefs had fallen away and faded into peculiar habits or *superstitions* within our own community. But the spiritual potency of the cooking pot lingered; it was baked into our cooking pots like the patina of a well-seasoned cast-iron skillet.

Cooking was sacred to Chase. Just like praying was intertwined with midwifery for women like her grandmother, Chase prayed without ceasing, and that praying was intertwined with cooking. *When I tell you about prayer I don't mean you have to get on your knees every day,* Chase explains. *You can offer up your work. That can be a prayer. You can say, "Well, I'll work this dish extra hard," and that can be like a prayer.* So it was known among those who worked with her that Chase was *always praying—when she's cooking, she's praying.*

I would venture to add that much like her ancestors did for centuries, she was praying to the spirit of the pot. The way she talks about pots suggests that she saw them as their own living entities. She tells us that to cook well, *you have to love that pot* and that *over the years, my pots, too, have become my friends.*[61,62] And in the midst of

Jim Crow, Chase's pots offered her refuge. *The pots don't care if I'm laughing or crying. They just sit there waiting for me to fill them.*[63] For this reason, Chase was *at home with [her] pots.*[64]

I think every cook has a favorite pot or pan to make certain dishes, Chase remarks. One of the ways that Black women have shown love to our pots was the dedication we put into caring for them. Chase talks about how she *[went] after [her] pots with a cleanser like religion*. After cooking a dish she scrubbed with all her might to make the pot *stay shiny, shiny, shiny both inside and out*. After decades of caring for a pot in this way, it becomes a part of you. Many a divorce has been started because a man was careless with his wife's cast-iron Dutch oven. And I know several Black women who won't let their men go anywhere near their sacred pots for that reason.

In her cookbooks, Chase regales us with stories of her family and how they think about their pots. She tells us about her sister who fell in love with the pot their aunt Lucy passed down to her.[65] Her sister was intimate with the spirit of that skillet, which is why her fried rice always turned out well when she used it. Her sister claimed that *rice just doesn't taste the same when [it's] cooked in anything else.*[66] Her sister *knows that skillet* in the same way that Chase *know[s] every inch of that gumbo pot*.[67] Chase's kindred connection with this pot gives her knowledge of how to coax the best gumbo out of it: *every ingredient that goes in there and just how much of it*.

When Chase was cooking, she was indeed praying. And when Chase stirred her gumbo pot in prayer, she was tapping into the legacy of her ancestors, which anchored her steadfast faith that we could, in the face of Jim Crow, continue to influence the course of America.

And so, Chase relied upon the spirit of her cooking pot in her restaurant to nurture the soul of Black communities as she plated dishes of red beans and rice and gumbo and greens for almost seventy years. When Chase talked about her restaurant's role in the Civil Rights movement, she often would say: *we changed the world over a bowl of gumbo.*[68] In the 1950s and 1960s, the fate of America was negotiated over steaming plates of soul food passed to civil rights leaders sitting in the booths of small Black eateries across the nation.[69] At Sylvia's of Harlem, Pascal's of Atlanta, Dooky Chases's of New Orleans, organizers of the Civil Rights movement strategized and received nourishment before and after hitting the streets in harrowing protests.[70]

In gumbo, in this New Orleanian take on greens, Chase not only saw a tool of survival, she also saw an America that had not yet come into existence. Having grown up in Jim Crow America, she and countless others were frequently humiliated and belittled through segregation in public spaces. But she understood that this was not the way our country *had* to be. Gumbo is a hallmark of the African American innovation that has always pushed American culture forward. With a distinctive West African base, gumbo is a dish that incorporates elements from the people who have historically played a crucial role in shaping our country: okra from the enslaved, sassafras from the Indigenous, a roux from the Europeans (the French). The gumbo that African Americans have created combines our West African heritage and traditions with an openness, willingness, and required ability to adapt to the new ingredients from other cultures we encountered. She tells us that *you can have gumbos of people, too, mixtures of people coming together, and that's the gumbo we need to make in this country.*[71]

Her analysis of the political climate of her time rings eerily relevant today: *You know we stay here and we don't talk*, Chase admonishes. *We don't talk to one another. So we don't mix that gumbo, it doesn't gel because we're not talking.*[72] Gelling did not mean assimilation, for Chase fiercely valued her Creole heritage. Gelling also did not mean agreeing with everyone. Chase was not afraid to disagree with people in her restaurant—even when they shared the same political goal, such as the liberation of Black people. Gelling meant that both sides see the value in the other person and recognize that they have something to bring to the table.

Chase saw that in action when civil rights activists from different races and social classes met in her restaurant and tried to address social injustice. They most certainly disagreed about policies and strategic tactics, even though they were all on the same team. Today, it's become a regular occurrence for political disagreements, no matter how slight, to destroy coalitions and dissolve allyships, to upend our friendships and familial relations (even, or perhaps especially, with other Black people). If that had been the attitude of these activists, we might have never seen the Civil Rights movement come into fruition.

Perhaps this is why Chase thought that this national experiment of democracy works only if we communicate with one another. Chase insists that *we have to talk about it to make it work. To make it work in our country, we have to come together.*[73] With her adherence to a gumbo-style politics, it is no surprise that Chase would open her restaurant doors to just these kinds of interracial conversations and meetings during Jim Crow.

Throughout the 1950s and 1960s, Chase defied the laws in Louisiana that forbade Blacks and whites to dine together in public spaces. In the upper room of her restaurant, hidden in the back, Black and white organizers strategized over how to bring down Jim Crow. For many of the organizers, Chase's restaurant was always the first place they went after a protest because she treated them with the dignity that had been stripped away from them when they faced down police batons and yapping dogs during their marches. And what they were doing in the upper room was no secret—even law enforcement knew.

Freedom riders like Rudy Lombard were amazed that the police never interfered with Chase's restaurant. As one of the hundreds of civil rights activists who embarked on perilous treks riding integrated buses from Washington, DC, down to New Orleans, he was well acquainted with the fury the police showed when segregation laws were violated. But when Lombard ate at Dooky Chase, *it was as though God threw a protective ring around the restaurant.* In the upper room, Blacks and whites dined together and *nobody ever bothered us there.*[74]

Our enslaved ancestors might say that this protection was provided by the spirit of Chase's gumbo pot, who had heard her cries for freedom. At her stove, she communed with the spirit that lives in her gumbo pot that allowed her to transform raw ingredients into a dish that could spiritually fortify weary protesters of the Civil Rights movement. So when Chase says that she *changed the course of America over a bowl of gumbo*, the valences of conjure ring out, calling in the community in need of strength and spiritual fortification. She stands in the long line of conjure women who have stood at their pots and altered the course of America for centuries.

CHAPTER TWENTY-NINE

Black Women Put Their Foot in This

IN AFRICAN AMERICAN FOOD TRADITIONS, CONJURE HAS SHOWN UP in many places: the praline lady's market, the pots of soul food restauranteurs, the Candy Lady's kitchen. Conjure women managed to turn all these spaces and tools of domestic labor into sites of freedom. But the most remarkable thing to me is that, sometimes, these conjure women transformed their very bodies—often denigrated by American culture as too Black, too strong, too sexy—into conduits of spiritual power. The Granny Midwife brought you into this world with the hands that caught babies. The hairdresser regulated your luck as she worked your strands into elaborate coiffures. The Candy Lady took hold of your soul with the feet she put in her food.

In the South, when someone tells you that you *put your foot* in your cooking, it is the highest compliment. It means you put your heart and soul into your cooking.[1] It means that what you cooked was beyond excellent. No one quite knows where the idiom came from, but our conjure practices offer salient clues.

Many African Americans once believed that the soul resided in our hands and feet.[2] In many West African religions, the hands and feet hold spiritual significance. Among the Yoruba, the big toes of our feet were revered. It was believed that a spiritual force resided there, called *ipori* (or *iponri*).[3] The *ipori* helps us to fulfill our destiny or soul's purpose by detecting evil or misfortune that lies ahead of us and steering us around it.[4] And the power of the *ipori* comes from our ancestors, whose lives steer the direction of our own journeys, just as the big toe leads every step we take.[5] (It's not a surprise I am writing about conjure, given that I am the namesake of my great-grandmother who was a Candy Lady.) Our ancestors' influence upon our lives was recognized in worship ceremonies, where libations were given to the big toe as representatives of our ancestral lines.[6]

African Americans maintained the reverence their Yoruba ancestors displayed for the big toe. During Jim Crow, conjure practitioners believed that *poison*—cursing or manipulating someone's luck for your own purposes—*went up* through the big toe.[7] It was the big toe that alerted victims they had been poisoned, through pain or tingling or swelling. Victims of *poisoning* would bathe in a downward manner to move the poison *right on out de toe*.[8] The thought was: [poison] come in [through the toe] and want it to go out from de toe.[9]

In our conjure traditions, the beliefs about the spiritual power of the big toe extended to the whole foot—the dirt from your foot tracks, socks or stockings that cover your foot, toenails, dead skin on the bottom of your foot. All of these things were used as proxies to conjure up a spiritual force like that of the big toe to command the luck, fortune, or destinies of your lovers.[10] Material taken from the foot could be incorporated into mojos that were nailed onto thresholds, buried under steps, or worn on the body.[11] And one special type of ritual involved putting toenails or the skin of your foot into your lover's food.

They say that if you *wanta rule* your lover or make them *jes as wild about you as somebody else is about dere baby*, here's what you do. Wash your foot real good, then clip your toenails or scrape the bottom of your foot. Grind the scrapings down to a fine powder. Then put the powder in a pot on the stove and roast it till its black like coffee grinds. Remove the black settlings from the pan and *put 'em in a pot of tea* or *mix it with yore sugar an' serve in [their] coffee* or *drop it intuh dere Coca-cola*. If you're cooking dinner, *mix [your foot grounds] with black peppah* and *put it ovah [their] grits or ovah [their] rice and put nice gravy over it*. Baby, just *crumble that in [their] food* and watch your foot *do the work*.[12]

In the conjure ritual, your foot is where part of your soul resides, so when you put your toenails or dead foot skin into someone's food, you are imparting your essence to them. Hence, to metaphorically *put your foot* in your cooking is to put your soul's stamp onto the food. These conjure rituals may be why we use this language in the South to describe someone who has cooked with their whole heart and soul.

I know this doesn't sound very appealing, your lover's toenails in your food. People would often say that a woman *put her foot in her food* in jest, as a way to draw attention to the something extra or special oomph that a woman puts into a dish, making it utterly delicious and uniquely hers. The kind of thing that could never be captured in a recipe. Which is why, even when you follow all of your mama's or grandmama's instructions for how to make your favorite food (if she is gracious enough to give them to you in the first place), it still won't turn out *exactly* like hers. To say a Black woman *put her foot in her food* is to appreciate our skills that have been honed by centuries of conjure that have taught us how to pray without ceasing, how to tap into the divine in whatever we do with our minds, our hearts, our voice, our hands, and, yes, our feet. In this context, every part of us is holy and deserving of reverence.

I know that many of us often do not feel that way. It can be hard to assert your worth when so much of the world belittles who you are. I know how dejecting it is to express the many ways that sexism and racism is killing your spirit and feel like no one is even bothering to listen to you—not your teachers, not your doctors, not your pastor, and maybe not even your lover. I know the incandescent rage that comes when you are passed over, yet again, for a job or career promotion that you are more than qualified for, simply because of your name, your skin, your hair, your heritage, or where you hail from. These feelings of dejection are not new to African American women, who have faced disappointment after disappointment in this country for centuries. But I do feel that Black women in America are having a particularly difficult moment right now. It seems like Vice President Kamala Harris's loss in the 2024 presidential election greatly amplified these collective feelings of anger and anguish.

I was with students at Spelman College the day after the election, when it seemed that America had, yet again, turned its back on Black women. So many of the students I met that day were crushed. They saw themselves in Kamala Harris, so seeing the nation reject her candidacy for presidency felt like a personal rejection of who they were—smart, competent, passionate leaders. And even those who were not outright or enthusiastic supporters still knew the importance of electing her over former president Donald Trump, a convicted felon, for the sake of maintaining our nation's democracy.

As I talked with these students about their frustration and despair and pain, I felt like an elder for the first time in my life. So I knew that it was my responsibility to pass on to them what I've passed on to you in this book. That no matter how small and unworthy and unloved this wayward country makes you feel, you need only meditate on the magic of Black women to know that there is no America without us. Our medicine has healed our countrymen for centuries. Our midwives brought thousands of Americans into the world, both Black and white. Our textiles gave this country the iconic pants that are beloved around the world. The music of America still moves to the rhythm of our blues. And if you ever feel paralyzed by all the forces in this world that are aimed against you, against a pantheon of Black girls, remember our stories of mermaids and mojos, because that's your ancestors reaching across four hundred years, sharing how you get free.

CONCLUSION

Where Did All the Conjure Women Go?

THE INCREDIBLE FLEXIBILITY OF CONJURE—ITS ABILITY TO ADAPT TO competing religious beliefs or integrate new scientific knowledge or simply hide in plain sight—has allowed it to survive for four hundred years. Zora Neale Hurston understood that as society changed, African Americans would find more resources to address the problems they usually turned to conjure for—physical ailments and heartbreak, protection and revenge. But our folk heroes and magical roots, like High John de Conquer, were not gone. Hurston observed that, in her lifetime, High John de Conquer simply *retire[d] with his secret smile into the soil of the South.* Black women's magic has slipped into the sediment of American life, and it is as ever present as the ground you walk upon—once you know how to see it.

Sometimes I see it in the discussions that unfold in my classrooms. Like the fall semester of 2022, when my Black women students wanted to know what I thought about Honey Pot, a line of plant-derived vaginal care products developed by entrepreneur Bea Dixon. My students in the Deep South had heard that Honey Pot was "demonic" and wondered: Doesn't that mean, as Christians, that they should toss this product out? This standpoint was mostly spread on social media through posts like that of Black microinfluencer Asia Salley on X: "[Black people] love witchcraft and demons lol its over for the honeypot. I knew there was a reason i didn't like this stuff."

Salley's accusation of "witchcraft and demons" seems to come from Dixon's origin story for her products, often placed on their labels: "I was suffering with bacterial vaginosis for 8 months when an ancestor came to me in a dream and gifted me with a vision to heal myself." Upon waking from this dream, Dixon took to the kitchen, mixing what she learned from her background in pharmacy with the ancestral botanical knowledge in conjure to create, as her website claims, "the first complete feminine care system powered by herbs." Considering her struggles with vaginal health, it is no wonder that Dixon named her products Honey Pot, a symbol of Oshun and a tool Yoruba practitioners use to summon her *ashe*.[1] Oshun reminds us that our genitals are holy and beautiful and deserving of pleasure—things that are hard to remember when we are in the throes of vaginal infections in a society that deems the by-products of our vaginas (healthy or not) to be icky and shameful and indecent for public discussion.

Salley's response to Dixon's story shows us how much Black attitudes toward conjure have changed. Posts like these have gotten thousands of likes and views. One TikTok video by Benita Ovwurie, "The Dark Truth About Honey Pot: Demonic Witchcraft and Spirituality," even gained over half a million views.

It's striking that over a century ago, Madame C. J. Walker claimed that she had received the formula for her hair-care products by way of an ancestral (African) vision-dream. And this story drove flocks of Black women *toward* Walker's products. The idea that Walker got her recipe from an African ancestor made Black women want the product even more. Walker's story suggested that her products were designed specifically for Black women—these products spoke to who they were and aligned with the spiritual traditions they had inherited from their mothers, which is ultimately why they trusted what Walker was selling. But ever since Honey Pot gained national attention in 2020 due to a swell of racist responses to a Target ad, several Black women have taken to their social media feeds to denounce the product as "witchcraft" for that very same ancestral connection.

A unifying source of these young Black women's dissent was their faith. Like nearly half of Americans today, these women were deeply influenced by Christian fundamentalism and Christian nationalism. Fundamentalists, a subset of evangelicals, tend to emphasize the importance of a conversion experience (the moment you "take Jesus as your Lord and Savior"); cultural separation from the nonbelieving world (you are to be "in the world, not of it"); and adherence to strict, literal interpretations of the Bible.[2] They take these spiritual beliefs to be the "fundamentals" of Christianity, but these principles have always had a political tenor as well. In the 1920s, fundamentalists railed against the liberalism of their Christian counterparts who embraced scientific theories like evolution and social change like women's suffrage.[3] And in the 1960s and 1970s, fundamentalists staunchly opposed desegregation and the Civil Rights movement.[4]

When Christian nationalism finds a foothold in Black communities, our conjure tradition often suffers. This is when we begin to hear, from the pulpit, that our conjure is "of the devil," a power that competes with, rather than complements, our faith in God. Dixon joins a host of Black women who have urged Black Christians of today not to fall for the ruses of this brand of evangelicalism, which forces us to abandon the practices and spiritual traditions of our ancestors, from our herb and root medicines to our mermaid goddesses to the prayers found in our tapestries and cooking pots. To those who denounce her products as demonic, Dixon responds that we need to "give love and respect and kindness and reverence and abundant appreciation to everything that fucking came before us. Because if it hadn't come, how would you be here? There'd be no you."[5] These leaders seem to be unable to grasp that when Black women like Dixon turn to conjure, they are upholding the principle of *sankofa* that their ancestors lived by: *go back and fetch it*.

Much of the conjure that Black women in the millennial and zoomer generations have gone back and fetched shows up in the health and wellness industry today. This industry was profoundly shaped by the New Age movement of the latter twentieth century, a mixture of a wide array of spiritual traditions and philosophies. New Age borrowed from theosophy (belief in the divine interconnectedness of the universe), New Thought (belief in the power of positive thinking), alternative medicine (like herbalism), East Asian religions, European mysticism, and African American church traditions like Spiritualism and the Sanctified Church.[6]

By the twenty-first century, aspects of our conjure—such as the herbalism of Granny Midwives and the veneration of the dead present in Spiritualism—had thoroughly blended with the astrology and tarot cards, Zen Buddhism and yoga, mindfulness and meditation that have become hallmarks of New Age spirituality.[7,8] So it's no surprise that scores of Black women in the millennial and zoomer generations now subscribe to the spiritual eclecticism of the New Age movement.[9] They have supplemented conventional Black churches with their healing crystals and a budding interest in ancient West

African traditions like Orisa.[10] Weary of evangelical sermons that pronounced their sexuality (straight and otherwise) as sinful and turned a blind eye to social injustice, these young Black women have begun to turn to a range of New Age practices to grasp some of the spiritual support that conjure once afforded their foremothers.

IN BLACK WOMEN'S SPIRITUALITY, CONJURE lives on as the superstitions many African Americans still abide by today. Advice like "men shouldn't eat a woman's red sauce dishes" or we should "eat black-eyed peas on New Year's for good luck" or we should season food "until our ancestors say 'that's enough, child.'" We still revere ancient divination practices, like when elder Black women predict pregnancies in younger women by dreams of fish. Even though many African Americans may not know the origins of these superstitions, these beliefs still speak to a relationship to the divine that we have inherited from our West African ancestors, who believed that the spirit world will always give us signs if we would only pay attention to it. And in Black communities, Black women's attunement to the signs, inherited from their conjure foremothers, is often captured by the phrase: "Black women be knowin'."

There are still conjure women among us, the mothers and aunties, friends and neighbors we know and love and rely on day to day. The mother who reached for Vicks VapoRub and ginger ale to manage our minor ailments when we were children. That friend who took up crochet and other textile arts during COVID. The neighbor who insists that her greens are the best because her collards are grown in her own backyard. These women in our communities have often shown up for us when we needed them most, just like Negro Mammies did during slavery and Granny Midwives did during Jim Crow.

Some modern-day conjure women are famous artists. Beyoncé Knowles channeled Oshun in her visual albums *Lemonade* and *Black Is King*, stoking nationwide interest in the Yoruba goddess. Music artist SZA summons Yoruba goddesses like Yemaya in her work, while poet and singer Tarriona "Tank" Ball (from Tank and the Bangas) hosted *Ritual*, a PBS documentary series on New Orleans conjure. Textile artists like Bisa Butler and Sonya Clark use their art to help us venerate our dead and revive the textile traditions of Granny Midwives, while visual artists like Alexandria Smith blend Voodoo, Yoruba worship, and social commentary in their art.[11]

Some carry conjure into their work in the health and wellness industry. Life coach and lawyer Iyanla Vazant is an ordained Yoruba priestess and a devotee of New Thought. Nurse-midwife Jeanine Valerie Logan claims that hoodoo inspired her to open the first Black-owned birthing center in Illinois.[12] And CEO and wellness expert Bea Dixon places conjure in the origin story of her Honey Pot products.

Some are gardeners and herbalists. Farmers and social justice advocates like Leah Penniman work to help Black people "restore their connection with the land of their ancestors."[13] CEO Maxine Manager corrals leading Black women doctors and herbalists to develop her line of Black Girl Vitamins. I'm tickled to see all the ads for the elderberry-based line of Black Girl Vitamins during cold and flu season—the same herb that Negro Mammies would dole out in teas around that time of year, hundreds of years ago.

And some of our modern-day conjure women are storytellers. Conjure has always been part of Black women's storytelling. During the 1970s and 1980s, Black women writers told stories of conjure women who defied the sexism and racism and classism they faced in America—poets like Nikki Giovanni and Lucille Clifton, novelists like Toni Cade Bambara and Toni Morrison, and essayists like Alice Walker and Audre Lorde. Contemporary Black feminist writers grasp the urgency of telling our conjure stories now, just as the previous generation of Black women storytellers did in the 1970s and 1980s.

Like generations of conjure women who rallied their communities to protest their oppression, activist-writers like Patrisse Cullors and Courtney Morris channel Yoruba *orishas* in their public events and art installations. Producers and screenwriters like Ava DuVernay gave us Nova, a Voodoo priestess, in the television show *Queen Sugar*, while Shonda Rhimes introduced mainstream American audiences to Marie Laveau in *American Horror Story*. Fantasy novelists like N. K. Jemisin (author of *The Hundred Thousand Kingdom* series) and Tomi Adeyemi (author of the *Legacy of Orisha* series) create spellbinding worlds based on Yoruba mythology. And Tracey Deonn (author of *The Legendborn Cycle* series) explores the southern roots of our conjure traditions.

I wrote this book, in part, for my students, who consume these stories today with no idea that the women depicted in them have had real, historical impact on our country. When I teach about conjure in my classes, my students always bring up *American Horror Story*, as the show's third season features Angela Bassett as Marie Laveau. My Black women students, time and again, look up in surprise and ask, with eyes that don't dare to hope, "Wait—was Marie Laveau a real person?" While I am saddened that they have been given so little of their history, hampering their abilities to navigate the complex and harsh world in which they live, their question gives me a chance to share their foremothers' legacy of power and resilience and joy. So I always smile and reply, "Yes, she was—and she is an essential part of the story of Black women in this country."

I wrote this book so that those who are feeling hopeless in the face of the overwhelming racism and sexism in this country will know how the Black women who came before them managed to craft a life that was not wholly swallowed up by their oppressors. So that the rebellion and faith that our foremothers' conjure fostered to make it through a world much different than ours (but that still has a long way to go) might inspire us and expand our imagination and offer us new ways to understand what it means to be free. I wrote this book so that you will see how Black women's conjure has touched your life and shaped your world. I wrote this book because it is *our* job to tend to the gardens of our foremothers—to till the four hundred years of Black women's magic that lie in the soil of this country and sow new dreams for the future of America.

Acknowledgments

A book like this takes a village, and I am so grateful for mine. I was so fortunate to have many hands help conceive, shape, and produce this book. Thanks to editor Katie Hall for all her advice when I was just beginning to bring this book to life. And thanks to my agent Victoria Sanders and her incredible team—Bernadette Baker-Baughman and Diane Dickensheid—for their faith in me and their steadfast encouragement. They were more than just business partners; they made me feel cared for in every way. Thanks also to their support staff Christine Kelder, for helping me keep all my paperwork in order. And a special shout-out to Benée Knauer—thank you for seeing my worth as a writer and what this book could be.

An abundance of thanks is due to my editor Amina Iro, for pushing my writing far beyond what I dreamed it could be. It was tough, and there were many tears, but I couldn't imagine this book without you! And thank you, Krishan Trotman, for bringing me into the Legacy Lit family. I'm so grateful for the mighty team at Legacy Lit—those I came into contact with directly and those I never met for their hand in producing this book.

I am also indebted to several academic institutions that made my research possible. Thanks to the University of Memphis for the variety of ways it has supported me through this project: the

ACKNOWLEDGMENTS

Ned R. McWherter Library, where I found most of the volumes of George P. Rawick's *The American Slave: A Composite Biography*; the Marcus W. Orr Center for the Humanities, whose program facilitated major developments of my research; the Department of Philosophy, where several colleagues supported my work from the very beginning; and, of course, my brilliant and beautiful and brave students—no one keeps me on my toes like y'all do!

Thanks also to the amazing librarians at the Eugene P. Watson Memorial Library at Northwestern State University, who went above and beyond to give me access to the unpublished Louisiana Federal Writers' Project interviews. Special thanks to the librarians at the Wilson Special Collections Library at the University of North Carolina at Chapel Hill and the researchers at Greensboro History Museum in Greensboro, North Carolina, for helping me to find invaluable resources on Lunsford Richardson and the history of Vicks VapoRub.

And I will never be able to thank Crystal R. Sanders, Juliet (Shepherd) Davis, and Velvaline (Shepherd) Sanders enough for their generosity of spirit and time in sharing their story. I will always be grateful that you responded to my Facebook post, Crystal!

Thanks to a bevy of scholars who continue to shape my work and make me grow as a thinker: Angela Davis, Regina N. Bradley, Janell Hobson, Deirdre Cooper Owens, Birgitta Johnson, Imani Perry, Yvonne Chireau, Denise Alvarado, Gladys Marie-Fry, Linda Janet Holmes, Nicholas Jones, and Katrina Hazzard-Donald. Special thanks to Kinitra Brooks and Kameelah L. Martin who put me on the long, long road to Oshun (and she completely took over this book!). And I could not have done this work without African scholars Jacob K. Olupona, Oyeronke Olajubu, Toyin Falola, and Margaret Olugbemisola Areo, who helped me go back and fetch the lost

ACKNOWLEDGMENTS

things. And where would I be without my intellectual muses: Zora Neale Hurston and Toni Morrison.

I also want to thank my family: my sister (Brittany Ardoin), mother (Alisia Stewart-Coleman), father (Emanuel Stewart), grandmother (Mary Ann Perkins), and grandfather (Lawrence Perkins) for all the wonderful stories they've shared throughout the years. And of course, my great-uncle Dan for all the incredible information he gave me about my great-grandmother Margaret "Booie" Lindsey Perkins.

I could not have done this without my support network of friends and extended family who have encouraged me through this marathon: Jameliah Shorter-Bourhanou, Kerri Malone, Mary Beth Mader, Maia Huff-Owen, Luvell Anderson, Verena Erlenbusch-Anderson, Leigh M. Johson, Myisha Cherry, Kris Sealey, Kathryn Sophia Belle, Jacque Rowe Fields, Ladrica Menson-Furr, Therí A. Pickens, Randal Maurice Jelks, Eric Michael Washington, and my husband's family, the Smiths.

And thank you most of all to Daniel Smith—you continue to be, in Toni Morrison's words, "a friend of my mind." Thank you for all the encouragement and comfort and advice you've given me freely throughout this whole process. Your support has meant the world to me these last three years. And this book is all the better for your presence in my life.

Bibliography

Author's Note

My primary source was the massive Federal Writers' Project Collection in two locations. First, many of the interviews I draw from can be found in *The American Slave: A Composite Autobiography*, a series of volumes edited by George P. Rawick. Second, much of the information about Marie Laveau can be found in the unpublished interviews by the Louisiana Federal Writers' Project, Folder 25, at the archives at Northwestern State University in Natchitoches, Louisiana. As noted earlier, I have italicized quotes that are historical primary sources and folklore and used quotation marks for contemporary writers and academics.

Abiodun, R. (2001). Hidden Power: Osun, the Seventh Odu. In J. M. Murphy & M.-M. Sanford (Eds.), *Òsun Across the Waters: A Yoruba Goddess in Africa and the Americas* (pp. 10–33). Bloomington: Indiana University Press.

Adeniyi, V. (2015). Portrayals of Indigenous Religion and Ifá Divination in Ola Rotimi's Gods Are Not to Blame. In D. O. Ogunbile (Ed.), *African Indigenous Religious Traditions in Local and Global Contexts: Perspectives on Nigeria*. Lagos, Nigeria: Malthouse Press.

Adepegba, C. O. (2001). Osun and Brass: An Insight into Yoruba Religious Symbology. In J. M. Murphy & M.-M. Sanford (Eds.),

BIBLIOGRAPHY

Òsun Across the Waters: A Yoruba Goddess in Africa and the Americas (pp. 102–112). Bloomington: Indiana University Press.

Adiji, B. E., Fagbenro, M. F., & Makinde, J. D. (2017, September). Sacred Textiles of the Yorubas in South Western Nigeria. *IOSR Journal of Humanities and Social Science, 22*(9), 47–51.

Akin-Adeboye, Mojalaoluwa. (2023, January 7). Hairdressing and Hairstyles in Yoruba Land: History, Nature, Dynamics, and Significance. Oriire. https://www.oriire.com/article/hairdressing-and-hairstyles-in-yorubaland-history-nature-dynamics-and-significance.

Albala, K. (2007). *Beans: A History*. New York: Bloomsbury.

Allen, C. (2002). *Listen, I Say Like This*. Gretna, LA: Pelican.

Alvarado, D. (2011). *The Voodoo Hoodoo Spellbook*. San Francisco: Weiser Books.

———. (2020). *The Magic of Marie Laveau: Embracing the Spiritual Legacy of the Voodoo Queen of New Orleans*. Newburyport, MA: Weiser Books.

———. (2022). *Witch Queens, Voodoo Spirits, and Hoodoo Saints: A Guide to Magical New Orleans*. Newburyport, MA: Weiser Books.

———. (2024). *The Marie Laveau Voodoo Grimoire: Rituals, Recipes, and Spells for Healing, Protection, Beauty, Love, and More*. Newburyport, MA: Weiser Books.

Andermann, R. R. (2018). *Brewed Awakening: Re-Imagining Education in Three Nineteenth-Century New Orleans Coffee Houses* (Vol. 4572). Baton Rouge: LSU Doctoral Dissertations.

Anderson, J. E. (2005). *Conjure in African American Society*. Baton Rouge: Louisiana State University Press.

Arablouei, R., & Abdelfatah, R. (2022, June 6). Abortion Was Once Common Practice in America. A Small Group of Doctors Changed That. National Public Radio. https://www.npr.org

/2023/01/19/1149924325/abortion-was-once-common-practice-in-america-a-small-group-of-doctors-changed-th#:~:text=In%20U.S.%20history%2C%20though%2C%2abortion,set%20out%20to%20change%20that.

Areo, M. O. (2015). The Visual Semantics of *Adire*. In A. Odebunmi & J. T. Mathangwane (Eds.), *Essays on Language, Communication, and Literature in Africa* (pp. 187–227). New York: Cambridge Scholars Publishing.

Arkansas Democrat. (1909, April 15). Newport Seeress Has Numerous Followers.

Arkansas State Parks Staff. (2016, March). The Hoo Doo Woman of Arkansas. Arkansas State Parks. https://www.arkansasstateparks.com/articles/hoo-doo-woman-arkansas.

Arnett, P., Cubbs, J., & Metcalf, E. W. (Eds.). (2006). *Gee's Bend: The Architecture of the Quilt*. Atlanta: Tinwood Books.

Asakitikpi, A. O. (2007). Functions of Hand Woven Textiles Among Yoruba Women in Southwestern Nigeria. *Nordic Journal of African Studies, 16*(1), 101–115.

Bach, A. (2004). Women's Lived Altars: Lived Religion from Now and Then. In E. S. Fiorenza (Ed.), *On the Cutting Edge: The Study of Women in the Biblical World* (pp. 21–35). New York: Bloomsbury Academic.

Badejo, D. L. (1996). *Òsun Sèègèsí: The Elegant Deity of Wealth, Power, and Femininity*. Trenton, NJ: Africa World Press.

———. (2001). Authority and Discourse in the Orin Odún Ósun. In J. M. Murphy & M.-M. Sanford (Eds.), *Òsun Across the Waters: A Yoruba Goddess in Africa and the Americas* (pp. 128–140). Bloomington: Indiana University Press.

Banks, I. (2000). *Hair Matters: Beauty, Power, and Black Women's Consciousness*. New York: New York University Press.

BIBLIOGRAPHY

Bascom, W. (1960). Yoruba Concepts of the Soul. In A. F. C. Wallace, (Ed.), *Men and Cultures: Selected Papers of the Fifth International Congress of Anthropological and Ethnological Studies*. Philadelphia: University of Pennsylvania Press.

———. (1992). *African Folktales in the New World*. Bloomington: Indiana University Press.

———. (1993). *Sixteen Cowries: Yoruba Divination from Africa to the New World*. Bloomington: Indiana University Press.

Beardsley, J., Arnett, W., Arnett, P., & Livingston, J. (2002). *The Quilts of Gee's Bend*. Atlanta: Tinwood Books.

Belluck, P. (2024, April 10). Arizona's 1864 Abortion Ban. *New York Times*. https://www.nytimes.com/2024/04/10/health/arizona-abortion-ban-history.html

Bennett, J. (1907, January 26). Mr. John Bennett Replies to Certain Criticisms of His Novel, "The Treasure of Peyre Gaillard"—That "Mermaid Riot." *New York Times*.

———. (1995). *The Doctor to the Dead: Grotesque Legends and Folk Tales of Old Charleston*. Columbia: University of South Carolina. First published 1943.

Berjonneau, G., & Sonnery, J.-L. (1987). *Rediscovered Masterpieces of African Art*. Art 135.

Berlin, I., Favreau, M., & Miller, S. F. (Eds.). (1996). *Remembering Slavery: African Americans Talk About Their Personal Experiences of Slavery and Emancipation*. New York: New Press.

Bicks, M., & Strachan, A. L. (Writers, Directors). (2022, February 7). Riveted: The History of Jeans (Season 24, Episode 1). *American Experience*. PBS (Producer).

Bird, S. R. (2021). *Sticks, Stones, Roots, and Bones: Hoodoo, Mojo, and Conjuring with Herbs*. Woodbury, MN: Llewellyn.

Blakemore, E. (2021, April 8). How an Enslaved African Man in Boston

Helped Save Generations from Smallpox. History. https://www.history.com/news/smallpox-vaccine-onesimus-slave-cotton-mather.

Bonaparte, A. D. (2024). Regulating Childbirth: Physicians and Granny Midwives in South Carolina. In A. D. Bonaparte & J. C. Oparah (Eds.), *Birthing Justice: Black Women, Pregnancy, and Childbirth*. New York: Routledge.

Bratcher, M. E. (2011). *Words and Songs of Bessie Smith, Billie Holiday, and Nina Simone: Sound Motion, Blues Spirit, and African Memory*. New York: Routledge.

Brown, E. R. (1980). *Rockfeller Medicine Men: Medicine and Capitalism in America*. Berkeley: University of California Press.

Brown, R. M. (2012). *African Atlantic Cultures and the South Carolina Lowcountry*. New York: Cambridge University Press.

Buel, J. W. (1883). *Mysteries and Miseries of America's Great Cities, Embraciing New York, Washington City, San Francison, Salt Lake City, and New Orleans*. San Francisco: A. L. Bancroft.

Bundles, A. (2001). *On Her Own Ground: The Life and Times of Madam C. J. Walker*. New York: Scribner.

Burlok, S., Burlock, M., & Burlock, S. (2024). *My Divine Natural Hair: Inspiration and Tips to Love and Care for Your Crown*. Minneapolis: Broadleaf Press.

Butler, S. (2020, December 22). Hoppin' John: A New Year's Tradition. History. https://www.history.com/news/hoppin-john-a-new-years-tradition.

Caldwell, E. C. (2017, October 26). The Assemblage Sculptures of Betye Saar. JSTOR Daily. https://daily.jstor.org/assemblage-artist-betye-saar/.

Callahan, N. (1987). *The Freedom Quilting Bee: Folk Art and the Civil Rights Movement*. Tuscaloosa: University of Alabama Press.

BIBLIOGRAPHY

Carney, J. A., & Rosomoff, R. N. (2009). *In the Shadow of Slavery: Africa's Botanical Legacy in the Atlantic World.* Berkeley: University of California Press.

Carter, C. J. (Ed.). (2009). *Freedom in My Heart: Voices from the National Slavery Museum.* Washington, DC: National Geographic.

Catalini, M., Smyth, J. C., & Shipkowski, B. (2024, September 11). Trump Falsely Accuses Immigrants in Ohio of Abducting and Eating Pets. AP News. https://apnews.com/article/haitian-immigrants-vance-trump-ohio-6e4a47c52b23ae2c802d216369512ca5.

Caudle, N. (2023, January 10). Mermaids of Charleston—Legends, Lore, and Riot. Medium. https://medium.com/@nicole.bcaudle/mermaids-of-charleston-legends-lore-and-riot-d6b9c4484946.

Cavallo, C. (2016, March 31). The Ancient Craft of Gullah Basket Weaving. Saveur. https://www.saveur.com/gullah-basket-weaving-charleston/.

Charles, D. (2015). *A Real Southern Cook in Her Savannah Kitchen.* Boston: Houghton Mifflin Harcourt.

Chase, L. (1990). *The Dooky Chase Cookbook.* New Orleans: Pelican.

———. (2003). *And Still I Cook.* New Orleans: Pelican.

———. (2007). Leah Chase on Callaloo/Gumbo Z'herbes: An Interview. *Callaloo, 30*(1), 182–185.

———. (2008). I Would Have Fed Him Gumbo Z'herbes. *Southern Quarterly, 46*(2), 152–158.

Cheers, K. (2020, July 14). Sweet Lady: An Ode to the Candy Lady. We Are Memphis. https://wearememphis.com/play/culture/sweet-lady-an-ode-to-the-candy-lady/.

Chireau, Y. P. (2006). *Black Magic: Religion and the African American Conjuring Tradition.* Berkeley: University of California Press.

BIBLIOGRAPHY

Clark, S. (2015). *The Hair Craft Project.* Sonya Clark [Website]. https://sonyaclark.com/project/the-hair-craft-project/.

Coleman, T. (2024, April 3). Doulas Are Filling in the Gaps in Maternal Care for Black Women. The Week. https://theweek.com/health/doulas-Black-mothers.

Collins, L. G. (2023). *Stitching Love and Loss: A Gee's Bend Quilt.* Seattle: University of Washington Press.

Commisso, D. (2020, January 22). When It Comes to Buying Jeans, Fast Fashion Leads. CivicScience. https://civicscience.com/when-it-comes-to-buying-jeans-fast-fashion-leads/.

———. (2023, February 6). Jeans Are Getting Faded Out by GenZ Shoppers and Remote Workers. CivicScience. https://civicscience.com/jeans-are-getting-faded-out-by-gen-z-shoppers-and-remote-workers/.

Correal, T. M. (2003). *Finding Soul on the Path of Orisa: A West African Spiritual Tradition.* Berkeley, CA: Crossing Press.

Cosette. (2023, May 12). Five Roads of Oshun, the Orisha of Love. Divine Hours. https://cosettepaneque.com/five-roads-of-oshun-the-orisha-of-love/.

Crowther, S. (1843). *Vocabulary of the Yoruba Language.* Oxford, UK: Oxford University Press.

Crumpton, T. (2024, January 2). Why Do We Eat Black-Eyed Peas on New Year's Day? Hoodoo. *Essence.* https://www.essence.com/culture/why-do-we-eat-black-eyed-peas-new-years-hoodoo/.

Dabiri, E. (2020). *Don't Touch My Hair.* New York: Penguin.

Dandridge, G. R. (2010). The Energy of People Passing Through Me. In F. S. Holsaert, M. P. Noonan, J. Richardson, B. G. Robinson, J. S. Young & D. M. Zellner (Eds.), *Hands on the Freedom Plow:*

Personal Accounts by Women in SNCC (pp. 273–298). Champaign: University of Illinois Press.

Davis, A. Y. (1983). *Women, Race and Class*. New York: Vintage Books.

———. (1999). *Blues Legacies and Black Feminism: Gertrude "Ma" Rainey, Bessie Smith, and Billie Holiday*. New York: Vintage Books.

Davis, P. A., Brown, S. A., & Lee, U. (Eds.). (1941). *The Negro Caravan: Writings of American Negroes*. New York: Citadel Press.

Deren, M. (2004). *Divine Horsemen: The Living Gods of Haiti*. Kingston: McPherson.

DeVoe, A. (2022, February 18). Black History Trailblazer: The Mobile-area Midwife Who Delivered Hundreds of Babies for More Than 50 Years. WKRG News5. https://www.wkrg.com/hidden-history/black-history-month/black-history-trailblazer-the-mobile-area-midwife-who-delivered-hundreds-of-babies-for-more-than-50-years/.

Dewitt, G. (1928). *The Picayune Creole Cook Book*. New Orleans: Times-Picayune.

Di Cola, J. M., & Stone, D. (2012). *Chicago's 1893 World's Fair*. Charleston, SC: Arcadia.

Domonoske, C. (2018, April 17). "Father of Gynecology," Who Experimented on Slaves No Longer on Pedestal in NYC. The Two-Way, National Public Radio. https://www.npr.org/sections/thetwo-way/2018/04/17/603163394/-father-of-gynecology-who-experimented-on-slaves-no-longer-on-pedestal-in-nyc.

Dorsey, L. (2020). *Orishas, Goddesses, and Voodoo Queens: The Divine Feminine in the African Religious Traditions*. Newburyport, MA: Weiser Books.

Douglass, F. (2010). *Narrative of the Life of Frederick Douglass* (A. Y. Davis, Ed.). San Francisco: Open Media Series.

Doumbia, A., & Doumbia, N. (2004). *The Way of the Elders: West African Spirituality and Tradition*. Saint Paul, MN: Llewellyn.

Drewal, H. J. (1990). *Yoruba: Nine Centuries of African Art and Thought*. New York: Harry N. Abrams.

———. (2001). Crowning Glories: Hair, Head, Style, and Substance in Yoruba Culture. In J. Harris & Pamela Johnson (Eds.), *Tenderheaded: A Comb-Bending Collection of Hair Stories* (pp. 227–236). New York: Pocket Books.

Drewal, H. J., & Drewal, M. T. (1990). *Gelede: Art and Female Power Among the Yoruba*. Bloomington: Indiana University Press.

Dunigan, J. S. (2024, October 30). How Hoodoo Inspired a Midwife to Open Illinois' First Black-Owned Birthing Center. Reckon News. https://www.reckon.news/black-joy/2024/10/how-hoodoo-inspired-a-midwife-to-open-illinois-first-black-owned-birthing-center.html.

Elliot, B. (2023). *White Coat Ways: A History of Medical Traditions and Their Battle with Progress*. West Chester, OH: Med Media.

Elliot, P. (2023, December 15). That Texas Abortion Case Is Even Worse Than You Think. *Time*. https://time.com/6510970/abortion-texas-case/.

Essex, M. (2024, March 28). Black Women's Complex Relationship with Religion and Spirituality. *Essence*. https://www.essence.com/lifestyle/spirituality-and-religion/.

Evans, F. W. (2011). *Congo Square: African Roots in New Orleans*. Lafayette: University of Louisiana at Lafayette.

Falola, T. (2022). *Decolonizing African Knowledge: Autoethnobiography and African Epistemologies*. New York: Cambridge University Press.

Fandrich, I. J. (2005). *The Mysterious Voodoo Queen, Marie Laveaux: A*

Study of Powerful Female Leadership in Nineteenth Century New Orleans. New York: Routledge.

Farlin, A. (1993). Maternal Goddess in Yoruba Art: A New Aesthetic Reclamation of Yemoja, Oshun, and Iya-Mapo. *Passages*, 6, pp. 7–8.

Fatunmbi, A. F. (1993). *Oshun: Ifá and the Spirit of the River*. Old Bethpage, NY: Original Publications.

Federal Writers' Project of the Works Progress Administration. (2009). *New Orleans City Guide 1938*. New Orleans: Garrett County Press.

Ferris, M. C. (2005). *Matzoh Ball Gumbo: Culinary Tales of the Jewish South*. Chapel Hill: University of North Carolina Press.

Fett, S. M. (2002). *Working Cures: Healing, Health, and Power on Southern Slave Plantations*. Chapel Hill: University of North Carolina Press.

Fieldhouse, P. (2017). *Food, Feasts, and Faith: An Encyclopedia of Food and Culture in World Religions* (Vol. 2). New York: Bloomsbury.

Fieldman, H. (2007). *Black Rhythms of Peru: Reviving African Musical Heritage in the Black Pacific*. Middletown, CT: Wesleyan University Press.

Finnigan, K. (2022, October 19). A Unique Fashion Collab Spotlights Artisan Quilters in the American South. *British Vogue*. https://www.vogue.co.uk/fashion/article/marfa-stance-gees-bend.

Fontenot, W. (1994). *Secret Doctors: Ethnomedicine of African Americans*. Westport, CT: Praeger.

Ford, T. C. (2015). *Liberated Threads: Black Women, Style, and the Politics of Global Soul*. Chapell Hill: University of North Carolina Press.

Foster, H. B. (1997). *"New Raiments of Self": African American Clothing in the Antebellum South*. New York: Berg.

BIBLIOGRAPHY

Fraser, G. J. (1988). *African American Midwifery in the South: Dialogues on Birth, Race, and Memory.* Cambridge, MA: Harvard University Press.

French, D. (2024, April 21). Evangelical America Is More Divided Than You Think. *New York Times.* https://www.nytimes.com/2024/04/21/opinion/christianity-fundamentalist-evangelical-pentecostal.html.

Fry, G.-M. (2002). *Stitched from the Soul: Slave Quilts from the Antebellum South.* Chapel Hill: University of North Carolina Press.

Fry, G.-M., Leone, M. P., & Ruppel, T. (2001). Spirit Management Among Americans of African Descent. In C. E. Oser (Ed.), *Race and the Archeology of Identity* (pp. 143–157). Salt Lake City: University of Utah Press.

Gates, H. L. (2013, March 4). *Did Black People Own Slaves?* The Root. https://www.theroot.com/did-black-people-own-slaves-1790895436.

George-Graves, N. (2019). Taking the Cake: Black Dance, Competition, and Value. In S. Dodds (Ed.), *The Oxford Handbook of Dance and Competition* (pp. 17–40). New York: Oxford University Press.

Glass, B. S. (2007). *African American Dance: An Illustrated History.* Jefferson, IA: McFarland.

Gore, L. L. (2007). *Memories of the Old Plantation Home.* Vacherie, LA: Zoe Company.

Gotthardt, A. (2017, October 26). How Betye Saar Transformed Aunt Jemima into a Symbol of Black Power. Artsy. https://www.artsy.net/article/artsy-editorial-betye-saar-transformed-aunt-jemima-symbol-black-power.

Graham, L. (2022, November/December). The Blue That Enchanted the World. *Smithsonian Magazine.* https://www

.smithsonianmag.com/arts-culture/indigo-making-come back-south-carolina-180980987/#:~:text=For%2050%20 years%2C%20starting%20in,even%20as%20barter%20 for%20slaves.

Griaule, M. (1975). *Conversations with Ogotemmêli: An Introduction to Dogon Religious Ideas*. London: International African Institute.

Haberman, C. (2015, March 8). Martin Luther King's Call for Voting Rights Inspired Isolated Hamlet. *New York Times*. https://www.nytimes.com/2015/03/09/us/gees-bend-alabama -martin-luther-king-voting-rights-1965.html.

Hall, G. M. (1992). *Africans in Colonial Louisiana: The Development of Afro-Creole Culture in the Eighteenth Century*. Baton Rouge: Louisiana State University Press.

Handy, W. C. (1991). *Father of the Blues: An Autobiography*. Boston: Da Capo Press.

Hansen, V. (2022, August 10). Denmark Vessey Is Honored. National Public Radio. https://www.npr.org/2022/07/19/1112040871 /denmark-vesey-is-honored-his-slave-revolt-was-thwarted -and-he-was-executed.

Harriot, M. (2021, February 18). 28 Days of Black Joy: Candy Ladies. The Root. https://www.theroot.com/28-days-of-black-joy -candy-ladies-1846232505.

Harris, J. B. (2003). *Beyond Gumbo: Creole Fusion Food from the Atlantic Rim*. New York: Simon and Schuster.

———. (2011). *High on the Hog: A Culinary Journey from Africa to America*. New York: Bloomsbury.

Hawgood, A. (2017, January 1). The Matriarch Behind Beyoncé and Solange. *New York Times*. https://www.nytimes.com/2017 /01/21/fashion/tina-knowles-lawson-beyonce-solange-matri arch.html.

Hazzard-Donald, K. (2011). Rethinking the Ring Shout: Dance of the Lost Hoodoo Religion. *Journal of Pan African Studies*, 4(6), 194–213.

———. (2013). *Mojo Workin': The Old African American Hoodoo System*. Urbana: University of Illinois Press.

Hazzard-Gordon, K. (1990). *Jookin': The Rise of Social Dance Formations in African-American Culture*. Philadelphia: Temple University Press.

Henry, L. A. (Host). (2020, September 24). Bea Dixon Talks Honey Pot, Being Accused of WitchCraft After Ancestral Dream, Her Upbringing, +More. Interview with Bea Dixon. *Leah's Lemonade* [YouTube channel]. https://leahahenry.com/2020/09/24/bea-dixon-talks-honey-pot-being-accused-of-witchcraft-after-ancestral-dream-her-upbringing-more/.

Herman, A. (2024, September 27). Vance to Speak at Tour Hosted by 'Prophet' Who Thinks Harris Practices Witchcraft. *Guardian*. https://www.theguardian.com/us-news/2024/sep/27/vance-lance-wallnau-event.

Higgins, W. C. (1885). *Historical Sketch Book and Guide to New Orleans*. New York: Will H. Coleman.

Hinds, K. (2020, July 23). Bisa Butler: Weaving the Stories of African Americans, Their History, Ancestry, and Culture. WMHT. https://www.wmht.org/blogs/arts-active/bisa-butler-weaving-the-stories-of-african-americans-their-history-ancestry-and-culture/.

History.com Editors. (2019, October 10). Cowboys. History. https://www.history.com/topics/nineteenth-century/cowboys.

———. (2022, August 8). California Gold Rush. History. https://www.history.com/topics/nineteenth-century/gold-rush-of-1849.

Holmes, L. J. (2023). *Safe in a Midwife's Hands: Birthing Traditions from Africa to the American South.* Columbus, OH: Mad Creek Books.

hooks, b. (1989). Straightening Our Hair. In b. hooks, *Talking Black: Thinking Feminist, Thinking Black.* New York: South End Press.

———. (1997). *Bone Black: Memories of Girlhood.* New York: Macmillan.

Hurston, Z. N. (1931). Hoodoo in America. *Journal of American Folklore, 44*(174), 317–417.

———. (1995). Characteristics of Negro Expression. In Z. N. Hurston, *Zora Neale Hurston: Folklore, Memoirs, and Other Writings* (pp. 830–845). C. A. Wall (Ed.). New York: Literacy Classics of the United States.

———. (1995). High John de Conquer. In Z. N. Hurston, *Zora Neale Hurston: Folklore, Memoirs, and Other Writings* (pp. 922–931). C. A. Wall (Ed.). New York: Literary Classics of the United States.

———. (1995). The Sanctified Church. In Z. N. Hurston, *Zora Neale Hurston: Folklore, Memoirs, and Other Writings* (pp. 901–905). C. A. Wall (Ed.). New York: Literary Classics of the United States.

———. (1995). Shouting. In Z. N. Hurston, *Zora Neale Hurston: Folklore, Memoirs, and Other Writings* (pp. 851–854). C. A. Wall (Ed.). New York: Literary Classics of the United States.

———. (2003). Letter to Langston Hughes, August 6, 1928. In Z. N. Hurston, *Zora Neale Hurston: A Life in Letters* (p. 124). C. Kaplan (Ed.). New York: Anchor Books.

———. (2006). *Dust Tracks on a Road.* New York: Harper Perennial Modern Classics.

———. (2006). *Their Eyes Were Watching God.* New York: Harper Perennial Modern Classics.

———. (2008). *Mules and Men.* New York: Harper Perennial Modern Classics.

———. (2022). How It Feels to Be Colored Me. In Z. N. Hurston, *You Don't Know Us Negroes: And Other Essays* (pp. 186–190). H. L. Jr. & G. West (Eds.). New York: HarperCollins.

Hyatt, H. M. (1970). *Hoodoo Conjuration Witchcraft Rootwork* (Vols. 1–5). Hannibal, MO: Western.

Jacobs, H. (2001). *Incidents in the Life of a Slave Girl*. N. Y. McKay & F. S. Foster (Eds.) New York: W. W. Norton.

Jarmon, L. C. (2003). *Wishbone: Reference and Interpretation in Black Folk Narrative*. Knoxville: University of Tennessee Press.

Joseph, M. B. (1978, January). West African Indigo Cloth. *African Arts, 2*(2), pp. 34–37.

Kail, T. (2016, December 28). The Mystery of the Memphis Nation Sack. Medium. https://memphishoodoo.medium.com/the-mystery-of-the-memphis-nation-sack-b3bfaf72aa8c.

———. (2017). *A Secret History of Memphis Hoodoo: Rootworkers, Conjurers & Spirituals*. Charleston, SC: History Press.

———. (2019). *Stories of Rootworkers and Hoodoo in the Mid-South*. Charleston, SC: History Press.

Katz-Hyman, M. B., & Rice, K. S. (Eds.). (2010). Textiles. In *World of a Slave: Encyclopedia of the Material Life of Slaves in the United States* (Vol. 2: K–Z, pp. 498–500). Westport, CT: Greenwood.

Kaufman, A. (2017). *The Little Blue Jar: A Family Remedy*. North Charleston, SC: CreateSpace.

Kendall, J. S. (1922). *History of New Orleans*. Chicago: Lewis.

Klibanoff, E. (2022, August 17). Texas Law Banning Abortion Dates Back to 1857. *Texas Tribune*. https://www.texastribune.org/2022/08/17/texas-abortion-law-history/

Kluchun, R. M. (2011). *Fit to Be Tied: Sterilization and Reproductive Rights in America, 1950–1980*. New Brunswick, NJ: Rutgers University Press.

Knowles, M. (2002). *Tap Roots: The Early History of Tap Dancing*. Jefferson, LA: McFarland.

———. (2012). *The Tap Dance Dictionary*. Jefferson, LA: McFarland.

Kumari, A. (2020). *Isese Spirituality Workbook: The Ancestral Wisdom of Ifa Orisa Tradition*. Self-Published.

Lane, P. J. (2008). The Social Production and Symbolism of Cloth and Clothing Among the Dogon of Mali. *Anthropos, 103*(1), 77–98.

Latrobe, B. H. (1905). *The Journal of Latrobe*. New York: D. Appleton.

Lee, M., & Lee, Ted. (2000, November 29). The Gumbo Variations: To Each His Own. *New York Times*. https://www.nytimes.com/2000/11/29/dining/the-gumbo-variations-to-each-his-own.html.

Lee, V. (1996). *Granny Midwives and Black Women Writers: Double-Dutched Readings*. New York: Routledge.

Leslie, F. (1888, January–June). Old New Orleans. *Frank Leslie's Sunday Magazine, 23*, pp. 450–455.

Lightfoot, N. (2019). *Good JuJu: Mojo, Rites, and Practices for the Magical Soul*. Woodbury, MN: Llewellyn.

Loewen, J. W. (1988). *The Mississippi Chinese: Between Black and White*. Long Grove, IL: Waveland Press.

Logan, O. L., & Clark, K. (2014). *Motherwit: An Alabama Midwife's Story*. San Francisco: Untreed Reads.

Long, C. M. (2001). *Spiritual Merchants: Religion, Magic, and Commerce*. Knoxville: University of Tennessee.

———. (2006). *A New Orleans Voudou Priestess: The Legend and Reality of Marie Laveau*. Gainesville: University Press of Florida.

Lord, D. (2013). *The Gentle Revolutionaries*. Bloomington, IN: WestBow Press.

Love, V. E. (2014). *Divining the Self: A Study in Yoruba Myth and Human Consciousness*. University Park: Penn State University Press.

BIBLIOGRAPHY

Luckerson, V. (2015, February 10). New Report Documents 4,000 Lynchings in Jim Crow South. *Time.* https://time.com/3703386/jim-crow-lynchings/.

Luibheid, E. (2002). *Entry Denied: Controlling Sexuality at the Border.* Minneapolis: University of Minnesota Press.

Luke, J. M. (2018). *Delivered by Midwives: African American Midwifery in the Twentieth-Century South.* Jackson: University Press of Mississippi.

MaCCNO. (2023, November). New Orleans Has a Long History of Street Vending—and Crackdowns. How Do We Stop This Cycle? *Antigravity.* https://antigravitymagazine.com/column/new-orleans-has-a-long-history-of-street-vending-and-crackdowns-how-do-we-stop-this-cycle/.

Mangam, C. R. (1971). The Magic of the Black-Eyed Pea. *New York Folklore Quarterly,* 27, 236–239.

Manring, M. M. (1998). *Slave in a Box: The Strange Career of Aunt Jemima.* Charlottesville: University of Virginia Press.

Marnach, M. (2024, June 5). Can Too Much Stress Cause Early Miscarriage? Mayo Clinic. https://www.mayoclinic.org/healthy-lifestyle/pregnancy-week-by-week/expert-answers/early-miscarriage/faq-20058214.

Martin, K. L. (2012). *Conjuring Moments in African American Literature: Women, Spirit Work, and Other Such Hoodoo.* New York: Palgrave Macmillan.

——. (2016). *Envisioning Black Feminist Voodoo Aesthetics: African Spirituality in American Cinema.* Lanham, MD: Lexington Books.

Martinez, R. J. (2018). *Mysterious Marie Laveau, Voodoo Queen: And Folk Tales Along the Mississippi.* Burke, VA: Borodino Books.

Matory, J. L. (2009). The Many Who Dance in Me: Afro-Atlantic Ontology and the Problem with Transnationalism. In T. J. Csordas

(Ed.), *Transnational Transcendence: Essays on Regional Globalization* (pp. 231–262). Berkeley: University of California Press.

Mbilishaka, A. M. (2021). PsychoHairapy Through Beauticians and Barbershops: The Healing Relational Triad of Black Hair Care Professionals, Mothers, and Daughters. In M. L. Lewis & D. J. Weatherston (Eds.), *Therapeutic Cultural Routines to Build Family Relationships: Talk, Touch, and Listen While Combing Hair* (pp. 173–182). New York: Springer.

McCormick. (2003, June 4). McCormick Completes Acquisition of Zatarain's. McCormick & Company. https://mccormickcorporation.gcs-web.com/news-releases/news-release-details/mccormick-completes-acquisition-zatarains.

McGaffey, W. (2000). *Kongo Political Culture: The Conceptual Challenge of the Particular*. Bloomington: Indiana University Press.

McGregor, D. K. (1998). *From Midwives to Medicine: The Birth of American Gynecology*. New Brunswick, NJ: Rutgers University Press.

McKenzie, P. (1997). *Hail Orisha!: A Phenomenology of a West African Spirituality and the Mid-Nineteenth Century*. Boston: Brill.

McKinley, C. E. (2012). *Indigo: In Search of the Color That Seduced the World*. New York: Bloomsbury.

McMillen, K. (2016). From Aunt Jemima to Aunt Marthy: Commodifying the Kitchen Cook and Undermining White Authority in "Incidents in the Life of a Slave Girl." In C. M. Sublette & J. Martin (Eds.), *Devouring Cultures: Perspectives on Food, Power, and Identity from the Zombie Apocalypse to Downton Abbey* (pp. 85–102). Fayetteville: University of Arkansas Press.

McPhail, T. (2014, June 21). New Orleans Invented America's First Fusion Cuisine. Vice. https://www.vice/com/en/article/new-orleans-invented-amercas-first-fusion-cuisine/.

BIBLIOGRAPHY

Miller, A. (2013). *Soul Food: The Surprising Story of An American Cuisine, One Plate at a Time.* Chapel Hill: University of North Carolina Press.

Monaghan, P. (2014). *Encyclopedia of Goddesses and Heroines.* Novato, CA: New World Library.

Morgan, J. (2017). *When Chickenheads Come Home to Roost: A Hip-Hop Feminist Breaks It Down.* New York: Simon and Schuster.

Morgan, J. L. (1967). She Put Newport on the Map. *Jackson County Historical Society: The Stream of History, 5*, 17–18, 28–32.

Morial, M. H. (2019, June 18). Leah Chase: 'We Changed the World over a Bowl of Gumbo. *New Pittsburg Courier.* https://newpittsburghcourier.com/2019/06/18/leah-chase-we-changed-the-course-of-the-world-over-a-bowl-of-gumbo/.

Morrison, T. (2008). A Knowing So Deep. In C. C. Denard (Ed.), *What Moves at the Margin: Selected Nonfiction* (pp. 31–33). Jackson: University Press of Mississippi.

———. (2008). Rootedness: The Ancestor as Foundation. In T. Morrison & C. C. Denard (Ed.), *What Moves at the Margin* (pp. 56–64). Jackson: University Press of Mississippi.

Moss, K. K. (1999). *Southern Folk Medicine: 1750–1820.* Columbia: University of South Carolina Press.

Mostafavi, B. (2020, August 8). Understanding Racial Disparities for Women with Uterine Fibroids. Michigan Medicine. https://www.michiganmedicine.org/health-lab/understanding-racial-disparities-women-uterine-fibroids.

Murphy, E. (2024, February 14). The Cymbee in South Carolina. *East Tennessean.* https://easttennessean.com/2024/02/14/the-cymbee-in-south-carolina/#:~:text=Imagine%20my%20surprise%20while%20looking,and%20survived%20the%20Middle%20Passage.

Musgrove, M. (2015). *The Spider Weaver: A Legend of Kente Cloth*. Baltimore, MD: Apprentice House.

Myrick, H. (1897). *Sugar: A New and Profitable Industry in the United States for Capital, Agriculture, and Labor*. New York: Orange Judd.

Myvett, K. (2020, November 23.). The Praline Ladies. *Country Roads*. https://countryroadsmagazine.com/cuisine/Louisiana-foodways/the-praline-ladies/.

Nassau, R. (1907). *Fetichism in West Africa: 40 Years' Observation of Native Customs and Superstitions*. New York: Charles Scribner's Sons.

Nittle, N. (2024, September 17). Trump's Claims About Haitians Draws from Centuries-Long Narrative. These Women Explain Why. Alabama Reflector. https://alabamareflector.com/2024/09/17/trumps-claims-about-haitians-draw-from-a-centuries-long-narrative-these-women-explain-why/.

Nunez, C. (2011). *Just like Ole' Mammy Used to Make: Reinterpreting New Orleans African-American Praline Vendors as Entrepreneurs* (Vol. 128). New Orleans: University of New Orleans Theses and Dissertations. https://scholarworks.uno.edu/td/128.

Olajubu, O. (2003). *Women in the Yoruba Religious Sphere*. Albany: State University of New York Press.

Oliver, P. (1997). *Conversation with the Blues*. New York: Cambridge University Press.

Olupona, J. K. (2001). Òrìsà Òsun: Yoruba Sacred Kingship and Civil Religion in Òsogbo, Nigeria. In J. M. Murphy & M.-M. Sanford (Eds.), *Òsun Across the Waters: A Yoruba Goddess in Africa and the Americas* (pp. 46–65). Bloomington: Indiana University Press.

———. (2004). Owner of the Day and Regulator of the Universe: Ifa Divination and Healing Among the Yoruba of Southwestern

Nigeria. In M. Winkelman & P. M. Peek (Eds.), *Divination and Healing: Potent Vision* (pp. 103–119). Tuscon: University of Arizona Press.

Onek, W. (2023). Race, Gender, and Hoodoo in the Arkansas Delta: The Case of Caroline Dye. *Arkansas Review: A Journal of Delta Studies, 54*(3), 173–180.

Opara, G. (2023, December 21). How Black Women Are Navigating Feminism Through African Spirituality. *Broadview*. https://broadview.org/black-women-feminism-african-spirituality/.

Oparah, J. C. (2024). Introduction: Beyond Coercion and Malign Neglect; Black Women and the Struggle for Birth Justice. In A. D. Bonaparte & J. C. Oparah (Eds.), *Birthing Justice: Black Women, Pregnancy, and Childbirth*. New York: Routledge.

Opie, F. D. (2008). *Hog and Hominy: Soul Food from Africa to America*. New York: Columbia University Press.

O'Sullivan, S. (2023, January 11). Wellness Culture Won't Save Us. It's Only Making Us More Sick. Refinery 29. https://www.refinery29.com/en-gb/wellness-industry-issues-perfectionism?callback=in&code=NJY2ZGE1ZMETMMNHNS0ZOGM2LTG2MJITMZVIMDFJOGE1NJAZ&state=e0731b6d35a0465d941024dbcf6f0e6f.

Owens, D. C. (2017). *Medical Bondage: Race, Gender, and the Origins of American Gynecology*. Athens: University of Georgia Press.

Owens, F. E. (1899). *Mrs. Owens' New Cook Book and Summary of Helpful Information*. Chicago: Owens' Publishing Company.

Padilioni, J. (2017, May 22). The History and Significance of the Kente Cloth in the Black Diaspora. Black Perspectives. https://www.aaihs.org/the-history-and-significance-of-kente-cloth-in-the-black-diaspora/.

Peek, P. M., & Yankah, K. (Eds.). (2004). *African Folklore: An Encyclopedia*. New York: Routledge.

Penniman, L. (2018). *Farming While Black: Soul Fire Farm's Practical Guide to Liberation on the Land*. White River Junction, VT: Chelsea Green Publishing.

Peress, M. (2004). *Dvorak to Duke Ellington: A Conductor Explores America's Music and Its African American Roots*. New York: Oxford University Press.

Perkins, Daniel, Jr., & Lawayne, C. (2023). *Perkins Rowe: A Piece of the Way*. Baton Rouge, LA: Catrell Lawayne.

Pine Bluff Daily. (1909, March 31). Voodoo Woman Has Large Following.

Prescott, V. (2019, February 9). How the Community of Gee's Bend Influenced the Famous Michelle Obama Portrait. Georgia Public Broadcasting. https://www.gpb.org/news/2019/02/08/how-the-community-of-gees-bend-influenced-the-famous-michelle-obama-portrait.

Press, K. (2011). *Hope in a Jar: The Making of America's Beauty Culture*. Philadelphia: First University of Pennsylvania Press.

Preyer, N. W. (1994). "Richardson, Lunsford." In William S. Powell (Ed.), *Dictionary of North Carolina Biography* (Vol. 5, P–S, p. 215). Chapel Hill: University of North Carolina Press.

Puckett, N. N. (2023). *Folk Beliefs of the Southern Negro*. Chapel Hill: University of North Carolina Press.

Pugh, M. (2015). *America Dancing: From the Cakewalk to the Moonwalk*. New Haven, CT: Yale University Press.

Raboteau, A. J. (2004). *Slave Religion: The "Invisible Institution" in the Antebellum South*. New York: Oxford University Press.

Ramos, M. W. (2014). *On the Orisha's Roads and Pathways: Oshún, Deity of Femininity*. Pembroke Pines, FL: Eleda.org.

Randall, M. (2023, March 22). Suffering Sassafras. *64 Parishes*. https://64parishes.org/suffering-sassafras.

Rawicks, G. P. (Ed.). (1972). *The American Slave: A Composite Autobiography* (Vols. 1–19). Westport, CT: Greenwood. First published 1941.

———. (1977). *The American Slave: A Composite Autobiography* (Supplemental Series 1, Vols. 1–12). J. Hillegas & K. Lawrence (Eds.).Westport, CT: Greenwood.

———. (1979) *The American Slave: A Composite Autobiography* (Supplemental Series 2, Vols. 1–10). Westport, CT: Greenwood.

Reagan, L. J. (2022). *When Abortion Was a Crime: Women, Medicine, and Law in the United States, 1867–1973*. Oakland: University of California Press.

Richardson, S. (1975). *The Early History and Management Philosophy of Richardson-Merrell*. Richardson-Merrell Inc.

Rigaud, M. (1985). *Secrets of Voodoo*. San Francisco: City Light Books.

Riley, J. (2024, May 31). Before Goop: The Radical 1970s Roots of Wellness. *BBC*. https://www.bbc.com/culture/article/20240530-before-goop-how-the-wellness-craze-originated-in-1970s-california.

Ripley, E. (1998). *Social Life in Old New Orleans: Being Recollections of My Girlhood*. Gretna, LA: Pelican.

Roberts, D. (2017). *Killing the Black Body: Race, Reproduction, and the Meaning of Liberty*. New York: Vintage Books.

Rooks, N. M. (1996). *Hair Raising: Beauty, Culture, and African American Women*. New Brunswick: Rutgers University Press.

Rubin, S. G. (2017). *The Quilts of Gee's Bend*. New York: Abrams Books for Young Readers.

Rucker, W. C. (2006). *The River Flows On: Black Resistance, Culture, and Identity Formation in Early America*. Baton Rouge: Louisiana State University Press.

Rutkow, I. (2010). *Seeking the Cure: A History of Medicine in America*. New York: Scribner.

Saar, B. (2020, April 1). Betye Saar: Mojotech. Issuu. https://issuu.com/robertsprojects/docs/saar_mojotech_robertsprojects

Salfino, C. (2023, February 19). After 150 Years, Here's Why Americans Are Still Pulling Their Jeans On. *Rivet*. https://sourcingjournal.com/denim/denim-business/150-anniversary-levis-501-jeans-cotton-incorporated-tiktok-byrdie-normcore-435634/.

Sampsell, C. A. (2023, November 15). Why Does Squeezing a Comb Help with Labor Pains? Ohio State Health and Discovery. https://health.osu.edu/health/womens-health/squeezing-a-comb-to-help-labor-pain#:~:text=Squeezing%20a%20comb%20during%20labor%20can%20reduce%20labor%20pain%20because%3A&text=Your%20hand%20has%20many%20acupressure,that%20can%20accompany%20physical%20pain.

Saxon, L., Dreyer, E., & Tallant, R. (2012). *Gumbo Ya-Ya: Folk Tales of Louisiana*. Gretna, LA: Pelican.

Sayej, N. (2019, July 18). "Forgotten by Society"—How Chinese Migrants Built the Transcontinental Railroad. *Guardian*. https://www.theguardian.com/artanddesign/2019/jul/18/forgotten-by-society-how-chinese-migrants-built-the-transcontinental-railroad.

Schwartz, M. J. (2006). *Birthing a Slave: Motherhood and Medicine in the Antebellum South*. Cambridge, MA: Harvard University Press.

Seacole, M. (2020). *Wonderful Adventures of Mrs. Seacole in Many Lands*. London: Macmillan Collector's Library.

Seed, S. (2024, September 29). Health Benefits of Black-Eyed Peas. WebMD. https://www.webmd.com/diet/health-benefits-black-eyed-peas.

Severson, K. (2019, June 2). Leah Chase, 96, Creole Chef Who Fed

Presidents and Freedom Riders. *New York Times*. https://www.nytimes.com/2019/06/02/us/leah-chase-died.html.

Shaw, B. J. (2020, March 11). More Black Millennials Are Turning Away from Traditional Religion to Find Their Spirituality. WCNC Charlotte. https://www.wcnc.com/article/features/black-millennials-moving-away-from-traditional-religion-to-spiritual-practices/275-99781bc1-a1a6-4989-b283-0bb4f91fcc33#.

Sherrow, V. (2023). *Encyclopedia of Hair: A Cultural History*. Santa Barbara, CA: Greenwood.

Shesso, R. (2014). *Planets for Pagans: Sacred Sites, Ancient Lore, and Magical Stargazing*. Newburyport, MA: Weiser Books.

Silva, M. (2022). *Haitian Vodou: The Ultimate Guide to an African Diasporic Religion and Its Influence on Louisiana Voodoo, Santeria, and Candomble*. Independently Published.

Smith, K. (2023, June 16). The Role of Charleston's 1867 Mermaid Riot. CHStoday. https://chstoday.6amcity.com/mermaid-riot-1867-charleston-sc.

Smith, M. C., & Holmes, L. J. (1996). *Listen to Me Good: The Story of an Alabama Midwife*. Columbus: Ohio State University Press.

Snodgrass, M. E. (2016). *The Encyclopedia of World Folk Dance*. Lanham, MD: Rowman & Littlefield.

Southern, E. (1997). *The Music of Black Americans: A History*. New York: W. W. Norton.

Stanonis, A. J. (2024). *New Orleans Pralines: Plantation Sugar, Louisiana Pecans, and the Marketing of Southern Nostalgia*. Baton Rouge: Louisiana State University Press.

Steinauer-Scudder, C. (2019, October 7). The Seeds of Ancestors: A Day at Soul Fire Farm. *Emergence*. https://emergencemagazine.org/essay/the-seeds-of-ancestors/.

Stone, S. (2019). *New Orleans Coffee: A Rich History*. Charleston, SC: American Palate.

Stuckey, S. (1987). *Slave Culture: Nationalist Theory and the Foundations of Black America*. New York: Oxford University Press.

Sullivan, J. (2007). *Jeans: A Cultural History of an American Icon*. New York: Avery.

Sumberg, B. (2010). *Textiles: Collection of the Museum of International Art*. Kaysville, UT: Gibbs Smith.

Sundquist, E. J. (1993). *To Wake the Nations: Race in the Making of American Literature*. Cambridge, MA: Belknap Press.

Sutton, M. A. (2019, May 25). The Day Christian Fundamentalism Was Born. *New York Times*. https://www.nytimes.com/2019/05/25/opinion/the-day-christian-fundamentalism-was-born.html.

Sweeney-Risko, J. (2020). Fashionable "Formation": Reclaiming the Satorial Politics of Josephine Baker. In I. Parkins & M. Denver (Eds.), *Fashion: New Feminist Essays* (pp. 498–514). New York: Routledge.

Tallant, R. (2017). *Voodoo in New Orleans*. Gretna, LA: Pelican.

Tann, M. C. (2018). *Haitian Vodou: An Introduction to Haiti's Indigenous Spiritual Tradition*. Woodbury, MN: Llewellyn.

Teish, L. (2023). *A Calabash of Cowries: Ancient Wisdom for Modern Times*. New Orleans: University of New Orleans Press.

Tharps, L. L. (2024). *Hair Story: Untangling the Roots of Black Hair in America*. New York: St. Martin's Griffin.

Thompson, R. F. (1984). *Flash of the Spirit: African and Afro-American Art and Philosophy*. New York: Vintage Books.

Thompson, R. F. (2001). Orchestrating Water and the Wind: Oshun's Art in the Atlantic Context. In J. M. Murphy & M.-M. Sanford

(Eds.), *Òsun Across the Waters: A Yoruba Goddess in Africa and the Americas* (pp. 251–262). Bloomington: Indiana University Press.

Thorne, J., & Thorne, M. L. (2000). *Serious Pig: An American Cook in Search of His Roots*. New York: North Point Press.

Tinsley, O. N. (2022). *The Color Pynk: Black Femme Art for Survival*. Austin: University of Texas Press.

Tobin, J. L., & Dobard, R. G. (2000). *Hidden in Plain View: A Secret Story of Quilts and the Underground Railroad*. New York: Vintage Books.

Truman, B. C. (1893). *History of the World's Fair: Being a Complete Description of the World's Columbian Exposition from Its Inception*. Chicago: E. C. Morse.

Turner, D. (2024). Queen Elizabeth Perry Turner: "Granny Midwife," 1931–1956. In *Birthing Justice: Black Women, Pregnancy, and Childbirth*. New York: Routledge.

Turner, J. W. (1994). *Collectible Aunt Jemima: Handbook and Value Guide*. Atglen, PA: Schiffer.

Turner, R. B. (2017). *Jazz Religion, the Second Line, and Black New Orleans After Hurricane Katrina: New Edition*. Bloomington: Indiana University Press.

Twitty, M. W. (2021). *Rice: A Savor of the South Cookbook*. Chapel Hill: University of North Carolina Press.

UN Educational, Scientific, and Cultural Organization. (n.d.). Slave Ship Mutinies. Slavery and Remembrance: A Guide to Sites, Museums, and Memory. https://slaveryandremembrance.org/articles/article/?id=A0035.

Villarosa, L. (2022, June 8). The Long Shadow of Eugenics in America. *New York Times*. https://www.nytimes.com/2022/06/08/magazine/eugenics-movement-america.html.

Wahlman, M. S. (1993). *Signs and Symbols: African Images in African-American Quilts*. New York: Studio Books.

Wallace-Sanders, K. (2009). *Mammy: A Century of Race, Gender, and Southern Memory*. Ann Arbor: University of Michigan Press.

Ward, M. (2004). *Voodoo Queen: The Spirited Lives of Marie Laveau*. Jackson: University Press of Mississippi.

Washington, T. N. (2005). *Our Mothers, Our Powers, Our Texts: Manifestations of Àjé in Africana Literature*. Bloomington: Indiana University Press.

———. (2015). *The Architects of Existence: Àjé in Yoruba Cosmology, Ontology, and Orature*. Oya's Tornado.

WebMD. (n.d.). Cotton—Uses, Side Effects, and More. https://www.webmd.com/vitamins/ai/ingredientmono-416/cotton.

Wedel, J. (2003). *Santería Healing: A Journey into the Afro-Cuban World of Divinities, Spirits, and Sorcery*. Gainesville: University Press of Florida.

Wells, I. B. (2014). Selections from The Reason Why the Colored American Is Not in the World's Columbian Exposition. In M. Bay (Ed.), *The Light of Truth: Writings of an Anti-Lynching Crusader* (pp. 125–145). New York: Penguin Books.

White, D. G. (1999). *Ar'n't I a Woman?: Female Slaves in the Plantation South*. New York: W. W. Norton.

White, S., & White, G. (1998). *Stylin': African American Expressive Culture from Its Beginnings to the Zoot Suit*. Ithaca, NY: Cornell University Press.

Whitley, R. (2019, December 13). Prayer and Mental Health. *Psychology Today*. https://www.psychologytoday.com/intl/blog/talking-about-men/201912/prayer-and-mental-health

Whooley, O. (2013). *Knowledge in the Time of Cholera: The Struggle over*

American Medicine in the Nineteenth Century. Chicago: University of Chicago Press.

Widjaja, M. (2001). *Nnöö—Welcome to Enugu: An Insight Guide to Igboland's Culture and Language*. Enugu, Nigeria: Congrats Press.

Widmer, M. L. (1991). *New Orleans in the Thirties*. New Orleans: Pelican.

Wilkie, L. A. (2003). *The Archeology of Mothering: An African-American Midwife's Story*. New York: Routledge.

———. (2004). Granny Midwives: Gender and Generational Mediators of the African American Community. In J. E. Galle & A. L. Young (Eds.), *Engendering African American Archeology: A Southern Perspective* (pp. 73–100). Knoxville: University of Tennessee.

Williams, F. (1918). Memories of New Orleans. *International Confectioner, 27*, pp. 37–40.

Willis, R. (1996). Africa. In R. G. Willis (Ed.), *World Mythology* (pp. 264–277). New York: Henry Holt.

Wolf, J. Q. (1969). Aunt Caroline Dye: The Gypsy in the "St. Louis Blues." *Southern Folklore Quarterly, 33*, 339–346.

Young, J. R. (2007). *Rituals of Resistance: African Atlantic Religion in Kongo and the Lowcountry South in the Era of Slavery*. Baton Rouge: Louisiana State University Press.

Notes

Introduction: How to Keep That Shit off You

1. For more on soul food as fusion food, see Harris, *Beyond Gumbo*, 4–7. See also McPhail, "New Orleans Invented America's First Fusion Cuisine."
2. Morgan, *When Chickenheads Come Home to Roost*, 58.
3. Morgan, 58.
4. I've adapted the two stories from Olajubu, *Women in the Yoruba Religious Sphere*, 27–29, 71–76, and 120–122.
5. Olajubu, *Women in the Yoruba Religious Sphere*, 71–76 and 120–122.
6. Drewal and Drewal, *Gelede*, 8.
7. Drewal and Drewal, 8.
8. Washington, *Our Mothers, Our Powers, Our Texts*, 14–15.
9. Washington, 14–15.
10. Drewal and Drewal, *Gelede*, 8.
11. Davis, *Blues Legacies and Black Feminism*, 155.
12. Hazzard-Donald, *Mojo Workin'*, 4. See also Fry, Leone, and Ruppel, "Spirit Management Among Americans of African Descent," 143–157.

Chapter 1: An Alternative History of Vicks VapoRub Salve

1. Preyer, "Richardson, Lunsford." See also Preyer, "Richardson, Lunsford," NCPedia, https://www.ncpedia.org/biography/richardson-lunsford-0.
2. Blakemore, "How an Enslaved African Man in Boston Helped."
3. R. McBlair, Notes on Draft of *Annals of an American Family*, Collection

04283: Henry Smith Richardson Papers, 1811–1999, Series 6: Richardson Family, 1882–1981, Subseries 6.6: *Annals of an American Family*, 1920–1937, Folder 270–288: R. McBlair Version, 1938, Wilson Library Southern Historical Collection, University of North Carolina at Chapel Hill, Chapel Hill, NC.

4 For more on mint found in North Carolina, see Melinda Heigel, "Specimen Spotlight: Mountain Mints," DurhamMasterGardeners, June 8, 2022, https://durhammastergardeners.com/2022/06/08/specimen-spotlight-mountain-mints/#:~:text=Mountain%20mints%20are%20native%20to,despite%20the%20alpine%2Dsounding%20name. For more on the turpentine forests on the Richardson's plantation, see Collection 04283: Henry Smith Richardson Papers, 1811–1999, Series 6: Richardson Family, 1882–1981, Subseries 6:2, Biographical Material, 1868–1978, Folder 223, Wilson Library Southern Historical Collection, University of North Carolina at Chapel Hill, Chapel Hill, NC.

5 Pharoah Richardson, Lunsford Richardson's uncle, helped Laurinda (Vinson) Richardson, Lunsford Richardson's mother, run the plantation upon the death of Lunsford Richardson's father. And Pharoah Richardson owned Wiley (along with her husband, Atlas) who passed this healing knowledge down through generations. Laurinda Richardson Carlson, "Biography of Lunsford Richardson, Sr.," Collection 04283: Henry Smith Richardson Papers, 1811–1999, Series 6: Richardson Family, 1882–1981, Subseries 6.2: Biographical Material, 1968–1978, Folder 223: Lunsford Richardson, including Laurinda Richard Carlson's Recollections of him, Wilson Library Southern Historical Collection, University of North Carolina at Chapel Hill, Chapel Hill, NC.

6 Richardson, *Early History and Management Philosophy of Richardson-Merrell*, 16–17.

Chapter 2: "An Old Woman, Who Doctored Among the Slaves"

1 Unless otherwise noted, all quotes by Harriet Jacobs are from Jacobs, *Incidents in the Life of a Slave Girl*.

NOTES

2. See the following interviews in Rawick, *American Slave*: Charlie Grant in Vol. 2, Part 2, 171–176; Dosia Harris in Vol. 12, Part 2, 103–114; Henry Towns Williams in Vol. 6, 385–393; Ruben Fox in Supplemental Series 1, Vol. 7, Part 2, 769–780; and Lucendy Griffin in Supplemental Series 2, Vol. 5, Part 4, 1607–1613.
3. Sarah Louise Augustus in Rawick, *American Slave*, Vol. 14, Part 1, 51–57.
4. George Womble and E. Driskell Whitley in Rawick, *American Slave*, Vol. 13, Part 4, 179–193. See also Fett, *Working Cures*, 128.
5. Fett, *Working Cures*, 147.
6. Fett, 147–150.
7. Mary Reynolds in Rawick, *American Slave*, Supplemental Series 2, Vol. 8, Part 7, 3284–3299.
8. See the following interviews in Rawick, *American Slave*: Charlie Sandles in Supplemental Series 2, Vol. 9, Part 8, 3441–3456; and Josephine Coxe in Supplemental Series 1, Vol. 7, Part 2, 525–528.
9. Mildred Graves in Berlin, Favreau, and Miller, *Remembering Slavery*, 103–104.
10. See the following interviews in Rawick, *American Slave*: Irene Robertson in Vol. 11, Part. 7, 232–234; and Mary Rhals in Supplemental Series 2, Vol. 8, Part 7, 3217–3220.
11. Thomas Foote in Rawick, *American Slave*, Vol. 16, Part 3, 14–16.

Chapter 3: Negro Mammies, Botany, and American Home Remedies

1. Carney and Rosomoff, *In the Shadow of Slavery*, 74–79.
2. Fett, *Working Cures*, 159.
3. Randall, "Suffering Sassafras."
4. Correal, *Finding Soul on the Path of Orisa*, 25.
5. Wedel, *Santeria Healing*, 65.
6. Olupona, "Owner of the Day and Regulator of the Universe," 112–117.
7. Olupona, 112–117.

8   Olajubu, *Women in the Yoruba Religious Sphere*, 110–112.
9   Washington, *Our Mothers, Our Powers, Our Texts*, 14.
10 Washington, 14.
11 Olajubu, *Women in the Yoruba Religious Sphere*, 110–112.
12 Wedel, *Santería Healing*, 113.
13 Wedel, 113.
14 Fett, *Working Cures*, 77.
15 Badejo, *Òsun Sèègèsí*, 1–2; and Tinsley, *Color Pynk*, 158.
16 Abiodun, "Hidden Power," 18–19.
17 Thompson, "Orchestrating Water and the Wind," 259.
18 Olajubu, *Women in the Yoruba Religious Sphere*, 79–80.
19 Olajubu, 79–80.
20 Dorsey, *Orishas, Goddesses, and Voodoo Queens*, 39–40.
21 Fett, *Working Cures*, 53; and Hazzard-Donald, *Mojo Workin'*, 141–142.
22 Dorsey, *Orishas, Goddesses, and Voodoo Queens*, 33.
23 See the following interviews in Rawick, *American Slave*: Eliza White in Vol. 6, 411–413; Harriet Collins in Supplemental Series 2, Vol. 3, Part 2, 883–893; and Walter Legget in Supplemental Series 2, Vol. 6, Part 5, 2319–2324.
24 Charlie Sandles in Rawick, *American Slave*, Supplemental Series 2, Vol. 9, Part 8, 3441–3456.
25 Anna Lee in Rawick, *American Slave*, Supplemental Series 2, Vol. 6, Part 5, 2273–2290.
26 See the following interviews in Rawick, *American Slave*: Nettie Henry in Supplemental Series 1, Vol. 8, Part 3, 975–987; Chales Hayes in Vol. 6, p.174–175; and Pierce Harper in Supplemental Series 2, Vol. 5, Part 4, 1642–1651.
27 See the following interviews in Rawick, *American Slave*: Lou (Granny) Williams in Supplemental Series 2, Vol. 10, Part 9, 4096–4101; and Henry Louis in Supplemental Series 2, Vol. 6, Part 5, 2336–2348.
28 Penniman, *Farming While Black*, 183–185.
29 See the following interviews in Rawick, *American Slave*: Irene Robertson

NOTES

in Vol. 11, Part. 7, 232–234; Emma Stone in Vol. 15, Part 2, 324–326; and Mary Johnson in Vol. 3, Part 3, 56–58.

30 Sampson Willis in Rawick, *American Slave*, Supplemental Series 2, Vol. 10, Part 9, 4161–4167.

31 Laurinda Richardson Carlson, "Biography of Lunsford Richardson, Sr.," Collection 04283: Henry Smith Richardson Papers, 1811–1999, Series 6: Richardson Family, 1882–1981, Subseries 6.2: Biographical Material, 1968–1978, Folder 223: Lunsford Richardson, including Laurinda Richard Carlson's Recollections of him, Wilson Library Southern Historical Collection, University of North Carolina at Chapel Hill, Chapel Hill, NC. See also Henry Smith Richardson, Charles Alphonso Smith, Mamie A. Richardson, and Mary Rawlins, "In North Carolina: A Dream Come True," Collection 04283: Henry Smith Richardson Papers, 1811–1999, Series 6: Richardson Family, 1882–1981, Subseries 6.5: Family History, 1934–1976, Folder 241: Drafts of Richardson family annals, Wilson Library Southern Historical Collection, University of North Carolina at Chapel Hill, Chapel Hill, NC.

Chapter 4: A Doctor's Visit in the Nineteenth Century

1 Lord, *Gentle Revolutionaries*, 89–91; and Rutkow, *Seeking the Cure*, 31–34.
2 Moss, *Southern Folk Medicine, 1750–1820*, 36–37.
3 Brown, *Rockefeller Medicine Men*, 61–63.
4 Brown, 61–63.
5 Nassau, *Fetichism in West Africa*, 106–108.
6 Fett, *Working Cures*, 61–62.
7 Fett, 64–65.
8 Fett, 64–65.

Chapter 5: What History Will We Choose to Remember?

1 Kaufman, *Little Blue Jar*, 42.
2 Laurinda Richardson Carlson, "Biography of Lunsford Richardson, Sr."
3 Preyer, "Richardson, Lunsford."

NOTES

Chapter 6: Why Can't Disney's Ariel Be Black?

1. Hurston, *Mules and Men*, 191.
2. Long, *New Orleans Voudou Priestess*, xvii–xx, 190–206; and Ward, *Voodoo Queen*, 93–107.
3. Tallant, *Voodoo in New Orleans*, 56.

Chapter 7: Juliette and the Voodoo Queen

1. Long, *New Orleans Voudou Priestess*, 13–15.
2. Long, 75–76.
3. Buel, *Mysteries and Miseries of America's Great Cities*, 535–536.
4. Gates, "Did Black People Own Slaves?"
5. Long, *New Orleans Voudou Priestess*, 75–76.
6. Long, 75–76.
7. Saxon, Dreyer, and Tallant, *Gumbo Ya-Ya*, 236.
8. Evans, *Congo Square*, 1–2.
9. Alvarado, *Witch Queens, Voodoo Spirits, and Hoodoo Saints*, 56.
10. Evans, *Congo Square*, 100–103.
11. Fandrich, *Mysterious Voodoo Queen*, 137–144.
12. Long, *New Orleans Voudou Priestess*, 104–118.
13. Long, 104–118.
14. Alvarado, *Magic of Marie Laveau*, 59–62; Fandrich, *Mysterious Voodoo Queen*, 139–140; and Long, *New Orleans Voudou Priestess*, 104–106.

Chapter 8: Mermaid History

1. Carter, *Freedom in My Heart*, 51–54.
2. Murphy, "The Cymbee in South Carolina."
3. Bennett, "Mr. John Bennett Replies to Certain Criticisms of His Novel." The folktale included in this chapter is adapted from the following sources: Bennett, *Doctor to the Dead*, 178–187; Brown, *African Atlantic Cultures*, 251–259; and Smith, "The Role of Charleston's 1867 Mermaid Riot." Although many report the incident as

NOTES

taking place in 1867, Brown notes that the event likely happened in the 1850s.

4 Cavallo, "Ancient Craft of Gullah Basket Weaving."
5 Caudle, "Mermaids of Charleston."
6 Schwartz, *Birthing a Slave*, 1–5, 14–28, 38–42.
7 Owens, *Medical Bondage*, 5–13, 21–26.
8 Hansen, "Denmark Vesey Is Honored."

Chapter 9: Conjure Fuels Rebellions

1 Rucker, *River Flows On*.
2 Martin, *Envisioning Black Feminist Voodoo Aesthetics*, xx–xxv.
3 Long, *New Orleans Voudou Priestess*, 95–96. See also Rigaud, *Secrets of Voodoo*, 75.
4 Catalini, Smyth, and Shipkowski, "Trump Falsely Accuses Immigrants."
5 Nittle, "Trump's Claims About Haitians."
6 Herman, "Vance to Talk at Tour."
7 Alvarado, *Witch Queens, Voodoo Spirits, and Hoodoo Saints*, 127.
8 Martinez, *Mysterious Marie Laveau, Voodoo Queen*, 56–57.
9 Fett, *Working Cures*, 167.
10 Long, *New Orleans Voudou Priestess*, 5–7, 12–15. See also Hall, *Africans in Colonial Louisiana*, 275–316.
11 For more on this point, see Hall, *Africans in Colonial Louisiana*, chapter 9.
12 Long, *New Orleans Voudou Priestess*, 12–15.
13 Long, 27–28.
14 Fandrich, *Mysterious Voodoo Queen, Marie Laveaux*, 1–3, 123–125.
15 Long, *New Orleans Voudou Priestess*, 19–20.
16 Hall, *Africans in Colonial Louisiana*, 275–316.

NOTES

Chapter 10: Oshun, Mami Wata, and a Pantheon of African Water Deities

1. Turner, *Jazz Religion, the Second Line*, xxii.
2. Brown, *African Atlantic Cultures and the South Carolina Lowcountry*, 111–126, 259–280.
3. Brown, 111–126, 259–280.
4. Alvarado, *Voodoo Hoodoo Spellbook*, 40–41, 36–37.
5. Hall, *Africans in Colonial Louisiana*, 275–316.
6. Rigaud, *Secrets of Voodoo*, 74–76; Silva, *Haitian Vodou*, 31–34, 40–41; and Tann, *Haitian Vodou*, 101–102, 112–113.
7. Alvarado, *Voodoo Hoodoo Spellbook*, 11–13, 40–41; and Alvarado, *Magic of Marie Laveau*, 55–56, 58–59.
8. Brown, *African Atlantic Cultures and the South Carolina Lowcountry*, 273–276.
9. UN Educational, Scientific, and Cultural Organization, "Slave Ship Mutinies."
10. Long, *New Orleans Voudou Priestess*, 5, 13.
11. Tallant, *Voodoo in New Orleans*, 62–63.
12. Hurston, *Mules and Men*, 193–194.
13. Alvarado, *Magic of Marie Laveau*, 45–47; and Long, *New Orleans Voudou Priestess*, xxxvii.
14. Long, *New Orleans Voudou Priestess*, 105–106.
15. Tallant, *Voodoo in New Orleans*, 67–68.

Chapter 11: The *Gris-Gris* of the Downtrodden

1. Ward, *Voodoo Queen*, 32–34.
2. See the following interviews in Rawick, *American Slave*: Peter Ryas in Supplemental Series 2, Vol. 8, Part 7, 3401; Mary Armstrong in Supplemental Series 2, Vol. 2, Part 1, 74; and Rose Mosely in Supplemental Series 1, Vol. 2, 14.
3. Seacole, *Wonderful Adventures of Mrs. Seacole*, 5.
4. Brown, *African Atlantic Cultures and the South Carolina Lowcountry*,

NOTES

111–126; Deren, *Divine Horsemen*, 116–119, 147–149; Olajubu, *Women in the Yoruba Religious Sphere*, 93–124; and Silva, *Haitian Vodou*, 28–29, 42–43.

5 Brown, *African Atlantic Cultures and the South Carolina Lowcountry*, 111–126.

6 Elliot, *White Coat Ways*, 9–10.

7 Tallant, *Voodoo in New Orleans*, 62–63, 90–93, 104–105.

8 *New York Times*, "The Dead Voudou Queen."

9 Ward, *Voodoo Queen*, 169–170.

10 It is from the Bambara people that we originally get the term *gris-gris*. As the largest and earliest group of Africans to have been brought to Louisiana, it makes sense that their phrase would gobble up similar West African practices that were also present in New Orleans. See Hall, *Africans in Colonial Louisiana*, 28–55; and Long, *New Orleans Voudou Priestess*, 93–94.

11 Correal, *Finding Soul on the Path of Orisa*, 25. See also Long, *New Orleans Voudou Priestess*, 93–94.

12 Fandrich, *Mysterious Voodoo Queen, Marie Laveaux*, 123–124; Hall, *Africans in Colonial Louisiana*, 156–200; and Long, *New Orleans Voudou Priestess*, 93–94.

13 Long, *New Orleans Voudou Priestess*, xxvi.

14 Alvarado, *Magic of Marie Laveau*, 9–13; Dorsey, *Orishas, Goddesses, and Voodoo Queens*, 150; Long, *New Orleans Voudou Priestess*, xxxvi; and Ward, *Voodoo Queen*, 80–82.

Chapter 12: "She Was Hard on the Men"

1 Marie Dédé in interview by Robert McKinney, Louisiana Federal Writers' Project, Folder 25.

2 Long, *New Orleans Voudou Priestess*, xxvi, 104.

3 I've adapted this story from the following sources: Tallant, *Voodoo in New Orleans*, 114–121; and Martinez, *Mysterious Marie Laveau*, 73–75. See also the following interviews from the Louisiana Federal Writers' Project, Folder 25: Camille Harrison, interview by Maude Wallace, January 9 and 11, 1940; Marie Dédé, interview by Robert McKinney;

NOTES

Oscar Felix, interview by Edmund Burke, March 4, 1940; and Charles Raphael, interview by Hazel Breaux and Jacques Villere.
4 Tallant, *Voodoo in New Orleans*, 100–102.
5 Morrison, "A Knowing So Deep," 32.

Chapter 13: Our Mermaids, Our Stories

1 Tallant, *Voodoo in New Orleans*, 67–68.
2 Alvarado, *Magic of Marie Laveau*, xi.
3 Fandrich, *Mysterious Voodoo Queen, Marie Laveauxs*, 133–134.

Chapter 14: Aunt Jemima's Grand Debut, the Chicago World's Fair of 1893

1 Di Cola and Stone, *Chicago's 1893 World's Fair*, 7–17.
2 Wells, "Reason Why the Colored American Is Not in the World's Columbian Exposition," 126–127.
3 Truman, *History of the World's Fair*, 63–69; and Di Cola and Stone, *Chicago's 1893 World's Fair*, 7–17.
4 Truman, *History of the World's Fair*, 273; Di Cola and Stone, *Chicago's 1893 World's Fair*, 7–8, 109; Manring, *Slave in a Box*, 62–78; and Wallace-Sanders, *Mammy*, 58–60.
5 Manring, *Slave in a Box*, 78; Wallace-Sanders, *Mammy*, 68–72; Turner, *Collectible Aunt Jemima*, 1–8; and Purd Wright, "Life of Aunt Jemima, The Most Famous Colored Woman in the World," https://archive.org/details/life-of-aunt-jemima-cc-harvard-d.-d.-teoli-jr.-a.-c.-16.
6 Luckerson, "New Report Documents 4,000 Lynchings in Jim Crow South."

Chapter 15: From Negro Mammy's Hoecake to Aunt Jemima's Pancake Mix

1 "Shortnin' Bread" lyrics from the Singalongasong Band, *The Nursery Rhyme Collection IV*, vols. 7 and 8, 2014, https://nurseryrhymescollections.com/lyrics/shortnin-bread.html.

NOTES

2 Snodgrass, *Encyclopedia of World Folk Dance*, 161.
3 Gus Feaster in Rawick, *American Slave*, Vol. 2, Part 2, 43–71.
4 For a discussion of the diets of enslaved children, see the following interviews in Rawick, *American Slave*: Prince John in Vol. 7, Part 2, 76–90, and Supplemental Series 1, Vol. 8, Part 3, 1167–1180; Needham Love in Vol. 9, Part 4, 292–296; Sabe Rutledge in Vol. 3, Part 4, 59–70; and William Williams in Vol. 16, Part 4, 114–116.
5 Lizzie Davis, in Rawick, *American Slave*, Vol. 2, Part 1, 288–298; and Supplemental Series 1, Vol. 11, Part 2, 107–114.
6 Willis Cofer in Rawick, *American Slave*, Vol. 12, Part 1, 201–211.
7 Hamp Kennedy in Rawick, *American Slave*, Supplemental Series 1, Vol. 8, Part 3, 1271–1277.
8 Carter J. Jackson in Rawick, *American Slave*, Vol. 4, Part 2, p. 180–181, and Supplemental Series 2, Vol. 5, Part 4, p. 1883–1887.
9 Chireau, *Black Magic*, 138–144; and Hazzard-Donald, *Mojo Workin'*, 90–104.
10 Long, *Spiritual Merchants*, 127–130; and Hazzard-Donald, *Mojo Workin'*, 94–95.
11 Chireau, *Black Magic*, 93–107; and Hazzard-Donald, *Mojo Workin'*, 90–96.
12 McMillen, "From Aunt Jemima to Aunt Marthy," 87–94.
13 Manring, *Slave in Box*, 74–76; and Wallace-Sanders, *Mammy*, 59.
14 McMillen, "From Aunt Jemima to Aunt Marthy," 89.
15 Wallace-Sanders, *Mammy*, 58–63.
16 Wells, *Crusade for Justice*, 58–66.
17 Turner, *Collectible Aunt Jemima Handbook and Value Guide*, 6.
18 Manring, *Slave in a Box*, 76–77.

Chapter 16: Sarah Byrd's Cakewalk

1 Pugh, *American Dancing*, 1–4.
2 Wallace-Sanders, *Mammy*, 58–59; and Pugh, *America Dancing*, 10–12.
3 For Sarah Byrd's interviews in Rawick, *American Slave*, see: Vol. 12, Part 1, 168–171; and Supplemental Series 1, Vol. 3, Part 1, p. 134–141.

NOTES

I also drew upon the following interviews for my discussion of Saturday night frolics from *American Slave*: Berry Clay, Vol. 12, Part 1, 189–194; Isabella Dorrah, Vol. 2, Part 1, 326–328; Sylvia Durant, Vol. 2, Part 1, 337–348; Malinda, Vol. 13, Part 4, 219–220; John Moore, Vol. 5, Part 3, 125–127, and Supplemental Series 2, Vol. 7, Part 6, 2736–2742; Andrew Moss, Vol. 16, Part 6, 49–54; Patsy Moses, Vol. 5, Part 3, 142–144, and Supplemental Series 2, Vol. 7, Part 6, 2780–2794; Reverend Wade Owens, Vol. 6, Pat 1, 306–308; Jake Terriell, Vol. 5, Part 4, 78–79, and Supplemental Series, Vol. 9, Part 8, 3772–3776; and Mary Veals, Vol. 3, Part 4, 167–169.

4 Evans, *Congo Square*, 105–107.
5 Evans, 105–107.
6 Douglass, *Narrative of the Life of Frederick Douglass*, 120–121; Hurston, "Shouting," 851–854; Stuckey, *Slave Culture*, 9–12; Hazzard-Donald, *Mojo Workin'*, 36–38; and Raboteau, *Slave Religion*, 68–75.
7 Hurston, "Shouting," 851–854, and "Sanctified Church," 901–905; and Raboteau, *Slave Religion*, 71–73.
8 For the song lyrics of "Promises of Freedom," see Davis, Brown, and Lee, *Negro Caravan*, 447.
9 Hurston, *Mules and Men*, 284–285.
10 Hurston, *Mules and Men*, 284–285; Hazzard-Donald, *Mojo Workin'*, 64–67; Young, *Rituals of Resistance*, 118–134; and Chireau, *Black Magic*, 47–48.
11 McGaffey, *Kongo Political Culture*, 89–90.
12 Hurston, *Dust Tracks on a Road*, 165. See also Thompson, *Flash of the Spirit*, 131.
13 Hazzard-Donald, *Mojo Workin'*, 85.
14 Manring, *Slave in a Box*, 69.

Chapter 17: Aunt Caroline Dye's Mojo

1 Martin, *Envisioning Black Feminist Voodoo Aesthetics*, xx–xxiii, xxx–xxxi.
2 Martin, xxiii.
3 Martin, xxi–xxii.

NOTES

4 Wahlman, *Signs and Symbols*, 105.
5 Young, *Rituals of Resistance*, 114–117.
6 Martin, *Envisioning Black Feminist Voodoo Aesthetics*, xxix.
7 Martin, xxxv.
8 Martin, xxix–xxxv.
9 Hurston, "Sanctified Church," 901–905.
10 Peress, *Dvorak to Duke Ellington*, 37.
11 Hurston, "Characteristics of Negro Expression," 841–842.
12 Hazzard-Donald, "Rethinking the Ring Shout," 200.
13 Southern, *Music of Black Americans*, 311–314.
14 Handy, *Father of the Blues*, 7–10.
15 Handy, 118–124.
16 Handy, 118–124.
17 Chireau, *Black Magic*, 145–146; Kail, *Secret History of Memphis Hoodoos*, 72–75; Martin, *Conjuring Moments in African American Literature*, 13, 129; Wolf, "Aunt Caroline Dye"; Onek, "Race, Gender, and Hoodoo in the Arkansas Delta," 173–180; Morgan, "She Put Newport on the Map"; *Pine Bluff Daily*, "Voodoo Woman Has Large Following"; *Arkansas Democrat*, "Newport Seeress Has Numerous Followers"; and Arkansas State Parks Staff, "Hoo Doo Woman of Arkansas."
18 Oliver, *Conversation with the Blues*, 98–100.
19 Hurston, "Hoodoo in America," 385.
20 Hazzard-Donald, *Mojo' Workin'*, 68–70.
21 Hurston, *Their Eyes Were Watching God*, 157.
22 Davis, *Blues Legacies and Black Feminism*, 123–124.
23 Davis, 157.
24 Arkansas State Parks Staff, "Hoo Doo Woman of Arkansas."
25 Davis, *Blues Legacies and Black Feminism*, 135–137, 261, 273–274, 330–331.
26 Bratcher, *Words and Songs of Bessie Smith*, 122–124.

NOTES

Chapter 18: Aunt Jemima, the Black Power Revolutionary

1. Mariah Robinson in *American Slave*, Supplemental Series 2, Vol. 8, Part 7, 3350–3358.
2. Gotthardt, "How Betye Saar Transformed Aunt Jemima."
3. Caldwell, "Assemblage Sculptures of Betye Saar."

Chapter 19: Our Ancient Textile Tradition

1. Commisso, "When It Comes to Buying Jeans."
2. Commisso, "Jeans Are Getting Faded Out." See also Salfino, "After 150 Years."
3. Sullivan, *Jeans*, xv–xix.
4. Sullivan, 4–6.
5. Sullivan, 4–6.
6. Sullivan, 15–18. For more on the racial makeup of the Gold Rush, see History.com Editors, "California Gold Rush."
7. Sayej, "'Forgotten by Society.'"
8. History.com Editors, "Cowboys."
9. Sullivan, *Jeans*, 5.
10. Sullivan, 5–8.
11. Ford, *Liberated Threads*, 4–5; Foster, "New Raiments of Self," 167–168; and Sullivan, *Jeans*, 32–34.
12. Katz-Hyman and Rice, "Textiles," 498–500. See also Bick's and Strachan's excellent documentary "Riveted: The History of Jeans," on PBS's series, *American Experience*.
13. McKinley, *Indigo*, 3–12.
14. McKinley, 3–5.
15. Joseph, "West African Indigo Cloth," 34.
16. Farlin, "Maternal Goddess in Yoruba Art," 7–8; Joseph, "West African Indigo Cloth," 34; Murphy and Sanford, *Òsun Across the Waters*, 53–54, 103–104; and Olajubu, *Women in the Yoruba Religious Sphere*, 65–93.
17. Washington, *Architects of Existencee*, 64–66.

NOTES

18 Musgrove, *Spider Weaver*; and Padilioni, "History and Significance of the Kente Cloth."
19 Griaule, *Conversations with Ogotemmeli*, 24–28; and Lane, "Social Production and Symbolism of Cloth," 77–78.
20 Davis, *Blues Legacies and Black Feminism*, 33.
21 Wahlman, *Signs and Symbols*, 25.
22 Fry, *Stitched from the Soul*, 7–8, 12–13. See also Wahlman, *Signs and Symbols*, 21–22, 25–35.
23 Asakitikpi, "Functions of Hand Woven Textiles," 101–103; and Wahlman, *Signs and Symbols*, 25.
24 Clark, *Hair Craft Project*.
25 Falola, *Decolonizing African Knowledge*, 411–412. See also Dabiri, *Don't Touch My Hair*.
26 Burlock et al., *My Divine Natural Hair*, 40–50; and Tharps, *Hair Story*, 4–5.
27 Drewal, *Yoruba*, 27–28. See also Sherrow, *Encyclopedia of Hair*, 516–517.
28 Drewal, *Yoruba*, 15–17, 27–28, 33–34.
29 Drewal, "Crowning Glories," 227–229.
30 Badejo, *Òsun Sèègèsí*, 1–5.
31 Badejo, "Authority and Discourse in the Orin Odún Òsun," 137–139.
32 Ramos, *On the Orisha's Roads and Pathways*, 168–172. See also Dorsey, *Orishas, Goddesses, and Voodoo Queens*, 36–37.
33 Ramos, *On the Orisha's Roads and Pathways*, 168–172.
34 Cosette, "Five Roads of Oshun, the Orisha of Love."

Chapter 20: Enslaved Midwives as Weavers

1 All quotes from Lu Lee are from her interview with the Federal Writers' Project. See also Lu Lee in Rawick, *American Slave*, Supplemental Series 2, Vol. 5, Part 6, 2291–2312.
2 Ed McCree in Rawick, *American Slave*, Vol. 13, Part 3, 56–65.
3 Annie Row in Rawick, *American Slave*, Vol. 5, Part 3, 258–261.
4 White, *Ar'n't I a Woman?*, 116.
5 Rose Adway in Rawick, *American Slave*, Vol. 8, Part 1, 17–18.
6 Fry, *Stitched from the Soul*, 67. See also Hurston, "High John de

NOTES

Conquer," 923. For examples of these stories in ex-slave interviews, see the following interviews in Rawick, *American Slave*: Mary Johnson in Supplemental Series 2, Vol. 6, Part 5, 2021–2030; and Aunt Clara Walker in Vol. 11, Part 7, 19–27.

7. See chapter 2, "Carrying History and Memory," in Collins, *Stitching Love and Loss*.
8. Adiji et al., "Sacred Textiles of the Yorubas," 48.
9. Areo, "The Visual Semantics of *Adire*," 191–192; and Falola, *Decolonizing African Knowledge*, 280–326.
10. Drewal, *Yoruba*, 14–15.
11. Thompson, *Flash of the Spirit*, 108–112.
12. Thompson, *Flash of the Spirit*, 117–120; and Young, *Rituals of Resistance*, 110–112.
13. Thompson, 117–131; and Young, 112–115.
14. McGaffey, *Kongo Political Culture*, 89–90.
15. Fett, *Working Cures*, 55–57, 79–80; and Young, *Rituals of Resistance*, 62, 112–113.
16. Berjonneau and Sonnery, *Rediscovered Masterpieces of African Art*, 60; and Thompson, *Flash of the Spirit*, 130–131.
17. Young, *Rituals of Resistance*, 112.
18. Thompson, *Flash of the Spirit*, 131.
19. See the following interviews in Rawick, *American Slave*: Solomon Caldwell in Vol. 2, Part 1, 170–171; Casey Jones Brown in Vol. 8, Part 1, 267–271; and Aunt Adeline in Vol. 8, Part 1, 11–16, and Vol. 13, Part 4, 212–213.
20. Harriet Collins in Rawick, *American Slave*, Supplemental Series 2, Vol. 3, Part 2, 883–896.
21. Fontenot, *Secret Doctors*, 115–116.
22. Fontenot, *Secret Doctors*, 53–54, 114–115; and Hazzard-Donald, *Mojo Workin'*, 143.
23. Hazzard-Donald, *Mojo Workin'*, 146–150.
24. Hazzard-Donald, *Mojo Workin'*, 146–150. See also Whitley, "Prayer and Mental Health"; and Marnach, "Can Too Much Stress Cause Early Miscarriage?"

NOTES

25 Cleveland Clinic, "Miscarriage," https://my.clevelandclinic.org/health/diseases/9688-miscarriage; and Cleveland Clinic, "High Estrogen," https://my.clevelandclinic.org/health/diseases/22363-high-estrogen.

26 Cleveland Clinic, "Miscarriage"; and Cleveland Clinic, "High Estrogen."

27 Burlock et al., *My Divine Natural Hair*, 40–50; and Tharps, *Hair Story*, 4–5.

28 Drewal, "Crowning Glories," 227–229.

29 Washington, *Our Mothers, Our Powers, Our Texts*, 24.

30 Asakitikpi, "Functions of Hand Woven Textiles," 103–105, 110–111.

31 Asakitikpi, 101–103.

32 Asakitikpi, 103–105, 110–111.

33 Asakitikpi, 110–111.

34 Asakitikpi, 110–111.

35 Adiji et al., "Sacred Textiles of the Yorubas," 47–49. See also Wahlman, *Signs and Symbols*, 25, 30.

36 I've adapted this story from Asakitikpi, "Functions of Hand Woven Textiles," 109–110. See also Peek and Yankah, *African Folklore*, 916–918.

37 Peek and Yankah, *African Folklore*, 916–918.

38 Sumberg, *Textiles*, 56–57. See also Areo, "The Visual Semantics of *Adire*," 198–203.

39 Asakitikpi, "Functions of Hand Woven Textiles," 105–106; and Peek and Yankah, *African Folklore*, 916–918.

40 Asakitikpi, 105–106; and Peek and Yankah, 916–918.

41 Tobin and Dobard, *Hidden in Plain View*, 9.

42 Areo, "The Visual Semantics of *Adire*," 195–210.

43 Areo, 199–200.

44 Areo, 202.

45 Falola, *Decolonizing African Knowledge*, 320–322.

46 McKinley, *Indigo*, 2–3.

47 Foster, "New Raiments of Self," 171, 199–204.

48 Fry, *Stitched from the Soul*, 74.

49 Eliza Washington in Rawick, *American Slave*, Vol. 11, Part 7, 49–56.

50 Fry, *Stitched from the Soul*, 12–13; and Wahlman, *Signs and Symbols*, 25–26, 60–61.
51 Wahlman, *Signs and Symbols*, 48.
52 Wahlman, 48.
53 Wahlman, 48.
54 George Washington Ramsey in Rawick, *American Slave*, Supplemental Series 1, Vol. 9, Part 1, 1775–1791.
55 Wahlman, *Signs and Symbols*, 48.
56 Tobin and Dobard, *Hidden in Plain View*, 75–77.
57 Wahlman, *Signs and Symbols*, 56.
58 Fry, *Stitched from the Soul*, 7, 44–46, 53; and Wahlman, *Signs and Symbols*, 75–88.
59 Peek and Yankah, *African Folklore*, 926; and Wahlman, *Signs and Symbols*, 91.

Chapter 21: Black Midwives and the Nineteenth-Century Brawl over Abortion

1 Owens, *Medical Bondage*, 42–73.
2 Bonaparte, Regulating Childbirth, 7; Owens, *Medical Bondage*, 4; and Schwartz, *Birthing a Slave*, 165–166.
3 Schwartz, *Birthing a Slave*, 85–86.
4 Davis, *Women, Race, and Class*, 9. See also Owens, *Medical Bondage*, 42–73; and Roberts, *Killing the Black Body*, 22–55.
5 McKinley, *Indigo*, 3–4. See also Graham, "The Blue That Enchanted the World."
6 McKinley, *Indigo*, 3–5.
7 Schwartz, *Birthing a Slave*, 16–19. See also Roberts, *Killing the Black Body*, 22–55.
8 Roberts, *Killing the Black Body*, 51.
9 Owens, *Medical Bondage*, 1–3, 26–28.
10 Schwartz, *Birthing a Slave*, 227–228, 237–239, 254; and Owens, *Medical Bondage*, 42–73.

NOTES

11 Domonoske, "'Father of Gynecology.'"
12 Schwartz, *Birthing a Slave*, 234–235.
13 McGregor, *From Midwives to Medicine*, 33–68.
14 Schwartz, *Birthing a Slave*, 93–95.
15 Schwartz, 144–145, 165–166.
16 Hazzard-Donald, *Mojo Workin'*, 136–145; and Holmes, *Safe in a Midwife's Hands*, 81–93, 113–123.
17 Holmes, *Safe in a Midwife's Hands*, xvi–xix.
18 Wilkie, "Granny Midwives," 83–89; and Holmes, *Safe in a Midwife's Hands*, 1–13.
19 Smith and Holmes, *Listen to Me Good*, 38–39.
20 Wilkie, "Granny Midwives," 83–89; Holmes, *Safe in a Midwife's Hands*, 111–124; and Hazzard-Donald, *Mojo Workin'*, 139–140.
21 Hazzard-Donald, *Mojo Workin'*, 139–140.
22 Hazzard-Donald, *Mojo Workin'*, 139–140. See also Aunt Clara Walker in Rawick, *American Slave*, Vol. 11, Part 7, 19–27.
23 Holmes, *Safe in a Midwife's Hands*, 111–124.
24 Holmes, 89–91.
25 Holmes, 13–26, 51–64.
26 Schwartz, *Birthing a Slave*, 93–100; and Reagan, *When Abortion Was a Crime*, 1–19.
27 Schwartz, *Birthing a Slave*, 99–100; and Fett, *Working Cures*, 64–65.
28 Lu Lee, in Rawick, *American Slave*, Supplemental Series 2, Vol. 6, Part 5, p. 2291–2312.
29 WebMD, "Cotton—Uses, Side Effects, and More."
30 All quotes from Mary Gaffney can be found in Rawick, *American Slave*, Supplemental Series 2, Vol. 5, Part 4, 1441–1457.
31 See the following interviews in Rawick, *American Slave*: James V. Deanne in Vol. 16, Part 3, 6–9; Julia Larken in Vol. 13, Part 3, 34–46; and Neal Upson in Vol. 13, Part 4, 48–70.
32 Schwartz, *Birthing a Slave*, 123–126.
33 David L. Byrd in Rawick, *American Slave*, Supplemental Series 2, Vol. 3, Part 2, 560–572.

NOTES

34 Byrd in Rawick, *American Slave*, 560–572.
35 Anna Lee in Rawick, *American Slave*, Supplemental Series 2, Vol. 6, Part 5, 2272–2290.
36 Fett, *Working Cures*, 64–66.
37 Schwartz, *Birthing a Slave*, 108–109; and Reagan, *When Abortion Was a Crime*, 1–19.
38 Elliot, "That Texas Abortion Case." See also Klibanoff, "Texas Law Banning Abortion Dates to 1857."
39 Arablouei and Abdelfatah, "Abortion Was Once Common Practice in America."
40 Arablouei and Abdelfatah.
41 Loewen, *Mississippi Chinese*, 1–6, 24–27.
42 Schwartz, *Birthing a Slave*, 111–113.
43 Davis, *Women, Race, and Class*, 204–205; Roberts, *Killing the Black Body*, 8–9; and Schwartz, *Birthing a Slave*, 111–113.
44 Owens, *Medical Bondage*, 44–46; and White, *Ar'n't I a Woman*, 106–107.
45 Davis, *Women, Race, and Class*, 208.
46 Kluchun, *Fit to Be Tied*, 3–5.
47 Luibheid, *Entry Denied*, 37–40.
48 Hazzard-Donald, *Mojo Workin'*, 139.

Chapter 22: The Quilt of Motherwit

1 All quotes from Onnie Lee Logan can be found in Logan and Clark, *Motherwit*.
2 Bonaparte, "Regulating Childbirth," 24–33.
3 DeVoe, "Black History Trailblazer."
4 Fraser, *African American Midwifery in the South*, 163–181.
5 Morrison, "Rootedness," 61.
6 Fontenot, *Secret Doctors*, 99–101.
7 Luke, *Delivered by Midwives*, 32–35.
8 Luke, 32–35.
9 Luke, 32–35.
10 Wilkie, "Granny Midwives," 83–89.

NOTES

11 Sampsell, "Why Does Squeezing a Comb Help with Labor Pains?"
12 Smith and Holmes, *Listen to Me Good*, 115–116.
13 Luke, *Delivered by Midwives*, 32.
14 Luke, 33, 152.
15 Kluchun, *Fit to Be Tied*, 12–20.
16 Lee, *Granny Midwives and Black Women Writers*, 41–42.
17 Luke, *Delivered by Midwives*, 26; and Lee, *Granny Midwives and Black Women Writers*, 27–30.
18 Lee, *Granny Midwives and Black Women Writers*, 36–37.
19 Fontenot, *Secret Doctors*, 53–54, 115.
20 Puckett, *Folk Beliefs of the Southern Negro*, 172.
21 Hazzard-Donald, *Mojo Workin'*, 140–142.
22 Kail, "The Mystery of the Memphis Nation Sack."
23 Hazzard-Donald, *Mojo Workin'*, 138–139; and Tallant, *Voodoo in New Orleans*, 101.
24 Drewal, *Yoruba*, 18; and Bird, *Sticks, Stones, Roots, and Bones*, 98.
25 See the following interviews in Rawick, *American Slave*: Alice Dixon in Vol. 8, Part 2, 153–156; Lizzie Farmer in Vol. 7, Part 1, 97–101; David Goodman Gullins in Vol. 12, Part 2, 78–90; and Robert Henry in Supplemental Series 2, Vol. 5, Part 4, 1706–1712.
26 Wahlman, *Signs and Symbols*, 105.
27 Bird, *Sticks, Stones, Roots, and Bones*, 13; and Alvarado, *Voodoo Hoodoo Spellbook*, 183, 233, 240–243, 255.
28 Fraser, *African American Midwifery in the South*, 181–212.

Chapter 23: The Midwife's Bag, a Tool of Rebellion

1 Turner, "'Queen Elizabeth Perry Turner,'" 20–23.
2 Hazzard-Donald, *Mojo Workin'*, 145–146; and Turner, "'Queen Elizabeth Perry Turner,'" 20–23.
3 Smith and Holmes, *Listen to Me Good*, 63; and Luke, *Delivered by Midwives*, 125.
4 Hazzard-Donald, *Mojo Workin'*, 145, and Holmes, *Safe in a Midwife's Hands*, 54–56, 112–115. See also Wilkie, *The Archeology of Mothering*, 138–139.

5. Fry, *Stitched from the Soul*, 44; and Wahlman, *Signs and Symbols*, 80–81.
6. Thompson, *Flash of the Spirit*, 101–109.
7. Hazzard-Donald, *Mojo Workin'*, 145. See also Wilkie, *The Archeology of Mothering*, 138–139.
8. Luke, *Delivered by Midwives*, 36–38, 87–88.
9. Luke, 48–50.
10. Luke, 48–50.
11. Parolee Daniels in Rawick, *American Slave*, Supplemental Series 2, Vol. 3, Part 4, 1028–1044.
12. Logan and Clark, *Motherwit*, 53.
13. Luke, *Delivered by Midwives*, 126–127.
14. Wilkie, "Granny Midwives," 85.
15. Smith and Holmes, *Listen to Me Good*, 134–145.
16. Luke, *Delivered by Midwives*, 125–130.
17. Kluchun, *Fit to Be Tied*, 4–5.
18. Roberts, *Killing the Black Body*, 8–10.
19. Roberts, 90.
20. Kluchun, *Fit to Be Tied*, 4–5, 101–106.
21. Mostafavi, "Understanding Racial Disparities."
22. Villarosa, "The Long Shadow of Eugenics in America."

Chapter 24: Black Women's Hair, the Everlasting Textile

1. Mbilishaka, "PsychoHairapy Through Beauticians and Barbershops," 178–179.
2. Mbilishaka, 178–179.
3. Akin-Adeboye, "Hairdressing and Hairstyles in Yoruba Land."
4. Dabiri, *Don't Touch My Hair*.
5. White and White, *Stylin'*, 55–56.
6. See the following interviews in Rawick, *American Slave*: James Williams in Vol. 11, Part 7, 170–171; Luck Key in Vol. 9, Part 4, 198–200; and Georgia Telfair in Vol. 13, Part 4, 1–10.
7. Tharps, *Hair Styling*, 111–113.

NOTES

8 See the following interviews in Rawick, *American Slave*: Tildy Collins in Vol. 6, Part 1, 83–86; and Georgia Telfair in Vol. 13, Part 4, 1–10.
9 White and White, *Stylin'*, 56–59.
10 See the following interviews in Rawick, *American Slave*: Frances Willingham in Vol. 13, Part 4, 151–160; and Katherine Eppes in Vol. 6, Part 1, 119–121.
11 Mahalia Shores in Rawick, *American Slave*, Vol. 10, Part 6, 154–156.
12 Amos Lincoln in Rawick, *American Slave*, Vol. 5, Part 3, 17–19.
13 Gus Feaster in Rawick, *American Slave*, Vol. 2, Part 2, 43–71.
14 Amos Lincoln in Rawick, *American Slave*, Vol. 5, Part 3, 17–19.
15 See the following interviews in Rawick, *American Slave*: Lina Hunter in Vol. 12, Part 2, 252–272; and Mary Williams in Vol. 11, Part 7, 179–188.
16 Willis Easter in Rawick, *American Slave*, Vol. 4, Part 2, 1–4.
17 Rosanna Frazier in Rawick, *American Slave*, Vol. 4, Part 2, 63–65.
18 Minnie Green in Rawick, *American Slave*, Vol. 12, Part 2, 64–65.
19 Hazzard-Donald, *Mojo Workin'*, 25.
20 Alvarado, *Magic of Marie Laveau*, 8–13, 53–54.
21 Press, *Hope in a Jar*, 66–68.
22 Press, *Hope in a Jar*, 66–68.
23 Rooks, *Hair Raising*, 51–74.
24 Rooks, 51–74.
25 Rooks, 51–74.
26 Bundles, *On Her Own Ground*, 60.
27 Kail, *Stories of Rootworkers and Hoodoo in the Mid-South*, 194–199.
28 Kail, 194–199.
29 bell hooks, "Straightening Our Hair," 1.
30 bell hooks, *Bone Black: Memories of Girlhood*, 55–57.
31 bell hooks, "Straightening Our Hair," 1.
32 bell hooks, 1.
33 Banks, *Hair Matters*, 129–133.

NOTES

Chapter 25: Oshun's Legacy in the New World

1. Kendall, *History of New Orleans: Vol. 3*, 1129–1130.
2. McCormick, "McCormick Completes Acquisition of Zatarain's."
3. Harris, *High on the Hog*, 207–208; Miller, *Soul Food*, 42–45; and Opie, *Hog and Hominy*, 124–137.
4. Crumpton, "Why Do We Eat Black-Eyed Peas on New Year's Day?"
5. Crumpton.
6. Harris, *High on the Hog*, 85; and Carney and Rosomoff, *In the Shadow of Slavery*, 182–185.
7. Olupona, "Òrìsà Òsun," 52–57.
8. Olupona, "Òrìsà Òsun," 45–48. See also Monaghan, *Encyclopedia of Goddesses and Heroines*, 23–24; and Teish, *A Calabash of Cowries*, 17–19.
9. Doumbia and Doumbia, *Way of the Elders*, 27–29; and McKenzie, *Hail Orisha!*, 301–303.
10. Morrison, "A Knowing So Deep," 32. See also Love, *Divining the Self*, 88–90.
11. My rendition of this tale is adapted from Fatunmbi, *Oshun*, 4–7; Teish, *Calabash of Cowries*, 49–52; and Love, *Divining the Self*, 88–90.
12. Willis, "Africa," 274–275; and Fieldman, *Black Rhythms of Peru*, 157–158.
13. Olupona, "Òrìsà Òsun," 45–48.
14. My rendition of this story is adapted from Bascom, *Sixteen Cowries*, 421–425.
15. Carney and Rosomoff, *In the Shadow of Slavery*, 70–72.
16. Carney and Rosomoff, 70–72.
17. Bascom, *African Folktales in the New World*, 1–16; and Teish, *Calabash of Cowries*, 77–102.
18. Olupona, "Òrìsà Òsun," 45–48.
19. Olupona, 45–48.
20. Olupona, 45–48.
21. Carney and Rosomoff, *In the Shadow of Slavery*, 177; Harris, *High on the Hog*, 129–130; and Miller, *Soul Food*, 121.
22. Harris, *High on the Hog*, 35.

NOTES

23 Harris, *High on the Hog*, 14, 32–33; and Carney and Rosomoff, *In the Shadow of Slavery*, 73–79.
24 Harris, *High on the Hog*, 32; and Opie, *Hog and Hominy*, 29.
25 Harris, *High on the Hog*, 32–33.
26 Carney and Rosomoff, *In the Shadow of Slavery*, 70–72.
27 Harris, *High on the Hog*, 11, 49–59; Harris, *Beyond Gumbo*, 6–9; and Opie, *Hog and Hominy*, 7–15.
28 Opie, *Hog and Hominy*, 19–20; and Miller, *Soul Food*, 148–149.
29 Carney and Rosomoff, *In the Shadow of Slavery*, 76–79.
30 Saxon et al., *Gumbo Ya-Ya*, 172.
31 Dewitt, *Picayune Creole Cook Book*, 1–4.
32 Harris, *High on the Hog*, 102–106.
33 Dewitt, *Picayune Creole Cook Book*, 1–4.
34 Harris, *High on the Hog*, 16–19, 105–106.
35 Carney and Rosomoff, *In the Shadow of Slavery*, 135; and Miller, *Soul Food*, 226–228.
36 Miller, *Soul Food*, 228–231.
37 Miller, 226–228.
38 Harris, *High on the Hog*, 232–236; and Miller, *Soul Food*, 3.

Chapter 26: The Candy Lady

1 Cheers, "Sweet Lady." See also Harriot, "28 Days of Black Joy."
2 Perkins and Lawayne, *Perkins Rowe*, 4.
3 Cheers, "Sweet Lady."
4 Perkins and Lawayne, *Perkins Rowe*, 4.
5 Saxon et al, *Gumbo Ya-Ya*, 30.
6 Saxon et al., *Gumbo Ya-Ya*, 28–29, 32–37, 43–46, 360–362. See also Widmer, *New Orleans in the Thirties*, 98.
7 Saxon et al, *Gumbo Ya-Ya*, 43.
8 Higgins, *Historical Sketch Book and Guide to New Orleans*, 13.
9 Harris, *High on the Hog*, 83–85; and Miller, *Soul Food*, 24–32, 35.
10 Alvarado, *Marie Laveau Voodoo Grimoire*, 56–57; and Long, *New Orleans Voudou Priestess*, 13–18.

NOTES

11 Alvarado, *Marie Laveau Voodoo Grimoire*, 56–57; Carney and Rosomoff, *In the Shadow of Slavery*, 182–185, Harris, *High on the Hog*, 127–129; and Stone, *New Orleans Coffee*, 33–37.
12 Stone, *New Orleans Coffee*, 33–37.
13 Saxon et al, *Gumbo Ya-Ya*, 43, 172; and Stone, *New Orleans Coffee*, 33–37.
14 Harris, *High on the Hog*, 102–105.
15 Myrick, *Sugar*, 27–28.
16 Ripley, *Social Life in Old New Orleans*, 16–22. See also Williams, "Memories of New Orleans," 37.
17 Harris, *High on the Hog*, 129; and Saxon et al., *Gumbo Ya-Ya*, 32–33.
18 Saxon et al., *Gumbo Ya-Ya*, 37.
19 Leslie, "Old New Orleans," 190; and Stone, *New Orleans Coffee*, 33–37.
20 Leslie, "Old New Orleans," 190.
21 Myvett, "The Praline Ladies."
22 Myvett.
23 John Moors in Rawick, *American Slave*, Supplemental Series 2, Vol. 7, Part 6, 2736–2742.
24 Saxon et al., *Gumbo Ya-Ya*, 37. See also Nunez, "Just Like Ole' Mammy Used to Make."
25 Joseph Alfred, interview by Robert McKinney, Louisiana Federal Writers' Project, Folder 25.
26 Hurston, *Mules and Men*, 223, 239.
27 Long, *New Orleans Voudou Priestess*, 98–99.
28 Alvarado, *Witch Queens, Voodoo Spirits, and Hoodoo Saints*, 203–208; and Saxon et al., *Gumbo Ya-Ya*, 45.
29 Olajubu, *Women in the Yoruba Religious Sphere*, 119–122; Love, *Divining the Self*, 82–83; and Washington, *Our Mothers, Our Power, Our Texts*, 22–24.
30 Alvarado, *Marie Laveau Voodoo Grimoire*, 121.
31 Saxon et al., *Gumbo Ya-Ya*, 144.
32 Hurston, *Mules and Men*, 1–3.
33 Hurston, "How It Feels to Be Colored Me," 828.

NOTES

Chapter 27: From Black-Eyed Peas to Red Beans and Rice

1. Chase, *And Still I Cook*, 32.
2. Opie, *Hog and Hominy*, 29.
3. Harriet Collins in Rawick, *American Slave*, Vol. 4, Part 1, 242–245.
4. Miller, *Soul Food*, 112–126.
5. Albala, *Beans*, 103–104; and Thorne and Thorne, *Serious Pig*, 289–298.
6. Mangam, "The Magic of the Black-Eyed Pea," 112–126.
7. Carney and Rosomoff, *In the Shadow of Slavery*, 186; Harris, *High on the Hog*, 129; and Miller, *Soul Food*, 121–122.
8. Mangam, "The Magic of the Black-Eyed Pea," 112–126.
9. Seed, "Health Benefits of Black-Eyed Peas."
10. Robert Shepherd in Rawick, *American Slave*, Vol. 13, Part 3, 245–263.
11. For an example of a black-eyed peas mojo to bring money, see Alvarado, *Voodoo Hoodoo Spellbook*, 230.
12. Hurston, *Mules and Men*, 186.
13. Butler, "Hoppin' John: A New Year's Tradition."
14. Twitty, *Rice*, 5–14.
15. Owens, *Mrs. Owens' New Cook Book*, 704.
16. Thorne and Thorne, *Serious Pig*, 289–298.
17. Owens, *Mrs. Owens' New Cook Book*, 814–815.
18. Dewitt, *Picayune Creole Cook Book*, iv.
19. Dewitt, iv.
20. Alvarado, *Voodoo Hoodoo Spellbook*, 29–30, 247. See also Alvarado, *Witch Queens, Voodoo Spirits, and Hoodoo Saints*, 145–149; and Willis, "Africa," 274–275.
21. Fieldhouse, *Food, Feasts, and Faith*, 535–536.
22. Ferris, *Matzoh Ball Gumbo*, 116–117.
23. Saxon et al., *Gumbo Ya-Ya*, 29.
24. Latrobe, *Journal of Latrobe*, 202.
25. Saxon et al., *Gumbo Ya-Ya*, 29.
26. Federal Writers' Project of the Works Progress Administration, *New*

Orleans City Guide 1938, 171; Saxon et al., *Gumbo Ya-Ya*, 29; and Thorne and Thorne, *Serious Pig*, 289.
27 Ripley, *Social Life in Old New Orleans*, 18–20.
28 Thorne and Thorne, *Serious Pig*, 289.
29 Mary Washington, interview with Robert McKinney, Louisiana Federal Writers' Project, Folder 25.
30 Alvarado, *Witch Queens, Voodoo Spirits, and Hoodoo Saints*, 145–149. See also Hurston, *Mules and Men*, 128–129; and Shesso, *Planets for Pagans*, 110–111.
31 Tallant, *Voodoo in New Orleans*, 94.
32 Cecil Hunt, interview with Zoe Posey, November 6, 1940, Louisiana Federal Writers' Project, Folder 25.
33 Hyatt, *Hoodoo Conjuration Witchcraft Rootwork*, Vol. 2, 1060–1075.
34 Alvarado, *Witch Queens, Voodoo Spirits, and Hoodoo Saints*, 145–152.
35 Charles Raphael, interview with Hazel Breaux, Jacques Villere, and Oscar Felix, March 14, 1940, in Louisiana Federal Writers' Project, Folder 25. See also Alvarado, *Marie Laveau Voodoo Grimoire*, 55–60.

Chapter 28: Wild Lettuce, the Greens in My Gumbo Pot

1 MaCCNO, "New Orleans Has a Long History of Street Vending."
2 Saxon et al., *Gumbo Ya-Ya*, 30.
3 Anderman, *Brewed Awakening*, 168–170.
4 Stanonis, *New Orleans Pralines*, 228–230.
5 MaCCNO, "New Orleans Has a Long History of Street Vending."
6 Harris, *High on the Hog*, 199–203; and Opie, *Hog and Hominy*, 101–118.
7 Harris, 199–203; and Opie, 101–118.
8 Harris, *High on the Hog*, 83–84, 95; and Miller, *Soul Food*, 19–32, 152.
9 Harris, 83–84, 95; and Miller, 19–32, 152.
10 Sarah Fuller in Rawick, *American Slave*, Supplemental Series 2, Vol. 4, Part 3, 1437–1439.
11 Alvarado, *Marie Laveau Voodoo Grimoire*, 63.

NOTES

12 Gus Feaster in Rawick, *American Slave,* Supplemental Series 2, Vol. 2, 55–67.
13 Fannie Moore in Rawick, *American Slave*, Vol. 15, Part 2, 128–137.
14 Smith and Holmes, *Listen to Me Good,* 29, 154.
15 Logan and Clark, *Motherwit,* 4–8.
16 Logan and Clark, 4–8.
17 Holmes, *Safe in a Midwife's Hands,* 90–93; and Logan and Clark, *Motherwit,* 52–53.
18 Miller, *Soul Food,* 31, 49–56; and Opie, *Hog and Hominy,* 81–82, 96–99, 118, 135.
19 Harris, *High on the Hog,* 183; Miller, *Soul Food,* 100; and Opie, *Hog and Hominy,* p. 90.
20 Harris, *High on the Hog,* 199–201, 174–175; and Opie, *Hog and Hominy,* 118.
21 Allen, *Listen, I Say Like This,* 149.
22 Unless otherwise noted, all quotes from Leah Chase come from Allen, *Listen, I Say Like This.*
23 Severson, "Leah Chase, 96, Creole Chef." See also Chase, *Dooky Chase Cookbook,* 11.
24 Chase, "Leah Chase on Callaloo/Gumbo Z'herbes," 182–132.
25 Chase, *Dooky Chase Cookbook,* 20.
26 Saxon et al., *Gumbo Ya-Ya,* 169–170.
27 Chase, *Dooky Chase Cookbook,* 22.
28 Chase, 36, 61.
29 Chase, 36, 61.
30 Carney and Rosomoff, *In the Shadow of Slavery,* 177–179; and Miller, *Soul Food,* 149.
31 Carney and Rosomoff, 179; and Miller, 149.
32 Harris, *High on the Hog,* 59; Miller, *Soul Food,* 157; and Opie, *Hog and Hominy,* 2–6.
33 Harris, *High on the Hog,* 11; and Opie, *Hog and Hominy,* 14–18.
34 Carney and Rosomoff, *In the Shadow of Slavery,* 179.
35 Chase, *Dooky Chase Cookbook,* 59–60; and Harris, *High on the Hog,* 49.

NOTES

36 Chase, "Leah Chase on Callaloo/Gumbo Z'herbes," 182–185.
37 Alvarado, *Marie Laveau Voodoo Grimoire*, 61–62; and Chase, *Dooky Chase Cookbook*, 59–60.
38 Chase, "Leah Chase on Callaloo/Gumbo Z'herbes," 182–183.
39 Chase, *Dooky Chase Cookbook*, 59. See also Alvarado, *Marie Laveau Voodoo Grimoire*, 61–62.
40 Lee and Lee, "Gumbo Variations." See also "Creole Gumbo," Cooking, *New York Times*, https://cooking.nytimes.com/recipes/7453-creole-gumbo.
41 Hyatt, *Hoodoo Conjuration Witchcraft Rootwork*, Vol. 1, 643, and Vol. 3, 2011–2012, 2233–2235.
42 Jarmon, *Wishbone*, 126–130.
43 Bird, *Sticks, Stones, Roots, and Bones*, 29–31. See also Thompson, *Flash of the Spirit*, 121.
44 Thompson, *Flash of the Spirit*, 121.
45 Raboteau, *Slave Religion*, 215–218, 372.
46 Betty Curlett in Rawick, *American Slave*, Vol. 8, Part 2, 82–87.
47 Jarmon, *Wishbone*, 122–126. See also the following interviews in Rawick, *American Slave*: Harriet Cheatam in Vol. 6, Part 2, 52–54; Anderson and Minerva Edwards in Vol. 4, Part 2, 5–9; Rachel Fairley in Vol. 8, Part 2, 258–261; Will Glass in Vol. 9, Part 3, 38–41; Cora L. Horton in Vol. 9, Part 3, 321–324; John Hunter in Vol. 9, Part 3, 359–366; Anna King in Vol. 9, Part 4, 201–206; Julia Malone in Vol. 5, Part 3, 43–44; and Wade Owens in Vol. 6, Part 1, 306–308.
48 Rachel Fairley in Rawick, *American Slave*, Vol. 8, Part 2, 258–261.
49 Julia Malone in Rawick, *American Slave*, Vol. 5, Part 3, 43–44.
50 See the following interviews in Rawick, *American Slave*: Anderson and Minerva Edwards in Vol. 4, Part 2, 5–9; Cora L. Horton in Vol. 9, Part 3, 321–324; and Anna King in Vol. 9, Part 4, 201–206.
51 Reverend John Moore in Rawick, *American Slave*, Vol. 16, Part 6, 47–48.
52 John Hunter in Rawick, *American Slave*, Vol. 9, Part 3, 359–366.
53 Jarmon, *Wishbone*, 122–126.

NOTES

54 Jarmon, 122–126.
55 Jarmon, 126–133.
56 Hurston, "Shouting," 851, and "Sanctified Church," 901–902.
57 Patsy Hyde in Rawick, *American Slave*, Vol. 16, Part 6, 33–36.
58 Jarmon, *Wishbone*, 133; and Raboteau, *Slave Religion*, 215–218.
59 Marie Dédé, interview with Robert McKinney, Louisiana Federal Writers' Project, Folder 25.
60 Saxon et al., *Gumbo Ya-Ya*, 172.
61 Chase, *Dooky Chase Coookbook*, 14.
62 Chase, *And Still I Cook*, 112.
63 Chase, 112.
64 Chase, 112.
65 Chase, 112.
66 Chase, 112.
67 Chase, *Dooky Chase Cookbook*, 250.
68 Morial, "Leah Chase."
69 Harris, *High on the Hog*, 199–206.
70 Harris, 199–206.
71 Chase, "I Would Have Fed Him Gumbo Z'herbes," 152–158.
72 Chase, 157–158.
73 Chase, 157–158.
74 Allen, *Listen, I Say Like This*, 84.

Chapter 29: Black Women Put Their Foot in This

1 Charles, *Real Southern Cook*, 40.
2 Hazzard-Donald, *Mojo Workin'*, 24–25, 101–102.
3 Bascom, "Yoruba Concepts of the Soul," 405; and Crowther, *Vocabulary of the Yoruba Language*, 137.
4 Matory, "The Many Who Dance in Me," 244–245.
5 Kumari, *Isese Spirituality Workbook*, 137–138.
6 Adeniyi, "Portrayals of Indigenous Religion and Ifa Divination," 179–180.
7 Hyatt, *Hoodoo Conjuration Witchcraft Rootwork*, Vol. 1, 196.

8   Hyatt, 351.
9   Hyatt, 376.
10 Alvarado, *Hoodoo Voodoo Spellbook*, 267–277.
11 Hyatt, *Hoodoo Conjuration Witchcraft Rootwork*, Vol. 4, 2951–2952, 2990, 3049–3059, 3068–3665.
12 Hyatt, 2990, 3050–3059.

Conclusion: Where Did All the Conjure Women Go?

1   Dorsey, *Orishas, Goddesses, and Voodoo Queens*, 50–52.
2   Sutton, "The Day Christian Fundamentalism Was Born."
3   Sutton.
4   Sutton.
5   Henry, "Bea Dixon Talks Honey Pot."
6   Anderson, *Conjure in African American Society*, 134–143.
7   Riley, "Before Goop."
8   Anderson, *Conjure in African American Society*, 134–143.
9   Essex, "Black Women's Complex Relationship with Religion and Spirituality." See also Gariella Opara, "How Black Women Are Navigating Feminism."
10 Shaw, "More Black Millennials Are Turning Away from Traditional Religion."
11 Hinds, "Bisa Butler."
12 Dunigan, "How Hoodoo Inspired a Midwife."
13 Steinauer-Scudder, "Seeds of Ancestors."

Index

abiku (born to die), 184
abortions, 10, 192
    birth rates relation to, 193–194
    cotton relation to, 185–186, 187–189, 193
    doctors and, 189–190
    knotted string relation to, 209
    midwife's bag relation to, 219–220
"Actually, Black Mermaid Folklore Has Been Around Long Before Disney's *The Little Mermaid*," 105
Adeyemi, Tomi, 300
adire fabric, 173–174, 227
agogo (hairstyle), 171
aje (magic), 5–6, 35
    of Candy Ladies, 252
    indigo dye relation to, 159–160, 175
    kijipa cloth and, 171–172
akara (black-eyed-pea fritters), 248
Alabama, 28, 222, 223–224
Alfred, Joseph, 259
Ali, Tatyana, 226
Alvarado, Denise, 82, 106
amala (porridge), 249

American Horror Story (television series), 105–106, 300
American Medical Association, 189–190
American Revolution, 179–180
Anansi, 160
Andersen, Hans Christian, 58–59, 104, 105
anger, 292–293
animal fat, 278
The Annals of an American Family (Richardson), 43
anti-Blackness
    hair straightening relation to, 229–230
    in medical establishment, 224
anti-immigration speech, 194
"The Apothecary and the Mermaid," 66–67
appropriation, 121–122
aquariums, 68, 74
Ariel (fictional character), 57–58, 104, 105
asafetida, 42, 169–170, 208, 255

INDEX

Ashanti people, 160
ashcakes, 128
ashe (divine energy), 34–35, 49, 244
   gris-gris relation to, 93
   of *kijipa* cloth, 172
   Negro Mammies relation to, 40
   of Oshun, 38, 295
   Yoruba healers relation to, 36–37
Augustus, Sarah Louise, 28–29
"Aunt Caroline Dyer Blues," 144
Aunt Diskie, 146–147
Aunt Jemima, 109, 123, 126, 135, 144, 148–149
   Civil War relation to, 124–125
   in "How to Make a Nonracist Breakfast," 150–151
   Saar relation to, 152–154
   at World's Columbian Exposition, 113–114, 115–117, 122
Aunt Nancy, 27, 28, 235
Aunt Patsy, 129–130, 131, 147
Aunt Prudence, 129–130, 131, 147
Aunt Sarah, 148–149
Ayida Wedo, 83, 100

babalawo (expert diviners), 35
Baby Yams, 226
Bailey, Halle, 58
BaKongo cosmogram, 163, 167–168, 212
   quilts relation to, 177–178, 216
   spiritual rituals and, 217
Ball, Tarriona "Tank," 299

Bambara people, 87
Bamboula, 97
Bantu people, 281
Barnett, Ferdinand Lee, 112
basket (*suku*), 171
basket-weaving, 69–70
Bass, J. B., 94
Bassett, Angela, 300
BB Super Gro, 17
beauty shops, 235–237
beauty standards, 228, 230–231
Bennett, John, 66–67
big toes, 290
birth rates, 193–194
birthing fire, 184
black cohosh, 32
Black eateries, 275
black-eyed-pea fritters (*akara*), 248
black-eyed peas, 266–268, 272
Black Girl Vitamins, 299
Black Is King (visual album), 299
Black market women (*marchandes*). *See* marchandes
black pepper tea, 183
Black Power movement, 242
black snake root, 39
Black women. *See specific topics*
blackface, 127, 150
#blackgirlmagic, 1
#BlackLivesMatter, 106
blended cosmology, 198
bloodletting, 20, 44–45, 46, 92, 119
blue notes, 141

INDEX

blues music, 138, 139, 145, 147
Board of Health, 199–200, 201–202, 203–204, 207, 213–214
born to die (*abiku*), 184
botanical knowledge, 33–34, 137, 234, 295
    of Negro Mammies, 120–121
    quilts relation to, 177
    of Yoruba healers, 35–37
Boukman (Priest), 76
braiding shops, 236
Brazos River, 38
breastfeeding, 185
Brent, Linda. *See* Jacobs, Harriet
Bre'r Rabbit (fictional character), 145, 166
brother *orishas*, 3–5
Brown, William H., 235
Brown v. Board, 223
Butler, Bisa, 226, 299
Byrd, Sarah, 128–129, 131, 147, 153

C-sections, 72, 182, 200
cakewalk, 127–128, 129, 131, 134–135, 138, 153
    See also "Old Aunt Jemima"
calabash (*koroba*), 171
calas (sweet fritters), 258
Calinda, 64
callaloo (stewed greens), 275, 280
calomel, 45
caminos (paths), 162
camphor, 42, 43, 50–51
candy business, 274–275

Candy Ladies, 13, 237, 242–243, 274–275, 278, 289
    aje of, 252
    Laveau relation to, 259, 261
    racism relation to, 260
    soul food of, 253–254
Caribbean Islands, 58, 83, 84, 162
    See also Haiti
Carney, Judith A., 280
"Carolyn Dye Special," 141
Charleston, South Carolina, 66–67, 70, 73
charms (*paquet Congo*), 137
Chase, Leah, 277–279, 284–285, 286–287
Chicago, Illinois, 110–112, 115–116
childbirth, 196, 200, 207, 216, 217
    See also Granny Midwife
Children's Bureau, 199
Chinese Exclusion Act (1882), 195
Chinese laborers, 192, 195
Choctaw people, 34, 99–100
Christian fundamentalism, 296
Christian nationalism, 296–297
Christianity, 6, 12, 37–38, 46
    Granny Midwife relation to, 199
    quilts relation to, 177–178
Christmas, 265
church, 276–277
Civil Rights Act, 224
Civil Rights movement, 11, 13, 223, 252
    Christian fundamentalism relation to, 296
    gumbo relation to, 286–287, 288

INDEX

Civil War, 47–48, 124–125
Clark, Sonya, 160–161, 299
"Climbing Jacob's Ladder," 165
coartación, in Spanish law, 60
Coastal Plain, 50
Coca-Cola, 252
Cockeysville, Maryland, 30
Code Noir, 79, 80
Codigo Negro, 80
Cofer, Willis, 120
coffee, 256, 257
cohosh bush, 39
colds, 39, 40–41, 44, 50, 208, 275
   inhalation for, 42
   potlikker for, 254
   salves for, 19, 43
Collins, Harriet, 34, 37–38, 39, 109, 169, 265
Columbus, Christopher, 110, 157
"Come On in My Kitchen," 210
common law, 80–81
community, 6, 36–37
Comstock Act (1873), 194
Congo, 6, 66, 83, 84, 87, 93
Congo Square, 63
Congo thigh-slapping dance (*nzuba*), 129
Congolese people, 168
congri (red beans and rice), 263–265, 266, 268, 270–273
conjure women. *See specific topics*
Constitution of the Carolinas, 25, 79–80
Cook, Will, 139
cooking pots, 281–286, 288
copper, in mojos, 212–213

cortisol, 170
cosmology, 160, 198
cotton, 159, 180–181, 191–192, 231
   abortions relation to, 185–186, 187–189, 193
   textile production of, 164–166
cotton gin, 180
cough syrup, 41, 50
coughs, 50, 278
Court of Honor, 113
Couvreure, Sanité, 62, 64
COVID-19 pandemic, 12, 298
Cow Alley, 70
cowrie shells, 161, 243
Creole women, 90, 91, 277, 278
Crescent City Quilters, 226
crossroads, 212, 221, 272
croup, 9, 21
Cullors, Patrisse, 300

Dahomey, 6, 83, 84
Damballah, 83, 85, 100
Danish people, 58
Danish West Indies. *See* Caribbean Islands
"The Dark Truth About Honey Pot," 295
Darrow, Louisiana, 253
Davis, Angela, 147, 152
Davis, Jacob, 158
Davis, Juliet, 49–50, 51, 52
Davis, R. T., 113–114, 124
Davis Milling Company, 113, 124
death, 217–218

INDEX

Dédé, Marie, 283
Dédé, Sanité, 259
deities (*vodun*), 6
delta land, 180
Demopolis, Alabama, 223–224
Deonn, Tracey, 300
Deslondes, Charles, 77
disease, 45, 46–47
divination, 10, 172, 243, 244–246, 298
Divine, 104
divine energy (*ashe*), 34–36, 93, 244
Dixon, Bea, 294–295, 296–297, 299
Dobbs v. Jackson, 12
doctors, 29–30, 72, 181–182, 189–190
    bloodletting by, 44–45, 46
    eugenics relation to, 224–225
    Granny Midwife relation to, 195, 201–202, 204–205, 223, 225
    at rural health clinics, 223–224
    slavery and, 179, 182–183, 192, 193
Dogon cosmology, 160, 281
domestic abuse, 96–97
Dominique, Rosine, 88
Dooky Chase, 277, 287–288
The Dooky Chase Cookbook (Chase), 278
Douglass, Frederick, 75, 112, 134
drugs, 46–47
DuVernay, Ava, 300
Dye, Caroline, 141–143, 144, 147, 195

Edison, Thomas, 111
efo yanrin (poisoned leafy greens), 249
egungun festival, 172
Eiffel Tower, 111

Elegue (*orisha*), 145
emancipation, 10, 195
emetics, 45
emmenagogues, 185
empowerment, 13
England, 179–180
enslaved Africans, 6–8, 9–10, 29, 146
    healing of, 19
    herbalism of, 22
    quilts and, 177–178
Episcopal Church, 46
Erzulie (*loa*), 76, 84, 85, 153
Eshu-Elegua (*orisha*), 269–270, 282
Eshu (*orisha*), 212, 234–235, 245–246
eucalyptus, 17
eugenics, 193, 202, 224–225
evil eye, 9
expert diviners (*babalawo*), 35

Fairley, Rachel, 282
fast fashion, 226–227
Feaster, Gus, 119–120, 232, 276
Federal Writers' Project, 28, 30, 87, 128, 212, 232
    Collins and, 34, 169
    Dédé and, 283
    Feaster and, 119–120
    Gaffney and, 186–187
    Hunt and, 272
    Laveau and, 94, 105
    Lee, A., and, 188
    Lee, L., and, 164
    Robinson and, 151–152
    Walker and, 123

INDEX

feet, 289–292
feminine mysteries, 64–65
fibroids, 225
Flint (Dr.), 23, 24, 25, 27, 44–45
Florida, 12, 32
flour-based breads, 120
Floyd, George, 12
Fon gods (*rada*), 84–85
Fon people, 83, 84–85, 87
foods, 276, 283
   black-eyed peas, 266–268, 272
   feet relation to, 290–291
   of *marchandes*, 269, 277
   of Oshun, 247–249, 251–252
   red beans and rice, 263–265, 266, 268, 270–273
   stewed greens, 275, 280
   of Yoruba people, 249–250
   See also soul food
Foote, Eliza, 30
foraging, 33
forests, 33–34, 49–50
   Ring Shout in, 37–38
   water in, 36, 39
fortune-telling, 121
four corners, of quilts, 212, 216
"Four Women," 148–149, 153
free people of color (*gens de couleur libre*), 80–81, 94–95
freedom riders, 288
fufu (pounded yams), 248, 250

Gaffney, Mary, 186–187, 188, 190, 191, 192, 193
Galen, of Pergamum, 46, 47
generational wealth, 22
gens de couleur libre (free people of color), 80–81, 94–95
Georgia, 28
German Coast, Louisiana, 77
germs, 45
gold rush, 158
Golden Brown Chemical Company, 235
goopher dust, 132
Granny Midwife, 13, 192, 196, 278, 289, 298–299
   Board of Health relation to, 203–204
   Candy Ladies relation to, 253
   death relation to, 217–218
   doctors relation to, 195, 201–202, 204–205, 223, 225
   during Great Depression, 276
   Logan, O., on, 197
   medical establishment relation to, 200, 206–207, 215–216, 222
   miscarriages relation to, 185
   motherwit of, 198–199
   nature sack relation to, 209–210
   Oshun relation to, 163
   quilts and, 212–214
   salves of, 208–209
   Spiritualism relation to, 297
   teas of, 219–222
   See also midwife-weavers
Great Depression, 276
Great Dismal Swamp, 26–27, 32

INDEX

Great Migration, 114–115, 242
Green, Nancy, 114, 122, 150–151
griot, 51
gris-gris (magical charms), 95, 132, 267
   of Laveau, 90, 93, 94, 99–102, 106, 233
   mojos compared to, 109
Gullah Geechee people, 66, 67, 69
gumbo, 269, 277–281, 285–287, 288
gumbo z'herbes, 280–281
gynecology, 11, 181–182, 199

hair straightening, 228, 229–230, 232, 234, 236
hairdressing, 160–162, 234, 235–236, 289
   during slavery, 230–233
   Yoruba people relation to, 170–171, 227–228
Haiti, 87, 112, 130, 137–138
   Saint-Domingue, 75–76
   United States relation to, 136
Haitian immigrants, 76
Haitian Revolution, 73, 75–76, 136–137, 153
Haitian Vodou, 8, 81, 84, 91, 144, 269
   Haitian Revolution relation to, 75–76, 136–137, 153
   United States relation to, 137–138
Hamer, Fannie Lou, 225
Handy, W. C., 138–139, 140–141, 147
Harris, Kamala, 76, 292
Harris, Zakiya Dalila, 228–229

healing, 6, 8–9, 19, 36–37, 67
   with botanical knowledge, 35–36
   with herbalism, 29–30
   by Negro Mammies, 32, 46, 47–48, 169–170
   water spirits and, 91–92
health and wellness industry, 297, 299
herbalism, 22, 27, 28, 30, 37, 295
   for abortions, 185
   with massage techniques, 183
   of Negro Mammies, 20–21, 29, 119, 122–123
   Osanyin relation to, 36
   Spiritualism relation to, 297
High John de Conquer, 51, 144–149, 153, 166, 294
Hightower, Zachary, 235
Hippocrates, 45–47
hoecakes, 118–119, 120, 121, 123, 124, 251
Holmes, William, 72–73
"holy trinity," 264
home remedies, 1–2, 200–201, 254
Honey Pot, 294–296, 299
hoodoo, 8, 109–110, 212, 299
hooks, bell, 236, 237
Hoppin' John, 265–266, 267–268
horsemint, 32, 39, 41
Houmas House Estate and Gardens, 255, 260–261
"How to Make a Nonracist Breakfast," 150–151
humors, 45–46
Hunt, Cecile, 272

INDEX

Hunter, Lina, 232
Hurston, Zora Neale, 59, 87, 138, 139, 146–147, 294
   on High John de Conquer, 144–145
   Mules and Men, 261–262
   on nature sack, 210
   on poison, 132
   on Ring Shout, 130–131
Hyatt, Harry Middleton, 272
hygiene practices, 8, 199–200
hysterectomy, 225

Illinois, Chicago, 110–112, 115–116
immigrants, Haitian, 76
Indigenous people, 7, 34, 84, 99–100
indigo dye, 159–160, 173–174, 175, 179–180
infertility, 181–182
inhalation, 43, 44, 48, 50
   of asafetida, 42, 169–170
   of turpentine, 208–209
"international foods," 241–242
interracial unions, 203
intro-communal conflict, 210
ipori (spiritual force), 290
irun biba (hairstyle), 171
irun didi (hairstyle), 171, 231
irun kiko (hairstyle), 171, 232
Islam, in West Africa, 6
itagbe cloth, 172–173, 174, 227
Iya Mapo (*orisha*), 159
iyami aje (secret witches), 5–6, 10–11, 35, 159, 171, 227
   LaBrique as, 260

   Mami Wata relation to, 84
   Oshun and, 102–103
   Voodoo Queens and, 61

Jackson Park, 112–113
Jacobs, Harriet, 23–25, 28, 29, 44, 71
   Aunt Jemima compared to, 109
   in Great Dismal Swamp, 26–27
Jacobs, William, 44–45
jalap plant, 145
jambalaya au congri, 266, 268, 272
James, Thomas "Papa Sing", 194
jeans, 157, 158, 159, 174–175, 186, 227
Jefferson, Thomas, 47
Jemisin, N. K., 300
Jim Crow, 11, 114, 125, 148, 215, 276
   cooking pots during, 285
   Dye during, 142–143
   Granny Midwife during, 195, 201–202, 298–299
   hair straightening during, 228
   lynching during, 262
   segregation relation to, 194
"Jim crow cards," 231
jimsonweed, 39
Johnson, Robert, 210
Jolly Batchelor (slave ship), 75
Jones, Pearl, 270–271
Jones (Doctor), 205–206, 207
jooks (Negro pleasure houses), 139
juba dance, 129–130, 131
Juliette, 59, 60–61, 63, 64, 106

INDEX

kente cloth, 160

Kersands, Billy, 116–117, 126, 127, 134–135, 149, 153

kijipa cloth, 171–172, 174, 209

kinetoscope, 111

Kleinfeldt family, 270–271

knotted string, 168, 170–171, 172, 209, 210

knotted string ritual, 170

Knowles, Beyoncé, 299

kola nut, 243, 248–249, 250, 251–252

koroba (calabash), 171

Ku Klux Klan, 148

LaBrique, Zozo, 259–260, 261, 262

lagniappe, 271

Lake Pontchartrain, 64, 87, 98, 106

landfills, in West Africa, 227

laundry, 264–265, 268–269

Lauryen, Kirby, 150–151

Laveau, Marie, 59, 62, 82, 88–89, 98, 300–301
    Candy Ladies relation to, 259, 261
    foods relation to, 283
    gris-gris of, 90, 93, 94, 99–102, 106, 233
    Mami Wata relation to, 87–88, 91–92, 103, 105
    marchandes and, 260
    nature sack relation to, 210
    Papa Legba relation to, 272–273
    romantic relationships and, 96–97

leafy greens, 249, 276, 279–280, 298

Lee, Anna, 188, 190, 196

Lee, Lu, 164, 165–167, 169, 176, 185

Lemonade (visual album), 299

The Liberation of Aunt Jemima (Saar), 152–154

licensing, 202, 204, 222
    during Jim Crow, 215
    midwife's bag relation to, 218, 219
    during slavery, 274

"Life of Aunt Jemima," 122

The Little Mermaid (Andersen), 58–59, 86

The Little Mermaid (film), 57–58, 104–105

loa (Voodoo deities), 61, 88, 91–92
    Erzulie, 76, 84, 85, 153
    Ogun, 137, 153
    Papa Legba, 145, 269–270, 272–273

Logan, Jeanine Valerie, 299

Logan, Onnie Lee, 196, 197, 199, 202–203, 205–208, 276
    on Board of Health, 204
    home remedies of, 200–201
    on midwife's bag, 219
    on motherwit, 198, 211–212, 214
    on Vicks VapoRub, 197, 209

Loko, 91–92

Lombard, Rudy, 288

Long, Carolyn Morrow, 64

Louisiana, 266
    Darrow, 253
    New Orleans, 63–64, 65, 77, 78–81, 87, 226, 256–257

Louisiana Purchase, 79

Lucas, Eliza, 159

INDEX

luck, 9–10, 177, 208, 269–270, 281
   cooking pots relation to, 284
   hairdressing relation to, 227
   mermaids relation to, 70
   mojos for, 212
   red brick dust relation to, 260
   spiritual rituals for, 263–265
lynching, 114, 143, 262

magic (*aje*), 5–6, 35, 159–160, 171–172, 175, 252
magical bundles (*nkisi*), 93, 132–133, 168
magical charms (*gris-gris*). See *gris-gris*
Makandal, Francois, 137
makolo (sacred knots), 168, 173, 210, 212
Malone, Annie Turnbo, 234
Mami Wata, 82–83, 84, 85–86
   Laveau relation to, 87–88, 91–92, 103, 105
   Ursula compared to, 104
Manager, Maxine, 299
manifest destiny, 158
Manring, M. M., 116
manumission, 80, 117, 261, 267–268
marchandes (Black market women), 256–258, 259, 260, 275
   foods of, 269, 277
   lagniappe of, 271
   See also Candy Ladies
maroon camps, 77
Maroon (Saint), 77, 94, 100
marronage (running away), 61, 62–63

Marshall, Rob, 58
Martin, Kameelah, 137
Maryland, Cockeysville, 30
massage techniques, 183, 200
maternity clinics, 198
Mawu-Lisa, 83
Mazaret (Captain), 82
McCormick and Company, 241
Medicaid, 223, 224
medical establishment, 163, 198–199, 213
   anti-Blackness in, 224
   Granny Midwife relation to, 200, 206–207, 215–216, 222
   midwife's bag relation to, 219, 222
medicinal herbs, 5–6
medicine, 29, 31, 46–48, 293
   See also herbalism; *minkisi*
medicine cabinet, 17
menopause, 217
menstrual blood, 102, 216–217, 283
menthol, 17, 21, 41, 51
mermaids, 58–59, 65, 76, 81, 88–89, 103
   Oshun relation to, 57, 70, 74, 162
   as *simbi* water spirits, 66, 74
   Trott relation to, 68–71, 72–73
#MeToo, 106
Midway Plaisance, 139
midwife-weavers, 165–167, 175, 179, 190, 196, 226
   abortions and, 185–186, 187–189
   doctors relation to, 183
   midwife's bag of, 218–219
   second sight of, 184

INDEX

midwifery, 161
midwife's bag, 218
    abortions relation to, 219–220
    two-bag trick and, 221–222
Miles, Charlotte, 62–63
Milstead, Harris Glenn, 104
minkisi (sacred medicines), 6–8, 137, 169, 281
minstrel shows, 113–114, 115, 116–117, 127, 138, 150
mint plants, 21
miscarriages, 170, 182, 185, 203–204
miscegenation, 203
Mississippi, 28
"Mississippi appendectomies," 225
mojos, 109, 117, 135–136, 138, 154, 290
    Aunt Jemima relation to, 149
    copper in, 212–213
    of Dye, 141, 147
    Golden Brown Chemical Company relation to, 235
    with High John de Conquer, 144–145, 146, 148, 153
    nature sack, 209–210
    of Negro Mammies, 110, 117, 133–134, 278
    red cloth in, 169
    Ring Shout relation to, 132
    Saar relation to, 152–153
    textile production relation to, 163
Monday, red beans and rice on, 264–265, 270–271, 272–273
Mondays, 269–270
moon, 39–40

Moore, John, 131–132
Morgan, Joan, 2
Morris, Courtney, 300
Morrison, Toni, 103, 198, 243, 260
Moss, Andrew, 130
mothballs, 42
motherwit, 198–199, 211–212, 214
Motte Fouqué, Friedrich de la, 59
Mrs. Owens' New Cook Book and Summary of Helpful Information (Owens), 268–269
Muir, Evie, 105
The Mulatto (play), 58–59
Mules and Men (Hurston), 261–262
mullein, 32, 39, 41–42

naming rituals, 184–185
nanny (*nounoute*), 62
nature sack, 209–210
Ne Kongo, 281
"negro cloth," 159
Negro Mammies, 13, 21–22, 49, 51–52, 53, 277–278
    Aunt Jemima relation to, 109
    botanical knowledge of, 120–121
    congri of, 268
    after emancipation, 195
    Federal Writers' Project and, 28, 30
    Flint and, 27
    foods of, 250–251
    in forests, 33–34
    Great Migration relation to, 115
    healing by, 32, 46, 47–48, 169–170

INDEX

Negro Mammies (*cont.*)
    herbalism of, 20–21, 29, 119, 122–123
    in "How to Make a Nonracist Breakfast," 150–151
    as *marchandes*, 256–257
    midwife's bag of, 218–219
    mojos of, 110, 117, 133–134, 278
    over-the-counter medicine and, 31
    potlikker and, 275–276
    pralines of, 258–259
    quick breads and, 118
    red cloth and, 169
    reproductive health relation to, 183
    Saar relation to, 152–154
    salves of, 42–43
    slave rebellions relation to, 77–78
    slavery relation to, 23, 298–299
    teas of, 40–41
    Voodoo Queens compared to, 61–62
Negro pleasure houses (jooks), 139
Nella Rogers (fictional character), 229
New Age movement, 297–298
New Orleans, Louisiana, 63–64, 65, 77, 78–79, 226
    free people of color in, 80–81
    marchandes in, 256–257
    water spirits in, 87
New Thought, 297, 299
New Year's Day, 265
New York, 75
New York Academy of Medicine, 182
New York Sun (newspaper), 94
New York Times (newspaper), 59, 66–67
Nicaud, Rose, 257–258, 260, 261, 262, 275
Nigeria, 2–3
1918 flu pandemic, 18
nkisi (magical bundles), 93, 132–133, 168
Nollywood, 236
North Carolina, 18, 21, 23, 26, 32
nounoute (nanny), 62
Nummo, 160
Nzambi, 85
nzuba (Congo thigh-slapping dance), 129

Obatala (*orisha*), 244–246
Obba (*orisha*), 249
obstetrics, 199
Ogun (*loa*), 137, 153
okra, 280, 286
Olajubu, Oyeronke, 36
"Old Aunt Jemima," 113, 116–117, 126–127, 135, 149, 153
Old Man Rutter, 72–73
Olodumare (*orisha*), 4, 5, 34, 93, 102–103, 162
one-drop rule, 80
Onesimus, 19
onisegun (specialized healers), 35
open kettle sugar, 257, 259
oppression, 3–5, 6, 102
ori (soul), 161, 227–228
orishas (Yoruba gods), 2–5, 12, 83, 300
    ashe of, 34–35

INDEX

black-eyed peas relation to, 266
Elegue, 145
hairdressing relation to, 161–162, 171
indigo dye relation to, 159–160, 173–174
rada relation to, 84–85
See also specific orishas
Orunmila (*orisha*), 172–173, 244
Osanyin (*orisha*), 36–37, 40
Oshogbo people, 247
Oshun Ibu Yumu (*orisha*), 162–163
Oshun (*orisha*), 2–5, 12, 40, 243
   ashe of, 38, 295
   divination relation to, 244–246
   Erzulie relation to, 85
   foods of, 247–249, 251–252
   Granny Midwife relation to, 163
   hairdressing relation to, 161–162, 171, 227
   herbalism relation to, 36–37
   indigo dye relation to, 159–160, 173–174
   iyami aje and, 102–103
   Mami Wata relation to, 83, 84
   mermaids relation to, 57, 70, 74, 162
Oshun Seegesi (*orisha*), 161
The Other Black Girl (television show), 228–229
ouangas (talismans), 93
over-the-counter medicine, 31
Ovwurie, Benita, 295
Owens, Frances Emugene, 268–269

Page Act (1875), 195
Papa Legba (*loa*), 145, 269–270, 272–273
paquet Congo (charms), 137
paths (*caminos*), 162
Peaches, 148–149
Pearl Milling Company, 109, 115, 122, 126, 151–152, 251
Pemberton, John S., 252
Penn, Irvine Garland, 112
Penniman, Leah, 299
peppermint, 51
PepsiCo, 151
Pergamum, Galen of, 46, 47
Perkins, Andrea, 233
Perkins, Daniel, Jr., 42, 255–256
Perkins, Margaret "Booie" Lindsey, 12, 42, 253, 255–256
Perkins, Mary Ann Wooden, 225
Peter (Saint), 100, 269–270, 272
pianos, in jooks, 139
Pilgrims, at Plymouth Rock, 157–158
placenta, 184
plagal chords, 141
plantations
   cakewalk on, 127–128
   Houmas House Estate and Gardens, 255, 260–261
   midwife-weavers on, 165–167
   Negro Mammies on, 20, 28–29, 48, 78, 119
Plymouth Rock, Pilgrims at, 157–158
Pneumonia Cure Salve, 17–18, 21

INDEX

poison, 132, 249, 290
poisoned leafy greens (*efo yanrin*), 249
poke leaves, 276
poke roots, 32
police, 13, 92–93
political disagreements, 287
poplar leaves, 120
Porcher, Francis Peyre, 47–48
Poroyen, 172–173
porridge (*amala*), 249
potlikker, 254, 275–276
pounded yams (*fufu*), 248
pralines, 258–259
The Princess and the Frog (film), 277
Proctor and Gamble, 18
progesterone, 170
"Promises of Freedom," 116–117, 131–132, 134–135
Protestantism, 7
puerperal fever, 181
purgatives, 45

"queen of the birds" (*reine des zozos*), 61
Queen Sugar (television show), 300
Queer Eye (television show), 1
quick breads, 118–120
quilts, 175–176, 213–214, 226
    BaKongo cosmogram relation to, 177–178, 216
    motherwit and, 211–212

rabbit tobacco, 43, 50
racism, 1, 292, 301
    Candy Ladies relation to, 260
    hair straightening relation to, 229
    during Jim Crow, 148
    in medical establishment, 163
    Sheppard-Towner Act relation to, 201
rada (Fon gods), 84–85
raffia, 174
ragtime, 139–141
Rainbow Row, 70
rape, by slave holders, 23, 24, 25
"The Reason Why the Colored American Is Not in the World's Columbian Exposition," 112
Reconstruction, 51, 190–191
red beans and rice (*congri*), 263–265, 266, 268, 270–273
red brick dust, 260, 284
red cloth, 133, 163, 166, 169
red meat, 250
"Red Mountain Blues," 148, 153
red sauce dish, 102
reine des zozos ("queen of the birds"), 61
Relf, Mary Alice, 225
Relf, Minnie Lee, 225
religious festivals, 167
reproductive autonomy, 185–186, 187
reproductive health, 10, 170, 181–182, 183, 190
    See also Granny Midwife; midwife-weavers
rheumatism, 39, 92
Rhimes, Shonda, 300
rice, 33

INDEX

Richardson, Lunsford, 18, 19, 209
   The Annals of an American Family, 43
   Negro Mammies relation to, 20, 21–22, 48, 51–52
   Stancil, M., relation to, 51
Richardson's Magic Croup, 17–18, 21
rickets, 182
Ring Shout, 37–38, 129–131
   High John de Conquer relation to, 145
   mojos relation to, 132
Ritual (documentary series), 299
Robinson, Mariah, 151–152
Roe v. Wade, 12
Roman Catholicism, 7, 8, 61
romantic relationships, 96–97
rootwork. *See* hoodoo
Rosalie, 88–89, 105
Rosomoff, Richard Nicholas, 280
roux, 279, 286
running away (*marronage*), 61, 62–63
rural health clinics, 223–224
Rutt, Chris, 113–114, 117, 122, 123, 127, 150

Saar, Betye, 152–154
sacred knots (*makolo*), 168, 173, 210
sacred medicines (*minkisi*), 6, 7, 8, 137, 169, 281
"sacred skin," 167
sage, 51, 234
Saint-Domingue, Haiti, 75–76
Salley, Asia, 295

salves, 42, 255
   for colds, 19, 43
   for coughs, 50
   of Granny Midwife, 208–209
   for vesicovaginal fistulas, 200
   See also Vicks VapoRub
San Malo, 77
Sanders, Crystal, 21
Sanders, Velvaline, 49, 50
Santería, 162
Sarah, 70
sassafras, 34, 278, 280–281, 286
Scandal (television show), 1
Sebastian (fictional character), 104
second sight, 184
secret witches (*iyami aje*). *See iyami aje*
secret worship sessions, 282–283
segregation, 194, 270, 287–288
self-rising flour mix, 113
sexism, 1, 229, 292, 301
   Aunt Jemima relation to, 150
   Candy Ladies relation to, 260
   during Jim Crow, 148
   in medical establishment, 163
sexual abuse, 96
Shade, Will, 144
Shango (*orisha*), 249
sharecropping, 191–192
Shepherd, Edward, 49
Shepherd, Victoria, 49
Shepherd, Wesley, 50–51
Sheppard-Towner Act (1921), 195, 199, 201, 204
shoes, 24

INDEX

shoestrings, 209
simbi water spirits, 66, 74, 83
Simone, Nina, 148–149, 153
Sims, James Marion, 181–182
sirens, 86
slave holders, 7, 11, 96, 130, 230–231, 251
    as doctors, 29–30
    mojos relation to, 133–134
    rape by, 23, 24, 25
    reproductive autonomy relation to, 187
    Voodoo relation to, 78
    wombs and, 71–72
slave rebellions, 26, 65, 75, 86
    in Charleston, 73
    gris-gris relation to, 93–95
    mermaids relation to, 81
    Negro Mammies relation to, 77–78
slave ships, 86
slavery, 25
    black-eyed peas and, 266–268
    in Caribbean Islands, 58
    cooking pots during, 282
    doctors and, 179, 182–183, 192, 193
    Dye relation to, 142
    foods relation to, 249–250
    hair straightening during, 228
    hairdressing during, 230–233
    healing in, 8–9
    jeans relation to, 159, 174–175
    licensing during, 274
    Mami Wata relation to, 82–83
    mermaids relation to, 74
    mojos during, 132, 133–134
    Negro Mammies relation to, 23, 298–299
    in North Carolina, 23
    Richardson relation to, 18
    sexual abuse in, 96
    sharecropping compared to, 191
    traditions in, 79
    Vicks VapoRub relation to, 19, 48
smallpox, vaccination for, 19
Smith, Alexandria, 299
Smith, Bessie, 147, 148, 149, 153
Smith, Margaret Charles, 215–217, 218
    on foods, 276
    on midwife's bag, 219–220
    on rural health clinics, 223–224
    two-bag trick of, 221–222
snake bites, 26
snakes, 85, 87
Snaky Swamp, 26
social discord, 4
social media, 1, 58
social rituals, 10
sore throat, 42
soul food
    of Candy Ladies, 253–254
    gumbo, 269, 277–281, 285–287, 288
soul (*ori*), 161, 227–228
South Carolina
    Charleston, 66–67, 70, 73
    Negro Mammies in, 28
Spanish law, 60, 257

INDEX

specialized healers (*onisegun*), 35
spinning looms, 165–166
spiritual force (*ipori*), 290
spiritual rituals
    BaKongo cosmogram and, 217
    for childbirth, 196, 200, 207, 216, 217
    cooking pots in, 282–283
    of hairdressing, 236
    for luck, 263–265
    quilts and, 177
    shoestrings in, 209
Spiritualism, 297
spirituals, 140–141, 165–166
St. John's Eve, 87–88
"St. Louis Blues," 140–141
Stancil, Alexander, 52–53
Stancil, Miley, 22, 49, 51, 52–53
Stancil-Shepherd family, 21–22, 48, 49, 51
statu liber (special designation), 60
"Steal Away to Jesus," 38
sterilization, 194–195
    eugenics relation to, 224–225
    "undesirable" births relation to, 203
stewed greens (*callaloo*), 275, 280
stimulation, 42–43, 44, 48, 50
Storer, Horace, 189–190, 192, 193–195, 203–204
Strauss, Levi, 158
suku (basket), 171
"Sundown Blues," 141
superstitions, 278, 281, 284

Sutton, Shady Anne, 146
sweet fritters (*calas*), 258
syncopation, 140–141
SZA, 299

"taking up the mother," 217
talismans (*ouangas*), 93
Tallant, Robert, 94
Tasie, 258
teas, 40–41, 278
    of Granny Midwife, 219–222
    for sore throat, 42
Texas, 186
    abortion in, 188–190
    Negro Mammies in, 28
textile production, 159–161, 187, 207
    of cotton, 164–166
    hairdressing relation to, 230
    midwife's bag relation to, 219
    mojos relation to, 163
    motherwit and, 211–212
    in West Africa, 167–168
theosophy, 297
Third Municipality Guards, 78–79, 82, 88
tignon, 81
TikTok, 150–151
Times-Picayune (newspaper), 63
tisanes, 61, 278
    See also teas
toenails, 291
Toledano, Betsy, 62

INDEX

traditions
  of *gris-gris*, 93
  of Hoppin' John, 265–266
  for quilts, 177
  in slavery, 79
  of West Africa, 34, 159–160, 166, 216, 297–298
transatlantic slave trade, 72
  cotton relation to, 180–181
  Mami Wata relation to, 82, 84, 86
  New Orleans relation to, 87
tripartite racial class system, 80–81
Trott, William, 67, 68–69, 70–71, 72–73, 74
Trump, Donald, 76, 292
Tubman, Harriet, 75
Tucker, Arminta, 66–67
Turner, Albert, 143
Turner, Nat, 26, 75
turpentine, 20–21, 41
  for colds, 50
  inhalation of, 208–209
  in salves, 43
Tuskegee Airmen, 281
two-bag trick, midwife's bag and, 221–222

"Under the Sea," 104
Underground Railroad, 38, 75, 94
Underwood, Charles, 113
"undesirable" births, 203
Undine (Motte Fouqué), 59

United States, 157, 226–227
  Haiti relation to, 136
  Haitian Vodou relation to, 137–138
  kola nut in, 251–252
updos, 232
Ursula (fictional character), 104–105
Ursuline nuns, 258

vaccination, for smallpox, 19
vaginal health, 295
Vaseline, 17
Vazant, Iyanla, 299
vengeance, 85–86, 106
Vesey, Denmark, 73, 75
vesicovaginal fistulas, 181–182, 200
Vick Chemical Company, 18
Vicks VapoRub, 17, 43, 52
  Candy Ladies and, 254
  Logan, O., and, 197, 209
  menthol in, 51
  in 1918 flu pandemic, 18
  slavery relation to, 19, 48
  Stancil-Shepherd family relation to, 21, 49
Virgin of the Vodous, 65, 82
Virginia, 26, 32
viruses, 45
vodun (deities), 6
Voodoo, 8, 59, 61, 63–64
  free people of color relation to, 81
  gris-gris relation to, 93
  gumbo z'herbes relation to, 280–281

INDEX

mermaids relation to, 65, 88
Mondays relation to, 269–270
red beans and rice relation to, 272–273
slave holders relation to, 78
See also loa
Voodoo deities (*loa*). *See* loa
voodoo dolls, 137
Voodoo Queens, 13, 63, 121, 134
Candy Ladies relation to, 259
Negro Mammies compared to, 61–62
slave rebellions relation to, 77
See also Laveau, Marie

Walker, C. J., 234–235, 295–296
Walker, Clara, 123
The Walking Dead (television show), 137–138
Warren, Bertie, 143
Washington, Mary, 260, 261
water, 32
in forests, 36, 39
moon relation to, 39–40
of Oshun, 4, 38, 40
water spirits, 173
hairdressing relation to, 161
healing and, 91–92
Mami Wata, 82–83, 84, 85–88, 91–92, 103, 104, 105
simbi, 66, 74, 83
Watts Delicatessen, 255

Wells, Ida B., 112, 115, 125
West Africa, 2, 12
black-eyed peas in, 266
gumbo relation to, 286
Islam in, 6
landfills in, 227
soul food relation to, 242–243
textile production in, 167–168
traditions of, 34, 159–160, 166, 216, 297–298
West Indies, 98
When Chickenheads Come Home to Roost (Morgan), 2
whippings, 30
"White City," 112–113
white flour, 123
white-owned restaurants, 275
white supremacy, 138, 144, 194
Why Not? (Storer), 192, 194
Wiley, Stancil, M., 49, 51
Winfrey, Oprah, 49
wombs, 71–72, 180, 182–183
World's Columbian Exposition, 110–112
Aunt Jemima at, 113–114, 115–117, 122
ragtime at, 139–140
Wright, Purd, 122, 123

yellow fever, 67–68, 90–91, 92, 100
Yemaya (*orisha*), 40, 159, 299
Yoruba gods (*orishas*). *See* orishas
Yoruba healers, 35–37, 91

INDEX

Yoruba people, 87
   adire fabric of, 173–174, 227
   big toes relation to, 290
   foods of, 249–250
   hairdressing relation to, 170–171, 227–228
   kijipa cloth of, 171–172
   on slave ships, 86
Yoruba religion, 5–6, 167, 212
   black-eyed peas relation to, 266
   indigo dye relation to, 159–160
   mermaids in, 74
   quilts relation to, 177–178
   Voodoo relation to, 8
   See also orishas

Zatarain, Emile A., 241
Zatarain's rice mixes, 241–242, 252, 264
zombies, 137–138